DISAFFECTED!

DISAFFECTED!

APATHY VS. ACCESS:
WHY EVERY ELECTION IS
THE ELECTION OF A LIFETIME.

by

SEAN PITTMAN

foreword by

DR. MYRON ROLLE

INKED
ELEPHANT
PUBLISHING HOUSE

Inked Elephant Publishing House, LLC
A Social Impact Publisher

Library of Congress Cataloging-In-Publication Names: Sean Pittman

TITLE: Disaffected. Access vs. Apathy; Why Every Election is The Election of a Lifetime / Sean Pittman; Foreword by Myron Rolle

DESCRIPTION: Castle Rock: Inked Elephant Publishing House, 2024

978-1-959694-07-6 HARDBACK

978-1-959694-08-3 PAPERBACK

978-1-959694-09-0 E-BOOK (LAYOUT FOR KINDLE)

LIBRARY OF CONGRESS CONTROL NO. 9781959694076

BISAC: POLITICAL SCIENCE/Political Process/Campaigns & Elections POLITICAL SCIENCE/Political Parties SOCIAL SCIENCE/Cultural & Ethnic Studies/African American and Black Studies

DESIGN AND COMPOSITION: Neon Pig Creative
COVER DESIGN: Neon Pig Creative
COVER IMAGES:
rawpixel.com / AdobeStock #340508814
vesperstock / AdobeStock #351034789

TYPOGRAPHY:
Headings set in Cheddar Gothic, designed by Adam Ladd
Body copy set in Masqualero, designed by Jim Ford of the Monotype Studio

Printed in the United States of America

Some names and identifying characteristics have been changed to protect the privacy of the individuals involved.

Inked Elephant Publishing House is committed to amplifying the works of quality and authenticity. In that spirit, we are proud to offer this book to our readers, however, the story, experiences, and words are the author's alone.

*I dedicate this book to the cherished family
that Audra and I have lovingly created, and their futures.*

*As a Girl Dad, it is because of Paloma, Pilar and Phoebe
that I truly began to care about the country and world we leave behind.
May the content of this book help shape a future of boundless possibilities.*

CONTENTS

Contents

FOREWORD

The year was 2005, I was an 18-year-old Freshman at Florida State University, fresh faced, wide eyed and full of ambition. As I walked into the house where the event was being held, the energy was electric. Gathered together were some of the most influential black leaders in Tallahassee and I was anxious to be in the mix.

At the time, I had an older teammate, Robert Hallback, who said he wanted to introduce me to someone. We walked across the room to this six-foot-tall, striking black gentleman in a well cut, nice blazer. He was holding court with a crowd of individuals and Robert turns to me and says, Myron, this is the man whose house we're in right now, Sean Pittman.

I was instantly impressed as he peppered me with genuine interest and questions. "It's a pleasure to meet you. I've heard about you. I've read about you. How do you like Tallahassee so far? How do you like Florida State?" It was just sort of small talk, but it was personal.

My teammate, a member of the Kappa Alpha Psi Fraternity, Incorporated, had a bit of an agenda in introducing me to Sean. He not only wanted to introduce me to the host, but also show me what success looks like coming from this particular black Greek organization. His sentiment; here is a living example of what you can become. And it worked.

I have always been attracted to possibility and potential. Whenever I can see people who are diligently living their purpose and doing well, those are the people I've always admired. Those people I want to be close to.

When I was young, I read a book by Ben Carson, Gifted Hands, and he became my academic hero. I watched Deion Sanders play football and baseball and do it with flash, style, grace, and a level of competitiveness that I've never seen before. He became my athletic hero.

Coming from the Bahamas my parents would often tell me stories about Sir Lynden Oscar Pindling, our first prime minister in the Bahamas after blacks took over as the majority rule. To listen to their stories of his leadership was awe-inspiring. He became my public service hero.

I've always been quick to set people as standards of excellence. Exalting them in my own head saying, "maybe one day, I don't know when, but one day I can be there."

Sean is one of the most successful lawyers in all of the state of Florida, and possibly even the Southeast region. He is remarkable and when you're in Tallahassee, Florida, and someone who wants to make a difference, not only in the classroom, or on campus, but in Leon County, the big bend area, all of Florida, maybe even all of the Southeastern America, you are going to want to know Sean Pittman.

And so, this was the lens through which I first began to know Sean. He immediately became the standard for what a successful black man looks like. The standard for what a successful brother of Kappa Alpha Psi looks like. What a black man with a family, multiple degrees, intelligent and suave and all of the things. He became the standard for what class looks like. And for me, at 18, he was a real-life embodiment of what I could be.

From then on, that's the role that Sean played for me. And ever since then, we've been inseparable. We are still very close to this day too. It is one of my personal beliefs God orders your steps and puts you in places and around individuals who can really guide your future.

I was at Florida state to play football and to be a student athlete, but then meeting Sean Pittman expanded my vision and my responsibility.

I said to myself, "You're not just a student athlete. You're not just making tackles and getting interceptions on the football field and getting A's in organic chemistry. You are now here to see what it's like to live as a role model, live as a leader and be an example. You are now here to set yourself up to make an indelible impact as an agent of change in the community because here's someone doing it and iron sharpens iron."

So fast forward, nearly twenty years later. I'm Dr. Myron Rolle, Chief Neurosurgery Resident at Massachusetts General Hospital, Harvard Medical School and Global Neurosurgery Fellow. I am the chairman of the Myron L. Rolle foundation, former Rhodes Scholar, former National Football League player, and a Florida State Seminole two-time grad and the author of *The 2% Way: How a Philosophy of Small Improvements Took Me to Oxford, the NFL, and Neurosurgery.*

When Sean asked me to consider writing the foreword for *Disaffected!*, I did not even let him finish the question. Not only because of our deep personal connection. But also, because of the messages in this work.

I believe that it's our duty to be actively involved in what happens to us, what happens to our family, to our friends. It is our privilege, a noble honor, to have the authority to make selections, to vote, to put people into places, and to put issues into places, and to put systems into places that can change lives, and affect all of us. This book reminds us of that privilege and challenges us to not take it for granted. Even when the odds seem against us or the road seems treacherous.

Disaffected! gets to the core of the issue, the sacrifices that individuals have made in order for us to have this privilege. He reminds us it did not come lightly. And for that responsibility, it's, our duty now to exercise this honor, this privilege that many people have died over, fought through, lost wages, lost reputation, or were simply excluded from. I believe Sean has done a beautiful job in highlighting the purpose, the power, and the responsibility of voting and its impacts.

The book begins with a reminder of how few votes can turn an election, and how powerfully different the policy aftermath can look based on that selected person's policy stances. It then takes you through a series of example policy areas where party elections have dramatically affected the everyday lives of individuals. Using these examples to bring these lofty topics right into our living rooms.

For me, the section on culture wars was very powerful. We have seen discriminatory labels begin to create structurally violent constructs that are then used to limit or deter someone's ability to exercise their right to vote. These kinds of labels are distracting to what's really important. American citizens, tax paying citizens, law abiding citizens, good faith citizens, those who believe in a promise of a country, promise of a city, of a County, someone who wants to do well, wants their families to do well, should never be denied access based on labels; because they're black or poor or LGBTQ or formerly incarcerated.

This is deeply ingrained in me as a brain surgeon. The brain is a phenomenal organ with intricate pathways running through it, around it, with a network of vessels with a complex structure of neurons communicating with each other through signals and electrical activity.

When I am in the midst of working on someone's brain, healing it or curing their disease, I do not have time to worry with these tags of culture; a last name, a skin color, a zip code, a sexual orientation. My mind zooms in on the fact that this is a life that I have to save. This is a life that needs intervening on. And it's a special moment to share that with colleagues in the operating room, because we're not distracted. We get the goal and we get it done. Anything else is an irrelevant distraction.

Disaffected! approaches this topic as well as the others examples as lens to see how powerful your vote can be and how intricately small decisions overlay one another and over time create huge impacts in people's lives.

I was also drawn to the overlay of messaging with my own book, *The 2% Way*. *The 2% Way* talks about small improvements as a way to achieve immediate or long-term goals. It highlights the fact that we often have this impractical vision of reaching a finish line very quickly, very robustly, because we're seeing social media or through friend networks that do not always tell the full story.

There is a societal sense that we have got to have it now, got to have it today. And it's got to be done quickly. But some of my greatest mentors, like my football coach at Florida State, challenged me and my teammates to just get a little bit better. You don't have to have everything today. You don't have to take over the world in one day, small little wins, small little victories. Over time these little things add up; six months, ten months, a year from now. And along the way pat yourself on the back for a job well have done, for little victories each and every day.

When I think about things, I typically put the *2% Way* glasses on to frame it in a way that is palatable for me. As the world is turning and a lot of things are happening and balls are in the air and people are doing this and that and we're going left to right. It can seem like endless chaos. But this methodical way of thinking and looking at the world, slows me down allows me to control my breath and focus on getting a little bit better every day.

This is the philosophy of Sean's call to action in Disaffected! We will not change decades of historical discriminatory policy or repressive voting in one day or one year. If you turn on the news you can easily be distracted, dissuaded, deterred from exercising your power and responsibility.

But every action counts. But we cannot become jaded and simply give in to inaction or apathy. We must start. One action at a time. One election at a time. One vote at a time. And together we open doors. We create change.

We must see the system for its beauty and positive power of having a voice, not its dark side of repression. We must stay locked in and zoomed in on those aspects and not get turned off by the background noise that sometimes fills up space on TV or social media.

This is what Sean is asking of us. What we should be asking of ourselves. Not only for today but for generations to come. I feel confident you will enjoy this work as much as I did. I hope it leaves you informed, thinking about the power of a vote in different, and more impactful ways. But I also hope it leaves you inspired. To join Sean, to join me and to join others who believe in the noble right we are granted as voting citizens. Let's take action.

— **Dr Myron Rolle**
Pediatric Neurosurgeon
at Johns Hopkins All Children's Hospital

"If the United States believes in the fundamental right to vote for every citizen, Election Day should be a federal holiday in this nation."

— Sean Pittman

INTRODUCTION

WHERE IT ALL BEGAN

I do not have a single memory of voting activity or elections from my childhood. Our Broadmoor apartment N-103—located in the mostly Black city of Riviera Beach, Florida—wasn't a place where you would see voter registration efforts or candidates canvassing to ask for support. I only recently learned that my mother was an avid voter, a fact she kept only to herself.

What is burned in my mind is that, in the 1970s and 80s, voting was not pushed forward as an important thing to do, anticipate, or work towards, in my neighborhood, my schools, nor at recreation centers or parks. It was far removed from the civil rights fight of the 1960s that involved voting rights and other corrective measures relating to past injustices, disparities, and inequities.

Some of my most vivid reflections from Broadmoor Apartments involve memories of Black people struggling to make ends meet and craft some sense of life. It was a reality of poor work, poor education, poor housing, limited transportation, and limited ability to better the situation. When your mind and life are preoccupied with consistent thoughts of how to get a couple decent jobs to pay rent and put food on the table, voting and concern for politics don't easily rise to the top of the priority list.

But as I reflect on those days and the people, I'm left wondering how things relating to voting and its placement on the priority list have changed over these many decades.

Unlike many of the families in Broadmoor, my mother had a steady job as a high school teacher in Palm Beach County. Black teachers in Black schools never made much money, but it was a stable profession. In some regard, my family should have been doing a little better than others in the neighborhood, living a little better, but my dad's long-term struggle with a consistent job, drained those possibilities to a great extent and lowered the playing field. And as I stated, black teachers in black schools didn't make much money.

Like low-income housing everywhere, Broadmoor was home to many big families in small living spaces. We had great families who lived there for a long time, made legendary because of the number of kids they had or how long they'd lived in Broadmoor and Riviera Beach in general. And while there were hardships, there were also small elements that brought joy to those who took advantage.

Broadmoor had a quarter-size basketball court with a rim and basket about half of the time. The apartment complex was located directly behind John F. Kennedy Jr. High School. The school's football field divided the apartment complex and the campus, offering a field to play football and other outside sports during closed school hours. Some kids, like my brother, Pokey, would hit tennis balls on the walls of the apartment complex—at least until the neighbor on the other side of that particular wall arrived home. The lone park in the complex never had the right equipment at any of the right times. Marbles, jump-rope, jumbo jacks, hide and seek, red light green light, and hopscotch were the everyday joys for the kids of all ages.

What seemed like big dreams then seem small now. Most of us didn't dream beyond graduating from high school, except perhaps the occasional few who considered a professional sports or entertainment career. Our lives were so full of scenes of poverty, crime, death, imprisonment, drug abuse, spousal and child abuse that setting your mind on being a doctor or lawyer or owning your own business seemed impossible. As a kid growing up, I never met a Black doctor or lawyer. I didn't have a Black male teacher until I was in high school.

Broadmoor was not a place filled with encouragement or mentorship or exposure to bigger things or people. A person's dreams are typically limited to what they learn or are exposed to, and Riviera Beach was no different. Today, social media can take a person outside of their limited surroundings and show them what's possible to achieve in life. The lack of exposure during the era I grew up in was a real detriment in Black and poor communities everywhere.

Just like everywhere in the world, exposing kids in Broadmoor to new and exciting things was important to broaden horizons and expand our knowledge. When kids experience different activities, cultures, and ideas, they develop a more comprehensive understanding of the world around them. Exposure to big and new things fosters creativity and critical thinking skills. It encourages children to explore, question, and come up with innovative solutions. Exposure helps young people develop their interests and passions. By seeing, experiencing, and feeling new things, kids can discover what they enjoy and excel in, leading to personal growth and fulfillment. Moreover, exposing kids to new and exciting experiences nurtures curiosity and personal development.

However, during that time—and in places like Riviera Beach—exposure to life and career choices were few. So, we created ceilings and floors based mostly on what surrounded us. Broadmoor was a place, like many others, where few people made it out to see, feel, and explore the rest of the world. While Broadmoor was a place full of good and beautiful families, most, unfortunately, spent each day just getting through the day, without the luxury of dreaming . . . much less preparing for a different future or bigger life. The impact of our votes was the farthest thing from our minds.

The 8.4-acre Broadmoor apartment complex was torn down in 2008, after being tarnished by crime over many years, most notably when a three year old was fatally shot there in 2004. Then, police responded to more than 150 calls there in 2006. However, Broadmoor will forever represent communities like it all over the world. And for me, it will forever inspire a personal call to action. In fact, as a daily reminder of how far I have come and that God is not finished with me yet, I named our 11-acre property in Tallahassee "Broadmoor."

I don't remember having a serious conversation about voting until my freshman year of college. As a new student at Florida State University, I was approached by a fellow student in our Student Union and lured to a table to register to vote. I had never been asked to register to vote before. I could not even recall the age requirement for registering, but that day in the union, I got all the information I needed. In fact, I was a little embarrassed not knowing much about the process or how I fit in it.

Here is how that scene played out.

Student Advocate: "Are you registered to vote?"

Me: "I don't think so."

Student Advocate: "Are you a Democrat or a Republican?"

Me: "Huh?" I had absolutely no idea.

Student Advocate: "Are you going to register as a Democrat or a Republican?"

Me: (staring blankly)

Student Advocate: "I'm sure you are a Democrat."

Her certainty came from the fact that I was clearly a Black American and it was well known that most Black people at this time in history identified with the Democratic Party.

She was right, I am a Democrat and align philosophically with their platform, but the point is, I had left Riviera Beach completely unaware of our entire political system.

I remember being so embarrassed that the people in line must have heard the conversation and realized I was the only one who did not know what the question meant or what a political party was.

Interestingly, I had run for Senior Class President in high school. I won that election but never really connected it to real politics. It was high school, and I was popular, so it seemed like the next step to creating lasting memories of my time at Suncoast Community High School. If I am honest, I was following what I had seen from older kids who I looked up to. I had a great slogan: "The seniors need someone to lead. Someone who is destined to succeed. So, look around and then you will see that the one to elect is Seany P!"

Clearly not a slogan that would work in any real political environment, but for the purposes of solidifying a teenage base, it worked. (By the way, Seany P was my nickname from sports and my short music career. There is no interesting story connected to the nickname, I just thought it just sounded cooler than Sean.)

And yes, I feel confident a class or two in high school mentioned voting, government, political parties, and politics in general. Yet none of these facts truly helped me understand the importance that voting has on the day-to-day lives of all Americans—especially for a demographic with more reasons to vote than most others. If those of us in Broadmoor were representative of similarly situated people across our nation, an entire generation of people, particularly Black people, were left largely uninformed about the impact of the ballot box.

The challenges of electoral process participation faced by poor and working-class people are numerous and very complex, often reflecting broader social, economic, and political inequities. I speak here about apathy, but there are other challenges—including lack of access—that exacerbate the apathy. These challenges can vary depending on the political system, but some common barriers include time constraints due to work inflexibility, having multiple jobs, lack of information, accessibility and availability of transportation, overreaching voter ID laws, systemic disenfranchisement, cynicism and distrust, social and cultural barriers, lack of resource investments, health concerns, the digital divide, and unnecessary law enforcement presence at the ballot box or other voter intimidation tactics.

The first time I voted was in 1988, during my sophomore or junior year in college. Jesse Jackson was on the ballot and running for President of the United States for the second time. Black people in general were enthusiastic about Jesse Jackson's run for president. He ran more than once, and the support for his candidacy continued to rise over the time frame of his political viability. Black registrations and Black votes increased significantly during this timeframe and are correlated with Jackson running.

He electrified his base, asking them to, "Keep hope alive."

Jackson was only the second Black American to run a nationwide campaign for the presidency, following Shirley Chisholm in 1972. Jackson was more successful than the Chisholm candidacy in terms of votes received and delegates won. His candidacy signaled to minority and Black voters that higher office, even the highest office in the land, should be the north star and goal for Black people.

It is clear that Jesse Jackson's presidential campaigns in the 1980s were instrumental in empowering and motivating Black voters, which emphasizes the importance of coalition-building in American politics and even shifting political discourse. Jackson's campaigns also set the stage for future Black and female candidates to run for and win higher political offices.

Additionally, Jackson helped push the Democratic Party to pay more attention to the concerns of Black voters. His policy positions were not fully adopted, but the sheer force of his campaigns and success in winning delegates pushed the concerns of the Black community to the forefront of Democratic Party platforms and discussions.

But what I remember most about this chapter of life is the ridicule I received for voting for him. Even in light of the great progress he made on behalf of the Black community, some of my White friends in college laughed when they learned I'd voted for him. Like many at the time, they didn't see Jackson as a political option; they only saw him as a preacher and a political caricature. I was so discouraged by this that I didn't return to the ballot box for years.

College began changing my perspective on life from my very first day on campus. Without much warning, indication, or idea of what to expect, college was a shock for me. I realized immediately that I was behind in so many ways—most prevalent was that I lacked exposure to things that seemed common knowledge to people I met, lived with, shared class with, worked with, and talked with.

The knowledge gap between different socioeconomic groups can vary significantly and be expressly exposed on college campuses. Florida State

University was no exception, and I received a front row seat. My lack of access to quality education, exposure, and opportunities made my college experience much more difficult on a day-to-day basis.

Students from higher income socioeconomic families have access at young ages to professional networks and connections that provide elite career exposures and opportunities, mentorships, and valuable information about industries, technologies, travel, internships, and job markets that better prepare them for college. Even their understanding of financial matters, political engagement, art, literature, history, and other cultural aspects can sharpen their perspectives and facilitate conversations and connections in certain social circles. These were all very helpful and common attributes in a traditional college setting that I very much lacked.

As with most college campuses, politics was alive and ever-present at Florida State University. The presence of a political and activist mindset on campuses directly reflects the young intellectuals' interest in changing the world. I immediately gravitated to student government. Other than wanting to join fellow students to change the world, it was also my way of figuring out how to start college from where I had ended high school. That thought alone indicates how naive I was.

Before classes even started in the fall of 1985, I was attending student government meetings and trying to get involved. I remember going to a Black student union information meeting. They were holding elections for committee chairs and some low level, worker bee type positions. My hand went up to run for a position. I was asked to stand, introduce myself, where I was from and why I was qualified to be elected to the position. To be completely honest, I was a total disaster. I was speechless. I didn't know anything about what I was running for. I didn't have a real reason for running other than wanting to be popular again, and fast, so I couldn't find the words to back up my interest.

Floundering, I said, "You should vote for me because I was senior class president in high school and, one day, I will be student body president here at Florida State University."

I lost that election and one other election with the Black Student Union not long after. But I was right about one thing: I did get elected Student Body President a few years later.

Before being elected Student Body President, I spent years in Student Senate and held very active roles in the Student Government Association. Florida State, like most large universities, had political parties that did not necessarily identify as Democrat or Republican. I joined the O.N.L.Y. Party—the Outstanding New Leadership for You Party. Let me tell you, I learned more from this process, this party, and this group of ambitious college kids than I learned in any classroom during my matriculation through undergraduate school.

Over time, I learned many of the things about life and the world that I didn't learn growing up in a poor, Black community. I began feeding off of my fellow student leaders like a sponge. Sadly, I felt ashamed of what I didn't know or understand and took great strides to ensure my ignorance wasn't exposed. I listened a lot. A whole lot.

Despite a strong Black Student Union, there were few Black students involved in overall student government during my time on FSU's campus. Just as they are now, Black students were a minority in school, consistent with the American population overall. When I talked to other Black students about why they didn't engage in the student government, they often cited a lack of confidence that they would make any difference—a bellwether for broader political apathy around the country.

Today, while Black students are still a minority on campus, they are much more active in student government. I am excited and humbled to know that the culture change had a lot to do with people like me showing that it is possible for a Black person to be elected to the highest office on campus, and to perhaps help them believe that their voice can be heard and make a difference for their community.

The first signs of this culture shift began with the elections of homecoming chief and princesses at FSU. We went through several years of Black students elected to one or both of the honorary positions. This effect took longer to impact student government elections, but Black students eventually began to use their block of votes to support minority candidates for student government positions.

The inner workings of real politics —be it University Student Government level or real life American politics—all fit the descriptive old adage of "sausage making." Politics are a complicated reality. Learning how the sausage is really made is a rite of passage for anyone dedicating their life to this work, and it is not without its challenges and hard knock lessons.

As a student at Florida State, I was on the fast track in university politics and the O.N.L.Y. party. My sophomore year, I was elected to the student senate for the second time. As the party continued to have success in student elections for a third cycle, they began to prepare for the next Student Body President race. The internal process of selecting a nominee was very similar to the national political party process, minus a convention.

One O.N.L.Y Party candidate, Todd Middleton, smartly decided he needed the Black votes within the party in order to win the nomination. Todd and his supporters believed if they promised to choose a Black person to run as his Vice Presidential running mate, he could count on Black votes and win. While it would not be the first Black student to run or be elected, it was still a rarity, and a big deal.

I was approached by Todd to serve as his Vice President should he win the O.N.L.Y Party nomination, as no formal selection of Vice President could be made until such time. I gave an exuberant and excited, "Yes," that led to my formal endorsement and a whisper to the Black members of the party about the deal we'd made.

As a Black kid from a low-income family in Riviera Beach, I was beside myself, unable to fathom the possibility that these smart, powerful and amazing people had selected me to join them in leadership at the predominantly White university in one of the largest states in America. I remember racing to my dorm inDeGraff Hall to share the news with my friends and hall mates. A few of us sat in the lobby of the dorm and talked for hours about the process, the issues, and how important this moment was—for me personally, but for Black students in general. This opportunity was special. It was a different time and a moment where these kinds of progressions in the Black community were milestones and pacesetting.

Todd Middleton won the O.N.L.Y Party nomination with overwhelming support from the Black members. I recall the thrill and excitement the night he won, for him and for what it meant for my own elevation and opportunities. I was a poor, Black student. A sophomore from Riviera Beach, Suncoast High School, and Broadmoor apartments. And I was about to run for high office at a major university in Florida.

Overnight, I had become a true leader of the Black members of the party. I believed this opportunity would amplify our movement and elevate our issues and concerns.

As I waited to congratulate our new nominee and party leader, I had a feeling of accomplishment and inclusion. After all, I was an important part of the strategy to ensure this amazing win. I remember my freshman roommate, Tim Jones, who had been impactful in convincing me that I had to accept the deal. He said to me that I had to take the opportunity to elevate beyond the illusion of inclusion and do my part to make it real and make it work.

More on the "illusion of inclusion" later.

As I walked up to Todd and reached out my hand, I said, "Congratulations." I expected him to say, "I could not have done it without you. Thank you for being a part of the team and the victory. Let's talk tomorrow. The work begins now," but he just said, "Thank you," and moved on to the next person in line. It felt very cold and dismissive, unlike the Todd I had become accustomed to talking to over the months of his campaign for the party nomination. Moreover, it was not at all representative of my part in the work, the accomplishment, or the deal. I was immediately worried but kept those feelings hidden, in part because I didn't want to speak my thoughts into existence.

I never heard from Todd.

A week later, at the next O.N.L.Y. Party meeting, I walked up to Todd and asked what the next step would be. He indicated that he and his team had decided to go in a different direction for the Vice President position. He did not give much more of an explanation.

I felt betrayed and very naïve. I made it very clear that this information would not be received well by Black members of the party or by Black students in general. But that no longer seemed to matter to Todd, his inner circle or the party.

There was so much I wanted to say to Todd and other party leaders, but I instantly felt like a foreigner: out of my league and, as Tim Jones would say, under the illusion of inclusion. I didn't realize at the time that this moment would begin to shape my feelings about politics, political parties, and government. And when we talk about political "sausage making," this is still a strong memory that resurfaces for me.

Todd Middleton would go on to lose his election for student body president largely because he was rejected by the Black student voters. He broke his promise but likely did not realize it would have a real impact on the outcome. For the first time in FSU's history, a transfer student won the presidency with an agenda that spoke to the marginalized and the outsiders. In general, Black students felt like the successful campaign and election of "the candidate who beat Todd Middleton" was a win for us, too.

There were other memorable moments of growth and political lessons as well. Lots of inside views of how the "sausage was made," as the old adage goes. The messy and complex nature of making sausage is very similar to politics; just as making sausage involves various ingredients, grinding, mixing, and stuffing, politics in general also entails multiple stakeholders, negotiations, compromises, and often opaque decision-making. Both processes can be messy, can involve behind-the-scenes activities, and the final product may not always reveal the full intricacies of how it came to be. The comparison illustrates the complexities, backroom dealings, and less savory aspects of political maneuvering and reflects the intricacies and sometimes less appealing elements of the political process.

As a freshman student senator slated and elected with the O.N.L.Y. Party, I ran for Pro Tempore and won, only to be shafted—against party policy—by an older, more established student leader. My opponent used backroom deals and some political maneuvering to get around me as the party nominee for President Pro Tempore of the Student Senate. She lost the party nomination but won the overall Senate vote and was seated as Pro Tempore.

MESSY. COMPLEX. REALITY.

History would suggest that an overturn of the party nominee was unprecedented and unlikely. I could not and still can't help but think this was allowed to happen because I am Black and was not a part of the White institution running student government. That aside, this political sausage-making process was painful and left a lasting impression that the rules in politics are conditional and, unfortunately, don't apply to everyone in the same manner.

There is a silver lining in this story, however. Roxanne Schunick, who defeated me for the position, was a great student senator and student leader. We would become close friends after the competition, and I learned so much from her.

While I definitely learned some hard lessons during this time in my life, college also dealt me some political highs. By my senior year in college, I ran and was elected Student Body President at Florida State University. It was a very difficult process and election, but I achieved the goal. I lived up to the promise I'd made to myself and that room of Black students when I stepped foot on campus.

As a Black man, achieving such an audacious goal at a predominantly White institution was not without its reality checks. The worst came the day after I was elected, and it brought me to tears.

I woke up to this shocking phrase spray painted all over campus: *Sean Pittman is a monkey.*

My freshman roommate, Tim Jones, would call this reality check the illusion of inclusion. According to Tim, the illusion of inclusion is defined as "a fallacious belief or assumption that your association with a system, organization, or professional or social group equates acceptance by the mere association." It is the misaligned—or mislabeled—assumption that familiarity affords real access and will transcend prejudices, traditional beliefs, and strong opinions about who you are and your value within the group.

I would be lying if I didn't admit that being a Black student and elected President at a predominately White institution was overwhelming. I certainly felt the illusion of inclusion, only to be harshly reminded that I was on foreign land because of the color of my skin. I have always described this moment as my best day at Florida State, directly followed by my worst day at Florida State. It was also my first time personally feeling disaffected with politics, position, process, governance, and people.

I entered law school at Florida State University not really knowing what to expect or if I would succeed. Law school is the kind of place that changes everyone at least a little. The first week of law school, you learn the two most important lessons for a lawyer to know and understand. First, don't ask a question that you don't know the answer to. Second, as lawyers we don't know everything, but law school will teach you where to *find* everything. I could talk endlessly about law school experiences and lessons that shaped my perspective on life and the law, but for the purposes of this book, I need only share about my Constitutional Law class.

Con Law was more akin to a legal history class, one focused on the fundamental principles by which the government exercises authority. These principles grant specific powers to the government—like the power to tax and spend, separation of powers for each branch of government, and ultimately protecting the rights of individuals and country. We learned and debated about some of the most pivotal moments in American History and American jurisprudence. We covered subjects like the Bill of Rights, Equal Protection, the right to bear arms, Freedom of Speech and Religion and, yes, Voting Rights in America.

In class, we engaged in huge argumentative debates due to the controversial nature of the subject matter, especially around the areas of race, gender, the Second Amendment, and abortion rights. But my most unusual interaction in Con Law would leave me flabbergasted, frustrated, and offended. We were studying the Voting Rights Act of 1965—which dealt with the removal of race-based restrictions on voting Federal law—and a student began to argue that voting was never meant for uneducated people. He argued that only people who are educated, or who can prove some level of awareness and competency, should have the right to vote. In his mind, we could not put the future of our country or political system in the hands of ignorant or unsophisticated people. He essentially said that disenfranchisement was a good practice, and that we needed laws to make sure that only the "right" people were voting.

Though extremely misguided, I believe his sentiment was sincere. He believed and argued that the fate of the country should not be left in the hands of voters who may be apathetic or limited in education, intelligence, or sophistication. As I look back and reflect on that conversation—which, by the way, almost led to a physical altercation, a fact that still bothers me deeply—I can't help but wonder if the sentiment expressed by my classmate is really what we are dealing with now as we witness the passage of voter suppression laws in many states across the United States, expressly making it harder for average and working class people to vote. After all, our country did not begin with everyone having the right to vote. Voting rights began with only people who owned property and were later expanded through the 15th, 19th, 24th and 26th Amendments to the United States Constitution. This combined with the sentiments of my law school classmate begs the question...

Did our forefathers ever really mean for our democracy to be democratic?

When I was weeks away from completing my third year in law school, I was contacted by Governor Lawton Chiles' office and asked to work as a regional director on his re-election campaign: the 1994 Gubernatorial Campaign. I didn't know much about the role, but it was clear it would expose me to very important people in the state and give me a crash course in politics at the highest level. Chiles was adored by Democrats in Florida, and they were the party in control at the time. They called him "Walkin Lawton" because, during his first campaign for U.S. Senate, he decided to walk the state from Century Florida to Key West's most southern point. Chiles' walking strategy worked to increase his name recognition and to create a grassroots campaign effort to win a seemingly unwinnable seat. The strategy is still one of the most iconic campaign tactics in Florida political history to date.

Even so, the decision to work on the Governor's campaign was not an easy one; I would have to defer taking the Florida Bar exam, relocate to Tampa, and hit the ground running for an already contested and close election. Even as a popular and sitting governor, Lawton Chiles had a difficult race ahead. While many statewide campaigns are difficult, Chiles was running against a young, resourceful, and ambitious Jeb Bush. It was a hard-fought campaign, as anyone can imagine, but Chiles ultimately prevailed by approximately 60k votes, or, roughly, one percentage point.

For me, however, the campaign lived up to all my expectations. I met incredible people all over state. I traveled with the governor on many occasions, and some of his friends became my close allies, mentors, and even good friends.

There are two important, poignant memories from my time with Lawton Chiles. The first almost killed me and the second gave me life.

The First—

While on the state plane over the west coast of Florida, we hit some very bad weather. At this point in my life, I had only been on a couple commercial flights, and I certainly had never been on a small, private plane. I was on the plane with Governor Chiles, a couple other staff members, and two FDLE officers who traveled everywhere with the governor. The flight got beyond bumpy. In fact, we were being tossed around the sky. Everyone on board was visibly terrified. The governor kept his cool for as long as he could, but eventually, he too was visibly shaken by the extreme turbulence and unexpected drops in altitude.

I started to think, "Why am I here? I should be studying for that damn bar exam which I pushed off to take this job." I closed my eyes and literally started thinking of dying in a plane crash with the Governor of Florida—I concluded that I would barely get mentioned in the news, and the stories would be all about Chiles and his storied career. With that in mind, l started to pray for traveling grace. I knew I wasn't the only one, but when I opened my eyes and looked across the small plane, I saw Chiles's gigantic blue eyes looking at me, full of the fear of God. In this moment, I no longer saw a powerful governor but just another very scared human in fear of losing his life.

This was an important moment in my young development, because it showed me that, no matter the title or the wealth or skin color, we are all the same when it comes to life and death situations. We all had the same thing in common at that vulnerable moment: wanting to live and survive. Obviously, we lived to tell this story, but that shared moment of humanity would change the way I viewed people and my outlook on life. In fact, it would set the stage for a version of me that was more confident when sharing my thoughts and opinions with others. It would become critically important to my work as a lawyer, my politics, and my life in general. This moment stripped the mysticism associated with successful and powerful people and allowed me to see the humility, humanity, and vulnerabilities that make us all equals.

The Second—

Ironically, the second moment of great impact during the Chiles years and on my life, needed the first moment. I needed to be able to strip successful people down so I could have the confidence to speak truth to power as necessary. As the election cycle was coming to a close, the campaign leadership decided Chiles was not doing as well with senior voters as he needed to beat the impressive and well-funded Jeb Bush. While Jeb's father, George W. Bush, had only served one term as President of the United States and was no longer in the White House at this point, the Bush name still meant serious business. The polls in the Chiles vs. Bush election were showing a dead heat, and the Chiles campaign was in a panic to get Democrats and Independents excited about the race and the sitting governor. The campaign decided to produce a television ad that would speak directly to seniors and motivate Democrats by bringing Rubin Askew and Bob Graham—popular former democratic governors—together for the commercial shoot.

These two legendary public servants were asked to sit around the conference table and respond to general questions about politics and democratic philosophy on important issues facing Florida. It was a lively conversation, as these guys had known each other since school at University of Florida and/or Harvard. They jovially discussed the early days of their individual and collective work in Florida's politics. They spent a lot of the time talking about issues impacting seniors: health care costs, crime prevention, transportation, cost of living, and patterns of work and retirement. Bob Graham and Rubin Askew talked about how important it was for Florida that Chiles was re-elected and how dangerous it would be for Jeb Bush to become governor.

As the youngest person in the room, I was fortunate enough to witness this incredible moment. Most in the room knew these men very well and had relationships with them. With the exception of my boss, Lawton Chiles, I had only seen the others on television and read about them in school. I couldn't believe I was in the same building with them, not to mention the same conference room.

Along with being the youngest, did I also mention I was the only Black person in the room?

When the taping concluded, many in the room began a conversation about polling, money, and efforts to get out the vote. At some point in the conversation, someone made a statement about African American turnout and how difficult it is to get that demographic to the polls. The prevailing sentiment was that shifting dollars to hopefully increase the Black vote was a lost cause. Someone even suggested that to spend any more money to optimize the Black vote was a potential "waste" of resources. "[Black people] don't really have an alternative place to go . . . they can't vote for Republicans because the GOP stances and positions on important issues to Black communities are all wrong..., so the money needs to be used in other persuadable areas and silos where the needle can be actually moved."

Chiles, Graham, and Askew nodded as if they understood the strategy and that the rationale was familiar and sound. But before I knew it, I blurted out, "If you know people will vote for you, why wouldn't you do everything possible to get as many of them as possible to the polls?"

The room went deafeningly quiet. I was pinching myself, trying to figure out if I'd really just blurted out what I was thinking. I looked around nervously and realized that I may have overstayed my welcome—every eye in the room was looking directly at me.

Yup, I'd said what I was thinking.

Askew looked sympathetic, perhaps withholding judgment based on our connection as former student body presidents at Florida State University. Graham reached into his coat pocket, took out one of his infamous mini notepads, and wrote something down; I don't think it was good. Chiles simply stared with blank contemplation.

Before anyone could utter a response, I continued. "You can't take Black voters for granted. You have to spend resources on the ground, with trusted voices, and in Black communities to get us to the polls and work intentionally to increase the numbers of black people registering and voting, especially because 9 out of 10of us will vote for the democratic party. If the party doesn't change this generalized way of thinking about the lack of options available to Black voters, we will slowly but certainly lose the allegiance and support of the Black population."

I didn't convince anyone of anything that day in Tampa, but looking forward to today—where an increasing number of black people are registering and voting outside of the democratic party, my words back then have become somewhat a reality. Especially as it relates to black men in particular. While still overwhelmingly registered as democrats, many are exploring alternative voting choices including growing support for Donald Trump over Joe Biden.

Chiles went on to win his reelection in a close and contentious race by roughly 60k votes, or one percentage point. The Republicans cried foul at his campaign for their last minute robo-calls to seniors that claimed Jeb Bush would take away social security benefits. The late Jim Krog was a genius campaign strategist and he served as chairman of the Chiles campaign. This kind of strategy, even more prevalent today and used by both parties, added to my education on the lengths people and parties will go to for the win.

In 1996, during Chiles' second term, the Republicans took control of the Florida House and Senate, and began solidifying their takeover and power in the state. Amplified by a long term strategy to pass laws under the umbrella of election reform that were designed to suppress votes and strengthen their positions.

Several factors led to the Republicans' majority in Florida. First, reapportionment led by the Democrats in 1990. The Black Democrats, experiencing internal frustrations, wanted to draw more minority-leaning seats in Florida. The White Democrats assuaged by drawing several super Black districts. The result of this process would weaken White districts, leaving close margins between Republican and Democratic voters. Current incumbencies made the close lines workable . . . in theory. What was not contemplated was what came next in Florida: term limitations and record migration to Florida.

When incumbent terms were over, Republicans had a chance to win these very close seats, and they did. While more Black candidates were elected to seats in the legislature as planned, the close non-Black districts went to Republicans. Since then, the number of Democrats in the House and Senate has continued to drop. In 1996, the Florida Legislature became the first of any of the former Confederacy states to come under complete Republican control. In addition, once Jeb Bush was elected as governor in 1998, the full Republican agenda began.

During these transformative years, super lobbyist Art Collins recommended I work with State Representative Willie Logan. This was an amazing opportunity for me to learn and work with the likes of people like Logan, Collins, Lobbyist John Thomas, Speaker John Thrasher, Attorney Ron L. Book, and former-house-member-turned-lobbyist Mike Abrams. Prior to my employment as a Staff Attorney at the Florida House, Logan gained national prominence after being removed as the democratic minority leader for failing to raise adequate dollars and because some White Democrats feared they could not win the state house back with a liberal Black leader at the helm.

Representative Logan went on to proclaim himself a free agent and convinced then-Speaker of the House, John Thrasher, to hire me in the Florida House as a Staff Attorney. From that position, I had a front row seat to view the strains of adjustment Democrats faced as the new minority party. Today, Republicans have grown their support in Florida, created super majorities in both chambers of the legislature, and have now significantly surpassed Democrats in registrations.

Another factor related to the Republican takeover in Florida is due to record migration to Florida. In recent years, Florida has experienced a significant influx of residents from the Midwest and the North, continuing its long-standing trend as a prime destination for relocation within the United States. The pandemic accelerated this trend, as remote work became more feasible, allowing people to live in desirable locations without the need to be near their workplaces. According to Census estimates, New York lost nearly 217,000 people to domestic migration from July 2022 to July 2023 and nearly 882,000 total since April 2020. New Jersey, Pennsylvania, Illinois, Wisconsin, and Michigan also lost thousands of residents in that time. At the same time, Florida gained more than 194,000 people from other states from 2022 to 2023, the largest influx in the nation.[1]

Since April 2020, nearly 819,000 people have moved to Florida from within the U.S.

While the movement has been fueled by people seeking the state's warmer climate, lower cost of living (compared to some northern states), and favorable tax policies, another factor has contributed to this evident migration: politics. Many Republican voters have seen the policies and philosophies of Governor DeSantis and have chosen to relocate here from Democrat-leaning states such as New York and California.

The impact of this Republican relocation has been enormous. Democrats in the past held a registration lead in the state, but Republicans overtook them in 2021 and have continued expanding the margin. During the 2000 Presidential Election, Democrats held a 379,086 voter lead over Republicans, but as of December 2023, the GOP has flipped that deficit—there are now 779,701 more Republican voters than Democrats.

STEPPING INTO THE RING

The culmination of these experiences from my youth left a burning desire to make a difference, and I decided to run for office myself. In 1996, shortly after my work with Governor Chiles' campaign, I declared my candidacy for County commission in Leon County. Leon County is home to Tallahassee, Florida's capital city.

As I look through the rear-view mirror, I can admit I was completely naïve in my effort to get elected. I ran that campaign as if I was running for Student Body President at Florida State. I didn't spend enough intentional effort seeking out Tallahassee's political insiders. I wasn't completely without counsel, however. I had people like Jon Ausman, who offered extremely helpful advice, in my corner. I remember him taking me to a neighborhood and teaching me how to canvass. Watching him work a door was like what I imagine Bobby Bowden was like in the living room with the family of a 5-star recruit: charismatic and relatable in every situation. Scott Maddox, my law school classmate and friend, was already in office as city commissioner and assisted with obtaining walking lists, etc. Other great minds that converged on my behalf included law school buddies, Mark Dunbar and Charlie Dudley, radio personality Joe Bullard, neighbors and friends Donald West, Pieter Swart, Jaya Davillier, and Attorneys John Marks and Tim Meenan.

Unfortunately, the wrong person was making decisions. Me.

My campaign manager was the recently deceased Ken Fowler; my best friend. Between me, Ken, Rufus Davis, and our visiting fraternity brother from Gainesville, Steve Baker, we knew just enough to be dangerous. Ken Fowler knew even less about campaigns than I did, but he was dependable and a great motivator of people. We ran a fun campaign that was, unfortunately, reliant on two very difficult demographics: the Black vote and students.

The student vote was tough. Pre-Andrew Gillum—who was one of the youngest elected officials in all the state of Florida—few students were ready or organized to show up in numbers and make a statement in the local community. We motivated our campaign workers by feeding them chicken wings and emphasizing that having a young person on the county commission to represent them was an attractive proposition. But in the end, it was very difficult to get the ever-migrating student population to register to vote or to change their registrations to Leon County from their home counties.

Additionally, there was continuous rain on election day. Rain or bad weather typically keeps people home—especially Black people, because they largely live in districts where there are few polling places and very long lines to vote.

When votes were counted, I landed in second in a six-person primary but lost the general election by 126 votes. If six more people per precinct had defied the rain and the long lines and shown up to vote in my favor, I would have won the race and perhaps had an entirely different trajectory and career. So, clearly, my sentiment that every vote counts is a personal one. Maybe if early voting existed during my time as a candidate, I could have made up the difference. Clearly it was a very close race, a majority of the district wanted our campaign to win, but the precincts with the less-diverse population showed up in force and the precincts most favorable to my candidacy did not.

EVERY VOTE MATTERS!

This experience on my own campaign, as well as my work with Willie Logan and Governor Chiles, made me realize a calling of managing or consulting campaigns in Tallahassee and across the state. Over the years, I and my ESP Media team built a reputation for developing and managing winning campaigns for underdog candidates. To this point, The Tallahassee Democrat said, "Pittman has a knack for knocking off incumbents, especially those who show any sign of weakness."[2]

John Marks for Mayor was my coming out party. John, a downtown Tallahassee Attorney and Former Public Service Commission Chairman, was well known by elite Tallahassee. However, he was fairly unknown across the overall community. He ran against several other candidates for Mayor, including two longtime sitting city commissioners, John Paul Bailey and Steve Meisenburg.

When Marks entered the race, no one but me and my assistant campaign coordinator Alan Williams thought he could win. But he had all the right stuff to penetrate the noise, provided he could raise money and build strong name recognition to get his message out. John checked a lot of boxes and was capable of raising early dollars and giving his own money to compete. While not the only Black person in the race, John was able to communicate to more Black people. His wife Jane Marks was able to organize a ground effort of women she called the Red Coats that created a swell of energy around the campaign that Marks opponents could not emulate or compete with. Marks' campaign television ads, created by Gary Yordon and the Zachary Group, was the first of its kind in Tallahassee, making Marks the new shiny object.

His campaign was impacted by the two sitting commissioners pulling votes from the same silo, which split that support in half, allowing John to secure the win and ultimately serve three terms as Mayor of Tallahassee. Mayor Marks would keep Alan Williams close to him as one of his two aides in the Mayor's office. John's influence and mentorship on Alan was significant. Alan would go on to win a seat in the Florida House of Representatives representing his home District. My bond of trust with Alan continued as he allowed me to lead his campaign effort and further my campaign consultant career.

I went on to run, advise or consult other highly visible local, state, and national races including: Brian Desloge for Leon County Commission, Willie Adams for Mayor of Albany, Georgia, Alan Williams for Florida State Representative, Nick Maddox for County Commission, Walt McNeil for Leon County Sheriff, Rocky Hanna for Leon County Superintendent, Andrew Gillum for Tallahassee Mayor, Jimmy Morales for Mayor of Miami-Dade, Oliver Gilbert for Miami Gardens City Council, Danielle Cohen Higgins for Dade County Commission, Ramon Alexander for State Representative, Trey Traviesa for State Representative, Cedrick Thomas for Riviera Beach City Council and State Representative, Willie Logan for U.S. Senate, Kasim Reed for Mayor of Atlanta, Chris Smith for State Senate, Perry Thurston for State Senate, Oscar Braynon for State Representative, Darryl Jones for Leon County School Board, Mack Bernard for Florida State Senate, Rufus Davis for Mayor of Camilla, Georgia, Marcus Nicolas for Leon County School Board, Gwen Graham for Congress, Andrew Gillum for Governor of Florida, Loranne Ausley for State Senate, and Christian Caban for Leon County Commission.

Most of these races were with candidates that initially were not favored to win the race. Most of these candidates didn't have the same amount of money or name recognition as their opponents. In having to win the hard way so many times, I learned that every single vote counts. Every opportunity to engage with voters or potential voters can make the difference in a close race. We didn't win them all, but we won a super majority of them.

The most solidifying example of "every vote counts" is shown in my work with Gubernatorial Candidate Andrew Gillum in the 2018 Florida Governor's race. Republican Ron DeSantis defeated Gillum by 33,383 votes in a state of twenty million people—that's 0.4% of the vote total. There were 6,096 voting precincts during the 2018 Florida Gubernatorial race. If one were to do the math, Gillum would have won this race if six more people had shown up to cast their ballots on his behalf at each precinct. If six more people at each precinct's location got off the sidelines and had their voices heard, history would be different.[3]

Under DeSantis, Florida passed laws to limit abortions and a woman's right to make decisions about her own body, stripped two Black-access congressional seats from their communities – including lifelong public servant Congressman Al Lawson - passed laws like "election integrity"—which created a police force designed to intimidate formerly incarcerated people from showing up to the polls—and enacted a curriculum to erase the evil of slavery, horrors of Reconstruction, and the devastation of Jim Crow Laws from our education system. They even went so far as to advocate for adding historical fiction that slaves benefited from the trades they mastered. The DeSantis campaign also banned certain books related to Black history, continuing their campaign of revising the past. Under DeSantis, Florida passed laws to eliminate Diversity, Equity, and Inclusion programs and remove positions from Florida's Colleges and Universities. It also attempted legislation aimed specifically to harm the Walt Disney Corporation for speaking out against the infamous "Don't Say Gay" legislation that was used in support of LGBTQ communities.

For anyone upset about these outcomes or wishing for a different direction in Florida, I will pose this question, how many people did not care to vote in the 2018 gubernatorial race? Picture them in your mind, and you can blame them—or thank them—for the success of the aforementioned issues. For anyone who is truly upset about the results above, keep in mind that only six more people per precinct could have led to a different outcome.

It's that simple: every single vote matters and counts. One vote can change many lives.

And as of this moment, only one party has been successful in convincing their constituencies of that.

WHY THIS BOOK?

After the Civil Rights Act of 1964 and the Voting Rights Act of 1965, the Black community felt pride to exercise the right to vote. After all, people had been jailed and had died for our right to vote in the United States. Black people in the United States of America are used to being uncomfortable to stand up for what is right, but even still, during events like the Montgomery Bus Boycott, Black people walked miles to work for months in solidarity and to stand up against the injustice and inequity of segregation in the public transportation system—specifically, forcing Black people to sit in the back of the bus.

We have not seen the same kind of sacrifice since, yet it has certainly been warranted especially as it relates to voting in America. We still live in a time where politicians continue to de-prioritize issues impacting Black families, Black businesses, and Black life in America. The responsibility to rectify or mitigate should not just be in the hands or interests of Black people alone. Forcing the Black community to fend for itself is a one-dimensional, single-minded response to a very complicated reality. If we truly are the Land of the Free and we believe everyone has a right to express themselves through the ballot box, this country must address the issues that run contrary to the freedom we espouse. We must all work to make the electoral process more inclusive and accessible for all. To do that, we need comprehensive policy changes that attack the symptoms and systems—not just the results—by prioritizing improving education, healthcare, economic opportunities, and criminal justice reforms.

This book will give us tools to speak directly, and hopefully effectively, to the non-voter—the one who doesn't believe their vote matters or even technically counts. The one who feels they can never affect the outcome of elections, changes in society, or even their own way of life. *Disaffected!* and its research on close elections and issues that impact our everyday lives will prove just the opposite: that your vote would have mattered in the past and still matters today. This message is important because recent history illustrates that every election is, indeed, the election of a lifetime.

Diving deep into the issues of disenfranchisement, redistricting, gerrymandering, and voter suppression in American politics today, *Disaffected!* examines how access to voting has been denied to many through restrictive laws and lack of resources, which has resulted in an apathy towards the electoral process. This book also looks at the effect of the aforementioned issues on election outcomes and, ultimately, our democracy as a whole.

Disaffected! engages the reader by using real-world examples and research-based evidence alongside my personal human experiences. We explore topics such as the alienation of American voters from government, why millions are denied the right to vote despite living in a democracy, meaningful engagement with Black and young voters, voting rights, close elections, culture wars in politics, non-partisan elections, and the disillusionment of the economically challenged cult following Trump.

Recent efforts to suppress the vote in some parts of our country remind us that the struggle for full enfranchisement is not a relic of history but a living, breathing challenge we are facing today. Let's be clear—when we put up barriers to vote, we chip away at the very foundation of our democracy.

This book strives to motivate, educate, and inspire the non-voter and voter alike, while also providing readers with an understanding of how every vote matters and how, when we work together, we create change and can better ensure that everyone's voice is welcomed and heard at the ballot box.

America has always been defined by a shared belief in the promise of this great nation, and it's in the act of voting that we make that promise real for every American. I encourage the reader to actively dive into *Disaffected!* and its contents. I hope it inspires you to work and advocate in the spaces that matter to you. I hope it illustrates to uninterested persons that voting matters and that choosing not to vote has real consequences for life, death, and quality of life.

I hope this book leads us all to continue wanting to work towards a more equitable future, one where our voices are heard and are representative of the real values of our country and all Americans.

The framers of our country created a democracy that initially allowed only property owners to vote. Disaffected will leave us with an ultimate question to be debated and answered: was democracy in America ever meant to be democratic?

To the young people who are skeptical about the political process, to the hard-working families wondering if their voices matter or if their vote will even make a difference, and to the communities of color who have felt the weight of history, I say this—

Your vote matters. Your voice matters.
What you do with that knowledge, is up to you!

*Close Only Counts
in Horseshoes and Hand Grenades*

We hear it repeatedly: "Your vote counts!"

But to many potential voters, it's just a slogan, something that political parties and politicians say to get themselves elected. People believe their votes don't matter for two primary reasons:

In a big election, there are thousands—and sometimes millions—of people casting their ballots, so how can one vote make a difference either way? This is a seductive emotional argument because there are many, many free elections where it's true that one vote wouldn't have mattered. But this misses the point. We live in a free democracy where the alternative to casting your one vote is to cast zero votes, ever. In many nations around the world, citizens get no vote, or they get a phony vote—the dubious privilege of casting their "vote" for the one party or candidate who has rigged the election and is guaranteed to win. This is why it's imperative that, to preserve our democracy—an ongoing experiment in rational self-governing—every eligible voter should participate.

The second reason we become disillusioned with voting is when we believe it doesn't matter who wins. We've all heard otherwise intelligent people say, "Who cares if a Democrat or a Republican wins? They're both the same. It's not a real choice."

That may have been true years ago . . . on certain issues. But since the election of Ronald Reagan to the U.S. presidency in 1980, anyone who thinks the Republican Party and the Democratic Party are equivalent is not living in the real world. The stark contrast between Republicans and Democrats was made more vivid in 2016 with the election of Donald Trump to the presidency. Critics believe the Trump Republican Party, with an ever-growing evangelical Christian and White nationalism bend, seeks to engineer a new era of minority rule.

Make no mistake about it; the policies of both parties can, and do, make a real difference in our daily lives.

In the recent past, we have seen some very close elections, and the consequences of such narrowly elected officials—who are so diametrically opposed to their opponents—have been devastating to many.

As these hair-thin victories prove, any citizen who forgoes their legal right to vote is giving up a chance to change not only their own wellbeing, but the wellbeing of many around them and generations to come. We should all ask ourselves, "What might have happened if the election had swung the other way? How might have the losing candidate's values and beliefs alter the lives of their constituents for the better? Based on the outcome of bringing out just a few more voters, what parts of history could have been changed?"

While we'll never know for certain, we can extrapolate from what we've learned about close-race candidates and the actions they took, as well as how the absence of those actions and the presence of good candidates in those seats could have made a real difference in people's lives.

1

THE ONES THAT GOT AWAY

Elections Won/Lost by a Hair

STATE RACE

Virginia House of Delegates, 2017

David Yancey

vs.

Shelly Simonds

Tied at

11,608

votes each

On January 24, 2018, Yancey won by a random lottery.[4]

THE CANDIDATES

David Yancey, a Republican, was 45 at the time of the 2017 Virginia House of Delegates race. At that time, he was the incumbent representative from the 94th District to the Virginia House of Delegates. He was first elected to that position in 2011. Before entering politics, he owned a property investment firm and was involved in a commercial fishing operation.

Shelly Simonds, a Democrat, was 49 at the time of the 2017 election. Simonds had previously run against Yancey for the same seat in 2015, as well. Though she lost both the 2015 and 2017 races, she would go on to beat Yancey in 2019 after redistricting changed the composition of the district. Before running for state office, she was an elementary school Spanish teacher. She also served on the local school board in Newport News, Virginia.

In the 2017 House of Delegates, Republicans had a narrow majority (51-49). Had Simonds been elected and the incumbent Yancey dismissed, the House of Delegates would have had a 50-50 split.

THE RESULT

As with the other races at this time, this was another example how thoroughly—but evenly—divided the United States had become. Ultimately, this race was decided by random draw from a bowl that ended up allowing Republicans to retain the majority.

None of the legislation David Yancey sponsored was particularly controversial. Most of it dealt with small changes to gun laws and court sentencing.

Shelly Simonds ran on a campaign that addressed multiple issues, including jobs, education, the environment, and civil rights. For example, given the influx of parental responsibilities that come after a parent's death, families require jobs that provide more flexibility. Additionally, expanding the public transportation system reduces the overall carbon footprint, which helps the environment. Despite these campaign policies, however, after voting concluded in 2017, Simonds tied with her Republican opponent and lost by a random draw.

In the 2019 rematch, Simonds soundly defeated Yancey with 11,556 votes to Yancey's 8,069 votes. Since Simonds took office, one can see some of the differences in their priorities, shown through legislation and appropriation requests. Much of the legislation and appropriations she has sponsored are based on her stated priorities and include bills providing increased public transportation, prison reform measures, and protections for renters.

STATE RACE

Kentucky House of Representatives, District 13, 2018

Jim Glenn

vs.

D.J. Johnson

6,319 VOTES

vs.

6,318 VOTES

One vote differential.[5]

THE CANDIDATES

Jim Glenn, a Democrat, was 70 years old at the time of the election. Prior to holding office, he was a community college instructor and adjunct professor. He ended up losing his seat back to D.J. Johnson in the 2020 Election.

D.J. Johnson, a Republican, was 66 at the time of the 2018 Election. Johnson was the incumbent in the race, having served from 2006 to 2018. Prior to his time in office, Johnson served in the army and was the general manager at a local car wash in Owensboro, KY. He ran as a Christian conservative with ties to the business community and local Baptist Church.

THE RESULT

Republicans held the Kentucky House, Senate, and governorship in 2018. Like several of the other races here, the voting apathy of conservatives after Trump's win in 2016 likely contributed to Glenn's narrow, one-vote victory, since the seat swung back on the next election.

No real consequential or controversial bills passed during Glenn's time in office. Since Kentucky was solidly red, Johnson's votes might have been different, but it would not have changed outcomes. But this election illustrates the fact that even in a district with over 12,000 votes cast, a candidate can win by *just one vote.*

GOVERNOR RACE

Governor of Washington, 2004

Dino Rossi

vs.

Christine Gregoire

1,373,361 VOTES

vs.

1,373,228 VOTES

133 vote differential.[6]

THE CANDIDATES

Christine Gregoire, a Democrat, is a former State Attorney General—the first and only female in this position. She is also the second female governor of Washington. She was 58 at the time of election. Prior to her position as State Attorney General, she was the Director of the Washington State Department of Ecology.

Dino Rossi, a Republican, served in the Washington State Senate from 1997 until 2003. He was 46 at the time of the governor's race. He served two more rounds in the Washington State Senate from July 2012 to November 2012 and again from December 2016 to November 2017. He ran again for Governor of Washington in 2008 and lost again against Gregoire. Her margin of victory was 53.2% to 46.8%.

At the time of the election, Democrats held the Washington House, Senate, and governorship—as they had for a long time.

THE RESULT

The race garnered national attention due to its legal complexities and remarkably close finish, making it one of the closest in U.S. election history. Initially, Republican Dino Rossi was declared the winner after an automated count and subsequent automated recount. However, a hand recount put Democrat Christine Gregoire ahead by just 133 votes.

Despite Gregoire being sworn in as governor on January 12, 2005, Rossi did not concede and called for a re-vote, citing election integrity concerns. The Republican Party's lawsuit in the Chelan County Superior Court was dismissed for lack of evidence of electoral sabotage. Rossi eventually conceded on June 6, 2005. Gregoire was re-elected in a 2008 rematch against Rossi.

The 2004 election was the first in Washington to use a party-line primary system. Both Gregoire and Rossi ran as centrists with a focus on job creation and economic growth. Despite controversy over her past sorority membership, Gregoire defeated Ron Sims and other minor candidates in the Democratic primary on September 14, 2004, winning over 60% of the vote. Sims focused on tax reform and a statewide income tax but dropped the issue after initial clashes with Gregoire.

In the general election, Gregoire advocated for increased state funding for embryonic stem cell research and promised to reform state government. The November 2, 2004 election saw Gregoire initially trailing Rossi by 261 votes, but then, a machine recount reduced Rossi's lead to 42 votes, and a Democratic-funded hand recount gave Gregoire a ten-vote lead. The State Supreme Court then allowed additional ballots from King County, increasing her lead to 130 votes, which was certified as a 129-vote lead after one ballot was disqualified.

Republicans claimed that ineligible votes—including those from felons and deceased individuals—were counted, but on June 6, 2005, Judge John E. Bridges ruled that there was insufficient evidence to overturn the election. Gregoire's campaign received substantial out-of-state donations, particularly from trial lawyers involved in the 1998 tobacco settlement, and nearly half of her 2004 campaign contributions came from out of state.

GOVERNOR RACE

Governor of Georgia, 2018

Brian Kemp

vs.

Stacey Abrams

1,978,408 VOTES

vs.

1,923,685 VOTES

54,723 vote differential.[7]

THE CANDIDATES

Stacey Abrams, a Democrat, is a former Georgia House of Representatives member who served from 2007 to 2017. At the time of the governor's race, she was 44 years old. She was also well-known as a lawyer and Voting Rights activist, and many have credited her with later efforts of getting out the vote for Joe Biden, Raphael Warnock, and Jon Ossoff in 2020.

Brian Kemp, a Republican, served as the Georgia Secretary of State from 2010 to 2018. He was 55 years old at the time of the 2018 election. He is also known for owning several businesses in the agricultural and real estate industries.

At the time of the election, Republicans held the Georgia House, Senate, and governorship, as they had since 2005.

THE RESULT

The changing demographics in the state of Georgia, particularly those in the suburbs of Atlanta, have been largely credited with narrowing the gap for Abrams. However, the influence of the Trump White House and divisions that formed among Republicans cannot be overlooked. In 2018, Kemp was fully aligned with and endorsed by President Trump, putting him clearly in the then-president's camp.

Brian Kemp's time in office has been marked by the passage of several controversial, conservative measures. On April 13, 2022, Governor Kemp signed legislation that makes it legal for Georgian gun owners to carry a concealed handgun in public without a license from the state. Kemp's signature on Senate Bill 319 etched "constitutional carry" into law.

"People don't have to carry if they don't want to," the governor said. "But this is a constitutional authority that people have, and they certainly shouldn't have a piece of paper from the government to be able to legally carry a weapon."

Before the law went into effect, if a gun owner wanted to carry a concealed firearm in public, they had to file an application for a weapons-carry license, a paper that would allow anyone to carry a concealed weapon except where it was expressly forbidden—ironically, one of those forbidden locations is the Georgia State House.

Kemp is also a radical on abortion denial. On May 6, 2019, he signed a bill that prohibited abortions once a heartbeat was detected. In July 2020, U.S. District Judge Steve Jones ruled against the state in a lawsuit filed by abortion providers and an advocacy group, but this was the beginning of a wave of actions by conservatives that helped lead to the overturning of Roe v. Wade.

Amazingly, a January 2022 *Atlanta Journal-Constitution* poll indicated that seven in ten Georgia voters said they were opposed to legislation that allows people to carry concealed weapons without a license, and more than two-thirds opposed overturning Roe v. Wade, the decades-old U.S. Supreme Court decision that guaranteed the right to an abortion.

So much for the "will of the people."

In a strange twist of fate after the 2020 presidential election, Kemp fell out of favor with then-President Trump over his refusal to decertify the election results, which put him on the opposite side of the conservative divide he'd been on in 2018. In a state like Georgia, Kemp's conservative policies had little impact on him. However, his response to Donald Trump's requests to decertify the 2020 election did have an impact. As a result, Trump endorsed his 2022 primary opponent, David Perdue. Kemp went on to handily win the primary, but tensions related to the Trump-Kemp fall out remain.

If Stacy Abrams had been elected Governor in 2018, it is certain that laws on abortion and weapons would have been vetoed—if they even gained enough support to move through the full legislative process. Because the legislature in Georgia is solidly Republican, it is hard to say how much of her agenda Abrams would have been able to get passed. However, she likely would have acted as a buffer, stopping or stalling bills like the abortion ban that was passed under Kemp.

If the "Heartbeat Bill" had not been challenged and overruled in the courts, there would have been a ban preventing abortions after six weeks, which is before some women even know they are pregnant. Additionally, many women face financial constraints or are coerced by their abusers because of a pregnancy. Now that Roe v. Wade has been overturned, women must seek protection at the state level. As a progressive Democrat, had Stacy Abrams been elected, she would have done everything she could to protect women's rights.

In the 2022 gubernatorial election, Abrams ran against the incumbent Kemp once again. Brian Kemp won re-election to a second term, defeating Democratic nominee Stacey Abrams in this rematch. Unlike the 2018 race, Kemp handily won the election, even though Democrats were hopeful that a last minute surge for Abrams would occur.

Stacey Abrams ran on a more progressive platform than most Democrats in Georgia. She talked extensively about her plans to expand Medicaid under the Affordable Care Act. She also used her identity and experience as a Black woman to set her apart. She campaigned about quality public education, a cleaner environment, and voting rights, "Because voting is a fundamental right, not a privilege for the wealthy few."

GOVERNOR RACE

Governor of Florida, 2018

Ron DeSantis

vs.

Andrew Gillum

4,076,186 VOTES

vs.

4,043,723 VOTES

32,463 vote differential.[8]

THE CANDIDATES

Ron DeSantis, a Republican, was elected governor in 2018 at the age of 40. Before his term, he served in the U.S. House of Representatives from 2013 to 2018. He also served in the U.S. Navy and, before entering politics, he was appointed by the U.S. Department of Justice to serve as the special assistant U.S. attorney in the Middle District of Florida.

Andrew Gillum, a Democrat, was 39 years old during the 2018 election. Before running for governor, he served on the Tallahassee City Commission from 2003 to 2014 and as the mayor of Tallahassee from 2014 to 2018. He was first elected to office at the age of 23.

Republicans controlled both the House and Senate in Florida in 2018, as they had since 1999.

THE RESULT

Before Florida went for Donald Trump in 2016, it was long considered a swing state. In fact, many analysts believe that, if Al Gore had not conceded in 2000, he would have won Florida. Perceived cracks in the conservative base and Trump's divisive influence seemed to make the 2018 race more competitive for Gillum. However, Democrats missed opportunities to turn out votes in South Florida gave DeSantis the edge in the end. Following the 2018 election, Florida has taken a sharp right turn and can no longer be considered a swing state. It is now a red one.

Despite winning by a razor-thin margin, DeSantis quickly moved to position himself as the radical right's alternative to Donald Trump. It became clear that he was not interested in governing Florida from a centrist, what's-best-for-the-most position, but instead in a manner more appealing to Republican primary voters in the 2024 presidential election.

Ron DeSantis has been a lightning rod of controversy for both his comments and policies during his time in office. From his moves to lift COVID-19 restrictions early to his anti-critical race theory rhetoric, DeSantis has pushed his administration and state further to the right. Of his controversial policies though, the widely nicknamed, "Don't Say Gay" bill has gotten the most attention and pushback. This bill—which prohibits teachers from discussing gender identity and sexual orientation—even drew criticism from the Disney Company, which rarely comments publicly on state policy. The law presents a clear risk to children who are LGBTQIA+ or who belong to families with same-gender or transgender parents.

Aside from policy, the 2018 gubernatorial race also had another lasting impact: the judiciary. Since DeSantis won the race for governor, he has appointed five of the seven judges to the Florida Supreme Court. During his administration, the DeSantis-created court has weighed in on many hot-button issues, including an alleged racially gerrymandered congressional map, an undocumented migrant relocation program, a six-week abortion ban, DEI prohibitions, books being removed in classrooms, and other controversial topics.

Andrew Gillum ran on a platform similar to Stacey Abrams in Georgia. He talked extensively about the $15 minimum wage and advocated for raising the corporate tax rate for educational funding from the current 5.5% to 7.75%. He sought to expand Medicaid to cover more people who didn't have access to health care. He was endorsed by Bernie Sanders, called for the impeachment of Donald Trump, and supported the removal of Confederate monuments. Unlike every Republican politician in Florida, he accepted the scientific consensus on climate change and warned that climate change causes sea level rise, something which will have disastrous effects for Florida; most of the state is only a few feet above sea level, and the state's highest point is a little rise called Britton Hill, just 345 feet above mean sea level. Gillum opposed President Trump's rash decision to withdraw from the Paris Agreement and said that, as Florida governor, he would work with other states in a state-based climate alliance.

His campaign policies were rational and progressive. Had he been elected, the "Don't Say Gay" bill would likely not have had the necessary support within the legislature to pass and it would have certainly have been vetoed if it did. Additionally, the makeup of Florida's Supreme Court would be unrecognizable compared to today's body. Governor Gillum would never have taken the rights of thousands of women across Florida, would never have rolled back decades of progress in equality and important progress toward understanding race and diversity, and never would have allowed LGBTQIA+ rights to be politicized in our school system.

As with Stacey Abrams, if Gillum had been elected, the differences would likely have been seen more in what he didn't pass. Because of the solidly Republican legislature, his agenda would have had to fight an uphill battle in Tallahassee. But as a Democratic governor, he would have dampened the radical excesses of the far-right conservatives and muted the "culture wars" that have become the bread and butter of today's MAGA Republicans. The support of then-President Donald Trump for DeSantis gave Republicans the edge they needed to win the election.

Compared to what we see today, a Governor Gillum would have drastically altered the electoral dynamics of Florida and prevented the "red wave" witnessed in 2020. One can reasonably assume that a Democratic governor would have excited the base, driven up voter turnout and registrations, and encouraged national donors to invest in the state these past few years. Instead, we witnessed a Republican onslaught in Florida following the 2018 gubernatorial race, one that shifted the state from a purple battleground to a red, conservative-dominated state.

GOVERNOR RACE

Governor of Arizona, 2022

Katie Hobbs

vs.

Kari Lake

1,287,891 VOTES

vs.

1,270,774 VOTES

17,117 vote differential.[9]

THE CANDIDATES

Katie Hobbs, a Democrat, made history as the first social worker elected governor of an American state and Arizona's fifth female governor. At 53 years old during her gubernatorial campaign, she previously served as Arizona's secretary of state from 2019 to 2023 and was a member of the Arizona State Legislature from 2011 to 2019.

Kari Lake, a Republican and former television news anchor, is currently running as a candidate in the 2024 United States Senate election in Arizona. She also contested as the Republican nominee in the 2022 Arizona gubernatorial election, where she was also 53 years old. In 2021, she declared her candidacy for governor and secured the Republican nomination with the endorsement of former President Donald Trump.

At the time of the election, a Republican was Governor, as they had been since 2006.

THE RESULT

In this closely watched 2022 Arizona gubernatorial election, Katie Hobbs, Arizona's secretary of state, secured victory with approximately 50.32% of the vote, winning by about 17,000 votes out of over 2.5 million cast. Her win marked a significant milestone as she became the first Democrat elected governor of Arizona since Janet Napolitano in 2006. The race, characterized by its narrow margin and intense competition, underscored Arizona's status as a battleground state in national politics.

Hobbs's campaign focused on protecting reproductive health rights and enhancing border security through state support for law enforcement, resonating with voters across the political spectrum. Her victory in a state where Republicans had previously dominated gubernatorial elections highlighted shifting political dynamics.

Her opponent, Kari Lake, who was endorsed by Donald Trump, refused to concede after the election and pursued a post-election lawsuit aimed at overturning the results. Despite her efforts, the majority of Lake's lawsuit was rejected across all levels of Arizona's state courts, with the remaining claims dismissed in May 2023.

The 2022 election also featured a diverse field of candidates from various political backgrounds, reflecting the state's complex electorate and the broad range of issues at stake. The outcome solidified Hobbs's position as Arizona's governor-elect, setting the stage for her administration's approach to governance and policy in the coming years.

CONGRESS

U.S. House of Representatives, Iowa, 2nd District, 2020

Mariannette Miller-Meeks

vs.

Rita Hart

196,964 VOTES

vs.

196,958 VOTES

6 vote differential.[10]

THE CANDIDATES

Mariannette Miller-Meeks, a Republican, was 64 years old when she first ran to represent the state of Iowa in the U.S. House of Representatives in 2020. Before running for office, she served in the military as a nurse and then as a physician for almost 24 years. Later, she went into private practice as an ophthalmologist.

Rita Hart, a Democrat, was 64 years old at the time of the election. Prior to her run, she served as the State Senator from the 49th District of Iowa from 2013 to 2019. She is co-owner of her family farm and was a teacher.

THE RESULT

Hart contested the election results, but on March 31, 2021, she formally conceded the election to the Republican, Miller-Meeks. In 2020, the Democrats retained control of the U.S. House of Representatives. The election was largely seen as a referendum on then-President Donald Trump's fitness for office, but it did not always transfer down the ballot. Since there was no incumbent in this particular race, it is harder to draw a line between Trump and the tightness of this race.

Many of the bills Miller-Meeks has introduced have not gained a lot of traction. However, it is notable that she has voted against all the major Democratic initiatives, including against the impeachment of Donald Trump and against Build Back Better.

On March 11, 2021, Miller-Meeks voted against the Background Checks Expansion Act, which would have prohibited firearm transfers between private parties unless a licensed gun dealer, manufacturer, or importer first took possession of the firearm to conduct a background check. The bill subsequently died in the Senate.

On August 12, 2022, Miller-Meeks voted against the Inflation Reduction Act of 2022. This landmark bill—whose provisions are supported by a majority of Americans—caps and lowers seniors' drug costs while sparing about 13 million low- and middle-income Americans from increases in their insurance premiums that otherwise would occur annually. It also secures the largest-ever investment to tackle climate change, dedicating roughly $370 billion to curbing harmful emissions and promoting green technology. For the first time, it levies a minimum tax on the many billion-dollar corporations that now pay nothing to the U.S. government. That, along with funding for the Internal Revenue Service to pursue tax cheats and another new tax on stock buyback, was expected to cover the costs of the bill and is expected to reduce the federal deficit by about $300 billion. Yet Miller-Meeks voted against all of these rational, necessary measures designed to help working families.

Rita Hart ran on a slate of issues, with many positions in line with the Democratic Party's platform. She wanted to build on the Affordable Care Act, allow students to refinance their debts, and tax corporations and the ultra-wealthy at a higher rate. It is safe to say that she would have been on board with more of the Democratic Party's priorities and likely would have voted for the impeachment of Donald Trump—however, her vote would not have changed the outcome of the Senate trial.

Rita Hart's campaign policies aligned with other Democratic candidates, but most importantly, she wanted to tackle the student debt crippling many American families. Her idea was to present the concept of, at least, refinancing student loans to reduce the amount owed. Many families cannot invest in homes or other consumer goods because of student loans. She is also for taxing the ultra-wealthy and the corporations at a higher rate.

CONGRESS

United States Senate, Minnesota, 2008

Al Franken

vs.

Norm Coleman

1,212,629 VOTES

vs.

1,212,317 VOTES

312 vote differential.[11]

THE CANDIDATES

Norm Coleman, a former Democrat (Democratic-Farmer-Labor Party)-turned-Republican, was 59 years old at the time of the 2008 election. He served as the mayor of St. Paul, Minnesota from 1993 to 2001 and was the incumbent, having served as the U.S. Senator from Minnesota from 2002 to 2008. Prior to his time in office, he was the chief prosecutor for the Attorney General's Office for the State of Minnesota.

Norm Coleman's platform was very much in line with George W. Bush and other Republicans of the time. He was a strong supporter of the War on Terror, and he saw himself as a "reformer" throughout his career, one who cut spending and taxes.

Al Franken, a Democrat (Democratic-Farmer-Labor Party), was 57 at the time of the election. Franken was well-known as a comedian, radio show host, and entertainer. He used his platform as a liberal activist until deciding to run for office himself in 2007.

THE RESULT

In 2008, enthusiasm for Barack Obama and the looming Great Recession brought voters to the polls, giving him a convincing win over Republican candidate John McCain and buoying down-ballot nominees. With the Franken/Coleman seat in the balance, this left Democrats within one seat of a super majority in the Senate.

It is safe to assume that Coleman would have been the polar opposite of Franken in terms of votes. With the massive loss of seats in the midterm election of 2010, every Democratic vote became more crucial.

During Franken's time in office, no legislation was more important to most Americans than the Affordable Care Act, also known as Obamacare. This law remains controversial in heavily Republican areas, has seen repeated repeal attempts by Republican lawmakers, and has been frequently challenged by Republican governors.

The Affordable Care Act (ACA) presented an opportunity to ensure that all Americans had access to health insurance through the Marketplace. Many progressive Democratic candidates, including Gillum (FL) and Abrams (GA), ran with policies to expand the ACA and provide further benefits through Medicaid in the Marketplace for the American people. However, these policies likely would have been considered a challenge for these candidates, as their respective states had strong Republican legislatures during the terms they served.

THE WHITE HOUSE

President of the United States, 2000

George W. Bush

vs.

Al Gore

50,456,002 VOTES

vs.

50,999,897 VOTES

543,895 vote differential

271 ELECTORAL COLLEGE VOTES

vs.

266 ELECTORAL COLLEGE VOTES

5 vote differential.[12]

THE CANDIDATES

George W. Bush, a Republican, was the former governor of Texas (from 1995 to 2000). His father, George H. W. Bush, served one term as the President of the United States from 1989 to 1992. At the time of the election in 2000, George W. Bush was 54 years old. Before his time as governor, he served in the Texas Air National Guard and worked in the oil industry.

Al Gore, a Democrat, was the former vice president of the United States for eight years (1992 to 2000) under Bill Clinton. Gore was 52 years old at the time of the 2000 election. Before his time as V.P., he was the U.S. representative from Tennessee (1977 to 1985) and served as their senator from 1985 to 1993. He has trained as a lawyer, served in the military during the Vietnam War, and is a renowned climate activist.

At the time of the election, Bill Clinton (a Democrat) had served two terms as president and could not seek re-election. The House and Senate were both controlled by the Republican Party.

THE RESULT

The scandal of President Clinton's affair with intern Monica Lewinski—as well as pent-up Republican resentment for Clinton's various sex scandals (including the Paula Jones accusation in 1994)—set the tone for the Republicans' "compassionate conservative" and "family values" messaging. This message resonated with moderates, especially in suburban areas. Clinton's perceived tendency toward infidelity contributed to an exceptionally tight race between Al Gore—Clinton's vice president—and Bush—respected for his family values over his intellect or policy prowess.

Al Gore campaigned on economic, social, and environmental issues, and looked to safeguard social safety net programs like Medicare. The relatively stable position of the U.S., both diplomatically and economically, left no key issue to dominate policy and debate discussions. Critics of Gore's campaign say he neglected to draw enough of a distinction between himself and Bush, leading to the popular vote win and electoral college loss.

We also know that every election is an appeal to the emotions of the voters. The reality is that Bush projected an image of folksy, comfortable confidence, while Al Gore—despite being on the popular side of the issues—projected an image of stiff, intellectual wonkiness.

Even so, Al Gore won the popular vote by a margin of over half a million votes. But due to the vagaries of our Electoral College system, which gives low-population Republican states an advantage, Bush needed only to capture Florida's 25 electoral votes to win the presidency. Ultimately, highly publicized and controversial voting recounts in Florida led to the Supreme Court ruling in favor of Bush—and of the election.

As the year 2001 unfolded, Bush's residency in the White House seemed to be progressing as any typical presidency would be expected to—that is, until the morning of September 11th. In response to the 9/11 terrorist attack on the United States, Bush declared the "War on Terror," and authorized a military operation in Afghanistan with the goal of eliminating the home base of Al-Qaeda, the organization behind the attack.

Then, for reasons that are still unclear but highly speculated, President Bush set his sights on the nation of Iraq, which was then ruled by the dictator, Saddam Hussein. Critics say it's possible that Bush really believed Saddam was a threat or, possibly, the president just wanted to "finish the job" that his father, President George H.W. Bush had wisely avoided after liberating Kuwait. The justification for going to war against Iraq was the claimed presence of "weapons of mass destruction" (WMDs) in Iraq. This assertion, made by the president himself, was never verified and was later admitted, under oath by General Colin Powell, as a fabrication. Also of note is that there were theories that George W. Bush invaded Iraq in retaliation for an attempted assassination of his father —an action which may have shaped the then-president's animosity toward Saddam Hussein. However, history now suggests that this so-called plot was a Kuwait fabrication.

This is where the voters and non-voters need to understand that when a president is elected, *so too is a vice president.* In the election of 2000, we got Dick Cheney. Most citizens were not aware—or didn't care—that, from 1995 to 2000, Cheney served as CEO of Halliburton, an oil-services company that also provided construction and military support services. This was the kind of company that could reap huge profits from a war. Cheney had deep financial ties to Halliburton; even while serving as vice president, he received as much as $1 million a year in deferred compensation from the company.

Cheney served as Secretary of Defense under George H.W. Bush, and he authorized payment of $3.9 million to the Halliburton subsidiary, Brown & Root (now KBR), to deliver a report on how private companies could help the U.S. Army during this time. Then, Brown & Root won a five-year contract to provide logistics for the U.S. Army Corp of Engineers all over the globe. In 1995, when Cheney (now out of the government) became CEO, Halliburton became a top Pentagon contractor. According to the Center for Public Integrity, the company raked in at least $3.8 billion in federal contracts and taxpayer-insured loans. This was the man the American people elected to serve as an experienced vice president to a relatively inexperienced president.

Over the course of the Iraq War—which cost U.S. taxpayers an estimated $2 trillion and caused nearly 7,000 American military deaths—Halliburton subsidiary, KBR, pocketed an estimated $39.5 billion in Iraq-related contracts; many of the deals were given without any bidding from competing firms, such as the $568-million contract renewal in 2010 to provide housing, meals, water, and bathroom services to soldiers. As reported by Bloomberg, that particular sweetheart deal led to a Justice Department lawsuit over alleged kickbacks.

Few Americans understood the authority Dick Cheney wielded over the White House. In 2011, the longtime aide and Chief of Staff to Secretary of State Colin Powell, Col. Lawrence Wilkerson, told ABC News, "[Cheney] wanted desperately to be President of the United States . . . he knew the Texas governor was not steeped in anything but baseball, so he knew he was going to be president and I think he got his dream. He was president for all practical purposes for the first term of the Bush administration." [13]

In contrast, consider Al Gore's running mate, the late Senator Joe Lieberman. While on many positions he was to the right of most Democrats, even his political opponents always characterized him as a decent and honorable man. If Al Gore and Joe Lieberman had won the presidential election of 2000, it's almost certain they would have taken military action in Afghanistan and not Iraq, because that's where Al-Qaeda was hiding. They likely would not have invaded Iraq, simply because there was never any rational reason to do so.

Bush's invasion of Iraq was a gift to Iran. Iraq and Iran were bitter military enemies, having fought a bloody war from 1980 to 1988. Saddam may have been a ruthless dictator, but he kept Iran's mullahs in check. With the collapse of Iraq's government in 2003, however, Iran was poised to step in.

As Jeremy Scahill and Murtaza Hussain wrote in *The Intercept* in 2019, "The chaos unleashed by the U.S. invasion allowed Iran to gain a level of influence in Iraq that was unfathomable during the reign of Saddam. Secret documents from the Iranian Ministry of Intelligence and Security, obtained by The Intercept, give an unprecedented picture of how deeply present-day Iraq is under Iranian influence." Thanks to the War on Terror, Iran, once an implacable adversary of Iraq, soon became its big brother.

Domestically, there were several important and controversial pieces of legislation passed during Bush's presidency, as well. The most well-known is the Patriot Act, which increased the powers of government surveillance and prosecution in pursuit of those who might commit terrorist acts. There was some resistance to this at the time, but in the atmosphere after 9/11, most Americans wanted to do whatever it took to keep the country safe. In hindsight, this act allowed provisions that were later addressed as overreaching, leading to the House refusing to renew the act in 2019. It expired in 2020.

Bush's record on the environment cannot compare to what Gore, an early and outspoken champion of the environment, would have done for the nation. On January 20, 2001—his very first day in office—Bush issued an executive order blocking regulations to reduce arsenic in drinking water, sulfur in diesel fuel, and raw sewage releases. As a member of a Texas oil-drilling family, Bush rejected any mandatory national limits on the greenhouse gas carbon dioxide emitted by vehicles running on fossil fuels—as well as coal-fired power plants—throughout his presidency. This put the United States on a path contrary to many other major-developed countries that had joined the carbon-capping Kyoto Protocol and were working to fight climate change. In his last months as president, Bush promulgated a long list of so-called environmental "midnight regulations" that overwhelmingly favored industry over human health and welfare.

"[The Bush administration officials] have been relentlessly opposed to clean energy solutions, climate change responsibility, and basic safeguards for air and water and land across all of their agencies over eight long years," said John Walke of the Natural Resources Defense Council to Reuters.

On Monday, August 29, 2005, Hurricane Katrina slammed into New Orleans and surrounding areas. This destructive Category 5 hurricane caused over 1,800 fatalities and $125 billion in damage, becoming the costliest tropical cyclone on record. The disaster was fully televised and, in growing horror, Americans across the country watched the images of people standing on rooftops waving their arms and pleading for help as the flood waters inundated their communities. Thousands of desperate people—mostly African American and low-income individuals—packed the Superdome, begging for aid in their time of need.

Simultaneously, President Bush was just 500 miles to the west, relaxing at his 1,600-acre Prairie Chapel Ranch in Crawford, Texas. According to a tabulation kept by CBS News, on the day Katrina made landfall, Bush had been on holiday there for 27 days. While it's true that everyone deserves a holiday, especially the most powerful person in the free world, Bush's staff did not want to disturb the president with bad news about the disaster on the Gulf Coast and only told him two days later—or so it was reported. After they told him, he flew back to Washington on August 31st.

Bush's blunders were then punctuated by his tour of the Katrina destruction with FEMA director, Michael Brown. During this time, the president cheerfully announced, "Brownie, you're doing a heck of a job." In reality, and in the court of public opinion, Brownie was doing a terrible job—and as an extension, so was Bush.

While we have no idea if President Gore would have acted more quickly to mobilize the resources of the federal government, we can estimate that his propensity to intensely follow environmental disasters would have led him to be, at a minimum, alert and ready to act at the moment of Katrina's impact.

If this moment in time impacted or affected you, and you are one of those who decided not to vote, your decision mattered—especially in states like Florida where the battle for electoral votes was close.

As for what Gore could have done differently to win in 2000—an election where he was the early favorite—theories abound. But this observation by Gerald M. Pomper in *Political Science Quarterly* is very much on point: "Turnout may have made the difference in the election results. Nationally, there was only a small increase over the last election in voter participation to 51% of all adults, although there were considerable increases in the most contested states, particularly by Union household members and African Americans. Usually, the preferences of nonvoters are not much different from those who actually cast ballots, but the 2000 election may have been an exception to that rule. CBS News polls immediately before and after the balloting suggested that, if every citizen *had actually voted*, both the popular and electoral votes would have led to an overwhelming Gore victory. The nonvoters, however, had less information about the election and less confidence in the political system, and they were less likely to see a difference between the parties."

Because Bush had adopted the mantle of a "wartime president" as 2004 approached, there was little significant opposition to his war effort. To win a second term, he easily rolled over Vietnam War veteran, John Kerry, in part by smearing Kerry's exemplary service record. But Katrina and the onset of what was to become the Great Recession damaged the Republican national brand and, in 2008, the Democrats fielded a brilliant young politician named Barack Obama as the party's candidate. He campaigned tirelessly, and the voters loved him and his wife Michelle, and he won decisively over his United States Senator colleague, John McCain.

THE WHITE HOUSE

President of the United States, 2016

Donald Trump

vs.

Hillary Clinton

62,985,106 VOTES

vs.

65,853,625 VOTES

2,868,519 *vote differential*

304 ELECTORAL COLLEGE VOTES

vs.

227 ELECTORAL COLLEGE VOTES

77 electoral vote differential.[14]

THE RESULT

This election, fresh in the collective mind of Americans, offers an even more dramatic demonstration of the challenges with the electoral college voting system. Hillary Clinton received 2.86 million more votes than Donald Trump—and yet decisively lost the electoral college by 77 votes.

To say there would have been vastly different outcomes for the nation under a Clinton presidency is an understatement. Clinton campaigned on a policy platform steeped in her deep, thirty plus years of governmental experience. Her proposals tended to be incremental in nature and they largely followed the policies set forth during the Obama presidency.

"She is well informed, has thought through and wrestled with a large number of issues and policy ideas, but arguably at the expense of having a big-picture orientation," said Mark Peterson, a public policy professor at the University of California, Los Angeles.

Her top campaign promises included free in-state tuition at public colleges for families making under $125,000 per year, expansive immigration reform that included a clear path to citizenship, infrastructure investment, and protecting Obamas' Affordable Care Act. From there, she focused on low-hanging fruit such as campaign finance reform, equal pay legislation and minimum wage increases, and additional tax reform that would place more burden on the wealthy. Her most controversial stances regarded unfair trade practices, such as the Trans-Pacific Partnership, and expanded background checks for gun sales.

In contrast to Clinton's 41-page research narrative, Trump's policy statements were a mere seven pages and were mostly filled with fluffy political buzzwords and unactionable promises, more akin to a high school class president promising a vending machine in every classroom than anything else.

But far more disheartening than campaign rhetoric is the very real dismantling of our democracy that took place under the Trump Presidency. According to David Rothkopf,

"The Taliban, all of them together, plus every Al Qaeda fighter in the world, do not pose the threat to the United States that Trump or Trumpist extremists do." And the Department of Homeland Security agrees, at least to the extent that Trump extremists fall into the official White supremacy category. Even Trump-appointed FBI director Christopher Wray has lamented that, while the threat posed by foreign terrorists is real, it has been vastly overstated in the wake of 9/11—in truth, the growing and more pressing threat is now domestic extremists.

One of the greatest threats by these extremists, outside of blatant violence, is the growing hostility to Democracy, and not just to Democrats. In his discussions with grassroots Republicans in the election-denial stronghold of Arizona, New York Times reporter, Robert Draper, found that the old John Birch Society battle cry—that America is "a republic, not a democracy"—is on many tongues:

> What is different now is the use of "democracy" as a kind of shorthand and even a slur for Democrats themselves, for the left and all the positions espoused by the left, for hordes of would-be but surely unqualified or even illegal voters who are fundamentally anti-American and must be opposed and stopped at all costs. That anti-democracy and anti-"democracy" sentiment, repeatedly voiced over the course of my travels through Arizona, is distinct from anything I have encountered in over two decades of covering conservative politics. [15]

Whether one would go so far as to say Trump endorses these extremists, it is indisputable that he has emboldened them and ushered in, at a minimum, a tolerance of acts that actively undermine democracy in America. The coup attempt on January 6th and the propagation of the Big Lie are examples of this. The efforts to directly repress or change votes are examples of this. The self-serving rhetoric of doubt around the COVID-19 pandemic is an example of this, one that cost thousands of people their lives. No terror group could ever hope to achieve such a level of damage.

Frightening to many, the Make America Great Again (MAGA) movement has now seeped deep into the Conservative psyche and has taken a life of its own. This sentiment is echoed by a Trump spokesman, Taylor Budowich: "The MAGA movement is the largest and most powerful political movement in modern American history, and it continues to be uniquely positioned to win major electoral victories because of President Trump, whose popularity and influence are unparalleled."[16]

While one might discount this grandiosity, there is no question that the movement has left a permanent mark on modern politics and on our civil society. A 2021 survey of approximately 300 Trump supporters found significant, disparaging alignments around race, immigration, and gender. They also strongly believed in complete delusions, such as "Antifa was responsible for the Capitol Riots" and "COVID-19 was a bio-weapon from China."[17]

DEMOCRACY FOR ALL

Whether we look at local elections or the national stage, the consequences for inaction are immense. During each and every election, candidates put their personal lives on display to win us over with rhetoric and promises of a better life under their leadership. There was once a time we could depend on candidates to represent the values of the people who put their trust in them, but that sentiment is now hard to authenticate.

Today, when some candidates ask, "Will you support me?" they are not asking to be a voice for us but rather, they are asking for blind faith that they will not become selfish, power-hungry dictators. As a society, we must continue to comb through the empty promises and elect candidates that innately mirror our values—candidates not bought by high-worth donors and powerful party insiders.

We must come together, as a group, as an electorate, to uphold the democracy and civil society we value. It is only through our diligent acts of voting at every opportunity that we'll rid our political offices of those who no longer stand for American values—of those who no longer stand for us.

SECTION

2

State of the Country
Uncovering Systemic Discrimination

While my passions run deep, I know they are not enough to inspire others to stand in the arena with me. So, I instead set out to dive deeper into the issues that matter and the places where policy intersects real life, the places where discrimination and systematic racism have been hiding for decades, and the places where, unfortunately, it is now not hiding at all.

This section begins with a historical perspective on voter supression before moving to the foundational issue of redistricting for free and fair elections. Next, we attempt to draw attention to those patterns with seven key issue areas: voting laws, redistricting, environmental justice, fair housing, transportation, the criminal justice and prison systems. While we will only be skimming the surface, these examples illustrate an important point, and while the seven issues may seem to be distinct from one another on the surface, in truth, they are intertwined like the roots of an aspen forest; where we find one, we will find a trail of breadcrumbs leading to political actors whose power was built on the back of discrimination.

The similar thread running through so many of the topics here is fear—fear of change, fear of losing power, and fear of being left behind. Before all the rhetoric that permeates today's society, there was a fear of change underlying American society, particularly in peripheral communities. This fear is felt strongest by the lower income White population residing particularly in the Midwest, who feel like they are losing opportunities and that the American Dream is no longer available to them. And yet, this country was literally founded on slavery and the repression of the Black population. A great deal of the wealth and opportunity that White people have experienced and still enjoy today was founded on the backs of enslaved people. They, quite literally, physically built most of the country and were pivotal to the economic structure.

While negative in its content, this section is not meant to point fingers or dissuade anyone from action. Rather, it is meant to inspire us to let our voices be heard so that our government can become truly reflective of the people it represents. It's important to the purpose of this book for the reader to see these issues on display in their true, raw nature to understand the magnitude of how these issues impact each and every one of us and can articulate who we are as a country. The raw nature of these issues will illustrate how the decisions being made by people who are elected have a direct impact on our lives. These issues will also show that voting is indeed a matter of life and death.

In recent years, there has been an uptick in the recognition of just how deep discrimination runs in our country. Very few can dispute the fact that it exists, but our ability to acknowledge its pervasive nature is still fledgling. We tend to isolate events as individualist rather than seeing their deeper patterns.

2

VOTING LAWS/RIGHTS, REDISTRICTING, AND GERRYMANDERING

There is no single issue most pressing on the Black community, but there is one obstacle whose solution is most elusive: voting rights.

There is no shortage of voting rights laws and amendments in America. The constitutional amendments affecting voting rights include the 15th, 19th, 24th, and 26th amendments. Federal voting rights laws include the Civil Rights Act of 1870 (amended in 1957, 1960, and 1964), the Voting Rights Act of 1965 (amended in 2013), the Voting Accessibility for the Elderly and Handicapped Act of 1984, the Uniformed and Overseas Citizens Absentee Voting Act of 1986, the National Voter Registration Act of 1993, the Help America Vote Act of 2002 (created U.S. Election Assistance Commission), and the Military and Overseas Voting Empowerment Act of 2009. [18]

The process and pitfalls of redefining political districts, particularly after reapportionment in the United States House of Representatives, has been studied extensively since the early 1900s. Until 1844, the House of Representatives only added seats to accommodate changes. However, as the country industrialized and populations shifted, the role of districts and how well each voter was represented became more important. When the number of House seats was capped in 1911, it also caused some districts, especially in the South, to stop reapportioning. By the 1920s, this led to large disparities between the size of districts, which was particularly disadvantageous for members of historically underrepresented groups.

In the 1960s, large redistricting efforts caught the attention of academic researchers who examined the larger phenomenon, its implications, and whether computers—a fairly new technology—might be a solution. In 1962, the Supreme

Court even weighed in on what redistricting meant for the idea of representation under the law. From political scientists to lawmakers and geographers, the debate over what physical and population characteristics comprise a fair district continues to occur on several fronts.

As scholars took time to reflect on the debates and legal changes of the 1960s, they began to gather data and understand the effects of redistricting based on race and on issues of district competitiveness. The consequences of the manipulation of districts, commonly referred to as gerrymandering, not only reduced the influence of competing political parties but also of new politicians who could've unseated incumbents. Reflecting the sentiment of the 1970s, Morris P. Fiorina notes that, "Congressmen are not merely passive reactors to a changing electoral climate. In no small part, they have helped to change that climate." [19]

Even with this knowledge, very little has changed in the way lawmakers approach redistricting over the last 40 years. In the 1980s, the Supreme Court intervened again in Karcher v. Daggett. The Court reaffirmed that redistricting must be done with population equality in mind. This furthered debates on the implications of the 1982 Voting Rights Act extension for redistricting and the efforts some lawmakers took to work around it. But 10 years later, ahead of the 1990 Census and 1992 redistricting, evidence of continued gerrymandering led to searches for better ways to redistrict and avoid gerrymandering, including using mathematical models and Geographic Information Systems (or GIS).

Moving into the 2000s, data shows that redistricting continues to happen based on the preferences of the party in power, but it may not have the intended effect. Research finds that even though biased redistricting efforts have stifled competition and given a slight advantage to Republicans, this multi-generational push has not had a great impact at the national level. But there are still many unanswered questions about the effects at subnational levels because, in large part, the idea of a "fair district" has never been fully defined or nationally agreed upon. States vary in who has the authority to draw new districts and most rely on their legislators; a smaller number rely on redistricting commissions or some combination of the two. Research by the National Conference of State Legislatures shows how the differences in requirements and procedures between states also adds to the challenge of drawing districts. This is especially true of the treatment of incumbents, who some states protect from running against each other, while others do not.

As the United States approached the 2022 midterm elections, the reapportionment from a controversial 2020 Census roll-out and a lack of concrete criteria meant lawsuits in multiple states, some that even delayed some primaries. With tight margins for Democrats in the House and Senate,

Republicans narrowly won the House due to their over-performance in the nation's four largest states: Texas, Florida, and the traditionally Democratic New York and California. While speculatory in nature, the effects of gerrymandering are likely to have played a role in these tight races. The added general sense that the Conservative-leaning Supreme Court has weakened provisions of the Voting Rights Act relating to redistricting and race makes the general stagnation in redistricting policy and progress even more troubling.

Most recently, on March 7, 2021—the 56th anniversary of Bloody Sunday—President Biden signed an Executive Order on Promoting Access to Voting, directing an all-of- government effort to promote information about the voting process as well as further the ability of all eligible Americans to participate in our democracy. The order urges Congress to pass the Freedom to Vote Act and the John Lewis Voting Rights Advancement Act, engage local Tribal leaders and Native communities to increase access to polls and registration, have U.S. postal services add routes on Tribal lands, and ensure that language assistance is provided to Native voters in relevant jurisdictions. Numerous federal agencies have already begun to enact changes. [20]

And yet, despite all these provisions, overcoming voting obstacles continues to be a challenge for millions of Americans.

In her book, The Voting Rights War: The NAACP and the Ongoing Struggle for Justice, Author Gloria Browne-Marshall brilliantly recounts 100 years of the National Association for the Advancement of Colored People (NAACP)'s history, starting from the organization's birth in 1909. [21]

Since its founding, the NAACP has fought viciously to end African American voter disenfranchisement in the United States. It has, however, been engaged in more than a mere struggle. Through the years, "the NAACP has fought longer for voting rights, brought more voting rights cases, and lost more members to violence than any other civil rights organization; it has been a war".

Today, more than 100 years later, significant advancements have been achieved, yet the issue of voting rights in the United States persists. In the early twentieth century for example, "White political leaders boasted about disenfranchising Black voters, and Ku Klux Klan members could shoot a Black voter in cold blood on the courthouse steps in broad daylight; now, legislatures quietly disenfranchise voters of color, and the criminal justice system incarcerates Blacks disproportionately", which disqualifies former inmates from participating in the electoral process without the difficult and cumbersome exercise of having their rights restored.

The Voting Rights Act of 1965, which guaranteed the African American citizens' right to vote, was largely a result of the NAACP's policy of protest.

The organization, along with other civil rights groups, was at the forefront of marches in Alabama, which spurred the government into action. In March 1965, the NAACP members "led a peaceful march protesting the denial of their right to protest for voting rights", only to face the violence of a White supremacist mob in an event that became known as the 'Bloody Sunday.' "Reporters and a television camera captured Alabama's all-White state trooper, some on horseback, wildly attacking Black men, women, and children with night-sticks and tear gas". Only after this incident, when people were horrified by the wave of violence, "on March 15, before the third attempt to march in Selma, President Johnson presented his demands for a voting rights law to both houses of Congress". The section 2 of what became known as the Voting Rights Act affirmed that "no voting qualification or prerequisite to voting, or standard, practice, or procedure shall be imposed or applied by any state or political subdivision to deny or abridge the right of any citizen of the United States to vote on account of race or color". Section 5, on the other hand, required "pre-clearance of districting plans affecting racial minorities; the act covered specific states and counties that had a history of discriminating against African Americans". Finally, while "the Voting Rights Act had not included a provision prohibiting poll taxes, [it] had directed the Attorney General to challenge their use".

Eventually, the states' right to administer poll taxes and literacy tests was revoked, then later challenged in the Supreme Court, which decided to uphold the federal legislation. These poll taxes and literacy tests were meant to discriminate against those who—as my law school classmate said back in Con Law class—were not meant to participate or be a part of making decisions for the wellbeing of our country or who should have a seat at the table. Proof that he was right!

CONTINUED REPRESSION

In the years since Donald Trump became president, there has been a continued effort to whittle down the votes from the Black and other underserved populations. As of October 2021, 19 states have enacted 33 separate laws that enforce greater restrictions in voting procedures, particularly for felons, people with disabilities, and those who choose to vote by mail. The pendulum has started to swing, however. As of October 2023, while 14 states have enacted 17 restrictive laws—all of which are in place for the 2024 general elections and that mostly target those who vote by mail—23 states have enacted 47 expansive laws, highlighted by comprehensive pro-voter legislation in Colorado, Michigan, and New York. [22]

The strictest laws are found in Georgia, Iowa, Kansas, Florida, and Texas, and they impose ludicrous criminal charges for innocuous actions such as handing out water or snacks to voters waiting in line at the polls.

In 2018, Florida voters approved the Amendment 4 ballot measure by a two-thirds margin, restoring voting rights to more than 1.4 million felons who have completed their sentences. However, the 2019 Florida Legislature, in a move that defied the will of the people, passed a law that put sharp restrictions on the passed ballot initiative. This law requires felons to pay fines, fees, and restitution before regaining their right to vote, effectively eliminating three-quarters of a million people who would have been eligible under Amendment 4.[23]

While implementing voter restoration amendment 4 has been controversial since its passage, there may be a light at the end of the tunnel. In May 2024, the Florida Rights Restoration Coalition dropped a federal lawsuit challenging how Florida passed a 2018 constitutional amendment to restore the voting rights of felons who have completed their sentences.

The decision came following an announcement from the state saying they intend to hold a rule-development workshop to update the process for felons to seek what are known as advisory opinions about their voting eligibility. Confusion about eligibility stems from a controversial 2019 law that Gov. Ron DeSantis and the Republican-controlled Legislature approved to carry out the constitutional amendment, which said voting rights would be restored "upon completion of all terms of their sentence including parole or probation."

Since its passage, more than two dozen people have been arrested for voting illegally. Many of the arrested people maintained that they were convicted felons who believed they were eligible to vote and were provided voter registration cards by elections officials.

Keeping in line with the theme of election integrity, the Florida Legislature passed a law creating a new election fraud investigative unit. A priority of Governor DeSantis, this police unit includes fifteen staff members who lead election fraud investigations and ten police officers who investigate election crimes. In January 2024, the election unit claims to have received over 1,300 complaints of election misdeeds over the past year.

However, this new unit has come under fire for those it has chosen to prosecute. In its first significant action shortly after being created, the office assisted law enforcement in mainly conducting early morning raids that resulted in the arrests of 20 former felons – just days before the August 2022 primary elections –for having illegally voted two years earlier. Most of those arrested were Black and had received government voter identification cards and were later dismissed or resulted in plea deals with no jail time.

These former felons included Ms. Marsha Ervin of Tallahassee, a 69-year-old woman arrested at her home at 3 A.M. for illegally voting in the 2020 and 2022 elections. Marsha Ervin had successfully registered to vote and was sent a government-issued registration card even though she was still on probation for felony charges and had not regained her voting rights. Following the police raiding her home and arresting her for voter fraud, the charges were dropped.[24]

This new law enforcement entity has been criticized as a suppressive unit that costs taxpayers millions of dollars annually. And it's a perception that is likely not far from the truth. The Florida legislature also considered measures that would prohibit voters with disabilities from casting a vote, expand restrictions on third-party voter registration, mail voting, drop boxes, and activities while voting, such as handing out water to voters waiting in lines at the ballot box.[25]

As of this writing, the Freedom to Vote Act and the John Lewis Voting Rights Act are the only national movements to thwart such state restrictions. Following both bills' failure to pass as standalone pieces of legislation, the bills were combined as an omnibus package in 2022. However, this combined bill failed to pass in 2023 after falling short of the 60 votes needed to invoke cloture in the Senate, a vote to exempt the bill from the Senate filibuster rules also failed.

But the news is not all bad. At least 25 states enacted 62 laws with provisions that expand voting access, including methods like automatic voter registration. In Florida, Federal Judge Walker struck down the aforementioned Senate Bill 90 as a bill that violates Section 2 of the Voting Rights Act of 1965 as well as the first and the fourteenth amendments to the United States Constitution. Florida now needs pre-clearance to enact any law concerning drop boxes or line relief without permission from the court.[26]

In Minnesota, Democratic Senator Amy Klobuchar introduced a bill to address voter registration and voting access, election integrity and security, redistricting, and campus finance to expand voter registration and limit purging of voter rolls. Unfortunately, expansion efforts like this tend to be in places where voter access is already a priority.[27]

In her seminal work, Our Time is Now: Power, Purpose, and the Fight for a Fair America, Stacey Abrams opens with a story of her grandmother who, during the Civil Rights movement "had faced the menacing growls of the massive dogs used to control protesting crowds, and she had been violently sprayed by the water hoses used to remind Blacks of their place; she'd gathered up the bail money to free her teenage son from jail when he got arrested registering voters; at one point, the local police were calling her regularly to interrogate her about the protest actions of her children".[28]

Today, nearly sixty years after the passing of the Voting Rights Act—which guaranteed the freedom to vote to all citizens—" would-be voters continue to turn away; their fear is again and again made real by stories of neighbors denied provisional ballots or lines that wind around city blocks because voting machines lack electrical cords". As a result, the voices of marginalized communities do not reach offices of power, further aggravating their already sub par living standards.

Abrams believes the threat of voter disenfranchisement in the United States is two-fold. First, while the United States Constitution guarantees its freedoms to all citizens, in reality, there is often a lack of implementation and enforceability. Through decades, people in marginalized communities fought for and achieved their right to cast a ballot: "people of color through the Fifteenth Amendment, women in the Nineteenth Amendment, and young voters in the Twenty-Sixth Amendment; but each of those amendments contained a loophole for suppression: leaving implementation to the states, particularly the ones most hostile to inclusion".

Second, the oppressed have become disillusioned with the system. Those who grapple with the -isms on a daily basis are less likely to vote. "They have come to expect suppression from the opposition and inaction from the winners; worse, the candidates who should engage them are afraid to reach out; campaigns typically decide to hunt elsewhere for votes" —remember Broadmoor?

Abrams goes on to outline many strategies of modern voter disenfranchisement including registration, access, ballot counting, and infrastructure. I find the most egregious of these to be voter registration and access.

VOTER REGISTRATION

For most Americans, the issue of voter registration never crosses their minds. Those "with a history of easy participation often take for granted the civic system's accessibility and relative ease; in 17 states plus the District of Columbia, voter registration occurs automatically, typically through the state's Department of Motor Vehicles; in almost every other state, registration when you get your license is an option". For minorities, on the other hand, voter registration can turn into a real battle. Because so many of them are unable to register, their issues rarely enter the political agenda of candidates in local and federal elections. In 2013 in Georgia for example, "more than 800,000 eligible people of color were not registered to vote, thousands of them in the most economically depressed parts of the state; so, they could never elect legislators and executives to put their needs first".

Multiple threats to minority voter registration remain in Southern states of the United States. Lack of transparency in state governments leaves rule violations hard, if not impossible, to prove. In 2014, for example, Stacey Abrams'

"New Georgia Project collected more than 86,000 registration forms; for each applicant, they went a step further and secured their permission to retain a copy of their form; in the end, nearly 40,000 of the applications disappeared from the process of registration". When questioned on those forms, the governor's office simply "claimed that the forms didn't exist, despite the evidence to the contrary".

Couple this with states' attempts to make it harder for third-party registration offices, which are largely used by minorities, to operate. For instance, "following the 2008 election, Florida Republicans targeted the process of voter registration, creating one of the nation's strictest laws for third-party registration; the law, which set tight restrictions, including a forty-eight-hour clock for turning in forms and a $50 penalty per form, had the desired effect of blunting registration efforts". As a result, "the New York Times found that 81,471 fewer voters registered in the period following the law's adoption than in the same period four years earlier; given that Florida statewide elections are often decided by fewer than 25,000 votes, the narrowing of the electorate matters".

While Florida has put voting restrictions in place for those eligible to cast a ballot, the legislature also passed restrictions on third-party organizations that traditionally have been active in voter registration efforts. Under the law passed in 2023, non-citizens and persons convicted of certain felonies are forbidden from "handling or collecting" voter registration applications ("felony and non-citizen volunteer restrictions"). Voter registration organizations are also required to re-register with the Division of Elections for every general election cycle. As part of the process, these organizations must list the names and addresses of every team member assisting with voter registration. Each listed member must not have been convicted of a specified felony or offense. These organizations could potentially be fined $50,000 per individual who was convicted of an applicable felony that is collecting or handling voter registration applications on its behalf.

The effects of these restrictions have been stark. In 2021 and 2022, the Leon County Supervisor of Elections Office, Mark Early, reported receiving approximately 10,000 voter registration applications. Since last year, that number has fallen to six (6).

With such a steep drop-off in the county that holds the state capital of the third largest state in the country, the impact cannot be ignored. In a state like Florida, where elections are decided at the margins, the near-complete stoppage of voter registration by outside groups will have an incredible influence on important races for decades to come. Furthermore, these organizations have generally worked to engage our most marginalized communities—further isolating them from the electoral process.

After registering to vote, further impediments to casting a ballot await those in marginalized communities. The very process of casting a ballot can sometimes be an insurmountable task. One example would be how some locations ask for specific ID—something meant to complicate the process. In North Dakota, when a Democrat candidate won a governor's race largely due to Native American votes, "Republicans looked to a tool they'd tried to use before, a policy of restrictive voter identification: the requirement that lawful voters in North Dakota must have residential street addresses on their IDs". This rule became an issue for many, as "for the several tribes who inhabit the vast lands of North Dakota, a verifiable residential address is a luxury and, for thousands, an impossibility".

All the above assumes you can even get to a voting location in the midst of increasingly challenging logistics. "One of the favored schemes during Jim Crow was making polling places so difficult to reach that voters simply gave up". Specifically, "if the location is too far away from public transit, those who have no access to vehicles may be unable to vote; if the location is non-ADA compliant, those with physical disabilities cannot reach the polls; when the polling place isn't in a neutral location like a school but rather a police station or judicial complex, the atmosphere can threaten a voter's confidence". Initially, citizens were protected from those kinds of situations through the Voting Rights Act, which required several states to notify the federal government of any changes to polling locations, however this requirement was revoked in 2013. Nearly 3,000 physical polling places across the United States were closed between 2012 and 2016 according to the Election Assistance Commission.

Another key underlying issue with voting rights today is unfair redistricting (aka gerrymandering).

REDISTRICTING BASICS

Redistricting is not sexy. It rarely garners more than a precursory mention on any news source. And yet it has profound implications on creating and maintaining a representative democracy.

At its most basic definition, states are required to comply with federal constitutional requirements related to population and anti-discrimination under Article 1, Section 2. However, states vary on the criteria relating to what data may be used in review processes, and also may have other districting concerns such as compactness, contiguity, preservation of counties and other political subdivisions, preservation of communities of interest, preservation of cores of prior districts, avoiding pairing incumbents, prohibition on favoring/disfavoring an incumbent, candidate, or party, competitiveness, and proportionality. In addition to population equality, Section 2 of the Voting Rights Act of 1965 prohibits plans that intentionally or inadvertently discriminate on the basis of race, which could dilute the minority vote.[29]

In most states, the state legislature holds primary control of the redistricting process—including 34 state legislatures with primary control of their own district lines—and 39 legislatures hold primary control over the congressional lines in their state. While some states require a supermajority, others approve maps via joint resolution.[30] The remaining states are split between politician commissions, advisory commissions, backup commissions, and independent commissions.

Seven states—Arkansas, Hawaii, Missouri, New Jersey, Ohio, Pennsylvania, and Virginia—draw state legislative districts with politician commissions. In a manner that closely mirrors standard legislative mapping, elected officials serve as members rather than a full legislative body.

Iowa, Maine, Utah, Vermont, and Maryland appoint advisory commissions and formally participate in the initial drafting body; however, the legislature maintains the final say.

Backup commissions, bodies that are brought in only if the legislature cannot successfully pass a plan, can be found in Connecticut, Illinois, Maryland, Mississippi, Ohio, Oklahoma, Oregon, and Texas. These commissions vary from state to state and can be used in addition to an advisory commission in the pre-drafting stage.

Finally—in arguably the most ethical and least partisan mechanism—independent commissions make up the remaining states of Alaska, Arizona, California, Colorado, Idaho, Michigan, Montana, New York, and Washington. Each of these states draw both state and federal districts using an independent commission, and they are bound by regulations limiting direct participation by elected officials. Members of these commissions are neither legislators nor public officials.

For states who decide their own legislative members to draw the redistricting plans, the extreme power alternates between whichever party sits atop the state throne at the time new plans are drawn. Many states take a gamble on the court system, preferring to ask for forgiveness rather than permission over any perceived Voting Rights Act violations. This was seen most recently in 2022 when the Florida legislature ceded redistricting for congressional districts to Governor DeSantis. While it is not the role of the Governor's office to draw maps, Governor DeSantis' drawn maps eliminated or weakened two African American voting districts: one in the Jacksonville-Tallahassee area and another in Orlando. Legal challenges were contested throughout the courts, however they have been unsuccessful to date.[31]

Most legislative opposition is left to organizations like the American Civil Liberties Union (ACLU), who recently challenged Arkansas's redistricting efforts. Research revealed expansive discrimination against Black voters—where 11 out of 100 House districts are Black majority districts, a reduction of one district from prior maps was seen, despite Arkansas' Black population increasing to 16.5%, according to the 2010 Census.[32]

In some states, like Texas, gerrymandering maps have skewed partisanship and prevented voters from casting meaningful votes. The lawmakers drawing maps create races which are considered too uninteresting to voters, or which seem noncompetitive, which effectively decreases voter interest and activity.[33]

While states like Florida and Texas seem focused on redistricting to restrict minority districts, gerrymandering is not only a tool for Republican interests. The Court of Appeals deemed New York's redistricting map, which was proposed by Democrats, unconstitutional, which resulted in a lessening of Democrats' ability to hold control in the U.S. House of Representatives. It also had sweeping impacts on upcoming statewide elections.[34]

Since 2011, California's new redistricting maps have been drawn by an independent commission that reflects the most recent population changes. While independence is considered popular with ethically minded voters, the resulting maps lessen disruption to incumbents, primarily Democrats, who have largely decreased in running across elections since 2012.[35]

After serving as the 82nd Attorney General of the United States, Eric Holder went on to found the National Democratic Redistricting Committee (NRDC). The mission of the NRDC is to challenge unfair maps and to advocate for more equitable political boundaries through the courts.

The fairness of the Electoral College congressional district apportionment system truly depends upon the fairness of how congressional districts are drawn.

For example, in the 2016 Clinton vs. Trump match-up, Clinton won the national popular vote by 2 percentage points but only claimed 205 congressional districts to Trump's 230. Much of this can be attributed to Republican-controlled state legislatures leading gerrymandering efforts. In these instances, the statewide congressional districts are drawn to virtually guarantee Republican victories despite having a minority within the overall statewide vote.[36]

In the example above, Clinton's win represents what is commonly referred to as "packing the districts." This is where Democratic votes have been "packed" into a few districts that the Republicans are willing to cede. Meanwhile, the remaining Democratic votes have been "cracked" and distributed among a wide number of Republican-leaning districts, ensuring that there is a minority of Democratic voters in each district. With today's digital data processing and deep knowledge of voter preferences—gleaned from social media sites like Facebook as well as from retailers' data—politicians in power can meticulously gerrymander districts to get exactly the results they want.

One question remains: despite being a minority party, how have Republicans been able to seize control of so many statehouses and ram through their gerrymandered maps? The answer is both simple and complex. Ahead of the 2010 redistricting cycle, Republicans worked feverishly to gain key legislative and governor's offices by that year's midterm wave. They impressively focused on local elections where outcomes are often measured by a handful of votes.

In 2010, Republicans were able to draw 55% of congressional districts to favor their party. Democrats—themselves no strangers to gerrymandering—managed to do the same, but only with 10% of all seats. The remaining 35% are swing districts.

In the 2012 presidential election, Republican gerrymandering gave candidate Mitt Romney an artificial boost, allowing him to capture 224 congressional districts while Barack Obama only took 211—even though Obama won the popular vote by almost 4% nationwide.

Here's the big picture. In January 2017, Daily Kos performed a simulation in which the 2016 electoral college votes were apportioned totally by congressional district. As we know in reality, Trump won 230 districts while Clinton only won 205, even though Clinton won the popular vote by a margin of 2.86 million votes.

After crunching the numbers for the 2016 election, Daily Kos concluded, "We can get a sense of how biased the districts are nationally by comparing that median margin to the national result, which Clinton won by 2.1%. Consequently, that 5.5% disparity in Trump's favor between the overall result and the median district indicates a strong pro-Republican bias. Clinton would have theoretically needed to win the national popular vote by 5.5% to carry a bare majority of districts if every seat swung her way by the same margin." In layman's terms, this means that if every state adopted an apportioned elector system for the electoral college—as Maine and Nebraska do—Hillary Clinton would have had to beat Trump by 5.5% in the popular vote to win the presidency in 2016.[37]

As FiveThirtyEight.com noted, "If . . . Republicans made a more concerted push to change the whole country's electoral college allocation rules to use congressional districts, it would make it very hard for Democrats to win the White House."

These examples are simply continued reminders of the importance of lower-level elections, and that these gerrymandered districts are drawn by state legislatures who are chosen in local elections where every vote counts. Republicans have done a better job than Democrats of realizing that, to get elected, it's not just a matter of how many votes you get; of equal importance is the system of voting and who controls that system.

This is an idea that Trump and his political operatives understand well, and it's why he used his charisma and positional power relentlessly to try and replace local government officials—people like states' attorney generals and election officials—with his own hand picked loyalists. He believes that his downfall in 2020 was not because he lost the election fair and square—which he did, decisively—but because local election officials were unwilling to "find" the votes he needed to win.

The rhetoric around this strategy continues to chip away at our collective democracy. A 2022 MSNBC poll showed nearly 47% of Americans were distrustful of the voting system. If this doesn't further convince every voter of the dire urgency to vote in every election—to vote for leaders who value ethics and transparency—then we have a problem.

What should further convince voters—especially Black voters—that there are people and politicians serious about achieving minority rule is that laws are being systematically passed to suppress the vote in low-income and Black neighborhoods. The formula is simple and brutally effective. History has shown the more difficult it is to vote, the more lower-income Black voters will be discouraged from voting at all. It's a strategy that Southern states used with great effectiveness during the period after Reconstruction and right up through the 1960s. It's a strategy that some politicians are working to revive today.

Political scientist Eric Schickler, co-director of Berkeley's Institute for Governmental Studies (IGS), remarked to Berkeley News that an "erosion of restraints" in a "racially polarized party system" has cleared the way for greater use of "stack-the-deck" strategies.

"You hear people talking openly about making it harder for groups to vote—whether it's young voters or Black voters or Latinx voters—in a way that echoes the Jim Crow South," said Schickler. "It's really something we haven't seen in recent American politics. It's out in the open, explicit."[38]

In an interview with Ken Lawler, I take a deeper dive to explore this not so hidden disenfranchisement tool. Lawler, a retired IBM consultant, who is now chairman of the all-volunteer Fair Districts Georgia Foundation, began as a politically astute policy wonk and blogger.

> *Lawler:* I worked for IBM for almost 40 years. Towards the end of my time, I said, "What am I going to do for an encore?" And I was getting very politically astute, reactive around how do we solve some of these

big challenges that the country has. And every time I looked at any particular policy issue, whether it was gun safety or health care or whatever, to me the problem always boiled down to there was some structural impediment in the way. Either it was the Senate's filibuster rules or the way the Supreme Court has lifetime appointments or gerrymandering.

He started a blog called *Our Imperfect Union* to address all these big, big problems. And before long he was compelled to move from writing to action. Fair Districts GA is a non-partisan, non-profit organization founded in 2018 that works to encourage a fair and transparent redistricting process in Georgia. Their focus is to fight gerrymandering—the practice of drawing legislative district lines to favor one group over another. Their ultimate goal is to reform Georgia's process for drawing state and federal electoral maps.

As one of the only strictly nonpartisan groups working on gerrymandering, they pride themselves on going beyond just following principles of fairness. Rather, they are chasing a full restriction on engagement in any electioneering.

Lawler: We don't take sides. We're just trying to fix the process.

When asked to talk through the history of gerrymandering in Georgia, Lawler exposed his deep expertise, truly bringing the issue into historical context. What follows is a rough paraphrasing of his explanation:

Prior to 2000 and the Newt Gingrich revolution, Georgia was a primarily Democratic-controlled state. However, the disposition of the party looked different than how we imagine "Georgia Democrats" today. Referred to as the Conservative Democrats of the Old South, Georgia was a conservatively run democratic state. After Newt Gingrich came along in the late 90s, many congressional districts turned Republican. Democrats saw the impending changes and made a last-ditch effort to hold on to power. Following the 2000 election, they executed a terrible gerrymander of the state maps. It was so bad, in fact, that it was thrown out and redrawn by the U.S. Supreme Court; to date, it is the only non-politically influenced map drawn and used in the previous 20 years in Georgia.

By the 2010 redistricting, Republicans were able to garner the gerrymandering power and carved out a supermajority in the state House and a near-super majority in the Senate, despite their vote share going down.

The Republican vote share peaked in Georgia around 2006. Since that time, it's been slowly coming down. By the 2018 governor's race, Republican Kemp won by 2/10ths of a% (50.2%) over Stacey Abrams. Then, in 2020, we elected

President Biden by the famous 11,000 votes as well as two Senate runoffs by a hair-fraction of a %.

A precursory glance at the 2020 U.S. Census Report and these election results should elicit no surprise. All of the growth in Georgia's population in the last ten years has been people of color—primarily African Americans, Hispanics, and Asians. With these changes in demographics, we should see all sorts of additional opportunities for minorities to be represented in the latest round of redistricting maps, and yet they're not. So, it's become the calling of organizations like Fair Districts Georgia to bring forth challenges of Voting Rights Act violations to the federal court.

> *Lawler:* So, you've got all these dynamics in terms of population changes and voting preferences. We're now officially a swing state. And that should mean that we have more competitive races for state House and Congress and state Senate, but we don't because of the way the maps are drawn. And that's one of the big bad things that has come out of this latest map cycle. They have drained the competitiveness out of these maps. These maps have been the maps are drawn to predetermine the outcome of the election. And that's where people get pissed off. Maps should be fair. Fair to us means to reflect the way Georgia voters really vote, not the way you want them to vote.

Beyond the lack of representation, gerrymandering, at its core, is a conflict of interest. Those in power, legislators or—in certain cases—the governor, draw their own maps. And while it is perfectly legal, it's also perfectly wrong. The Supreme Court has said they are not dealing with partisan gerrymandering at a federal court level and are, instead, leaving it to the states. More than 30 states have a provision in their constitution that protects free and fair elections, and in states like North Carolina and Pennsylvania, courts have rejected blatantly gerrymandered maps as a violation of free and fair elections. Georgia, on the other hand, does not have strong laws to deal with partisan gerrymandering.

> *Lawler:* And so, we are fighting a long game here because we don't have some of the tools.

When asked what keeps him up at night, Lawler was quick to answer, "the Supreme Court." This is due to federal lawsuits like the one in Alabama where a three-judge panel concluded the map violated the Voting Rights Act and ordered it be redrawn. However, rather than abiding, the state appealed to the U.S. Supreme Court, who agreed to take the case. Normally the Supreme Court will let a lower court ruling stand while it moves through the process at the higher level but in this case, they rejected the lower court's ruling—to fix the map—giving Alabama the advantage of re-framing the case. Alabama then argued that the Ritual v. Common Cause case (2019) proves gerrymandering is legal as long as it does not discriminate against people on the basis of race, which they claim did not happen.

> *Lawler:* There's a possibility that the Supreme Court takes this case and with the current mood of the court says, well, you're right, Alabama, you can partisan gerrymander all you want as long as your intent wasn't racial gerrymandering in court. But no one knows the intentions. It's all behind closed doors. The damage is done in secret. Suddenly there's a map that does no good. It keeps me up at night that the Supreme Court could pull the rug out from under the Voting Rights Act.

So how do we make change? Like so many of the stories in this book, we are beginning to see a pattern of power behavior that hearkens for change. But where does society or an organization like Fair Districts Georgia begin to chip away at change?

Lawler begins with the small wins, like the 2019 surprise gathering at a last-minute committee meeting set to pass mid-cycle redistricting maps without any public notice.

> *Lawler:* In Georgia, we have this phenomenon called mid-cycle redistricting, which means you can redistrict any time you want, without waiting on a census. Over the last 15 years, the Republicans, as majority party, have gerrymandered 64 different districts without the insights of a census. So, our group, in 2019, got wind of some of a new map being passed and showed up in force at the hearing. Even though gerrymandering has been around as an issue, no one in Georgia was really watching. And all of a sudden, a group of 50 people showed up in a hearing room at 8:00 in the morning when a last-minute hearing was called, and the politicians were completely taken aback. And they basically were shamed into not passing the bill.

That sort of grassroots activism is slowly starting to make a difference as more research is produced on the widespread issue of gerrymandering as well as its negative consequences. Fair Districts Georgia partnered with the Princeton Gerrymandering Project to reexamine and re-validate the 20 years of election research started by Fair Districts. They examined trends to see what happens to these elections before and after a map is adjusted. The data was telling. Despite voting share decreases, seat shares were rising for the majority party. From there, the team created simulations and drew hundreds of hypothetical maps, recreating what the seat shares should look like if they properly represented the vote share, revealing the bias of the existing maps beyond a doubt.

When the 2020 U.S. Census data was released in August of 2021, this joint team was already poised to create new maps to serve as benchmarks for advocacy. Holding legislative and media briefings as well as one-on-one legislator meetings, they were able to bring more awareness and education to the issue than ever before.

Unfortunately, this fell on deaf ears.

> *Lawler:* We said to the legislature, you're about to draw maps. We're going to tell you in advance what fair looks like. We can help you demonstrate that your maps are fair. Let us be the independent checks. They did not take us up on that offer. They had no interest in being fair.

Despite this legislative snub, Fair Districts Georgia and partners like the Princeton Gerrymandering Project serve as a model for other organizations around the country. Using mathematical research and showing up to the table to advocate for true fairness, they were able to change the conversation and bring in independent experts. They changed the game in terms of how people evaluate redistricting maps and they spread the information through town halls, newsletters, and social media. They wrote hundreds of letters to editors around the state. They made sure the legislature was aware they were watching. And through those efforts, they inspired others. They continue to move the needle on what free and fair elections are supposed to be, but it remains an uphill battle.

> *Lawler:* In the summer of 2021, prior to the release of 2020 census data, the Senate and the House committees jointly held hearings at 11 different locations around the state. They invited citizens to stand up and ask, "What would you like to see in these maps?" And in every single hearing, in every single location, we had citizens, not a part of our group, standing up and saying, "You should pay attention to what Fair Districts Georgia and the Princeton Gerrymandering Project is saying." So, we knew our message was getting out there. We take pride in that fact.

While Georgia is a microcosm for this work, as we saw earlier in this chapter, other states are in need of similar reform efforts. I asked Lawler about the promising trends he is seeing around the country, and he highlighted that some states have made quicker progress than they have managed in Georgia, primarily due to better tools of legislation, oversight, and general understanding of the issue.

He also pointed to some of the great grassroots efforts going on around the country. For example, in 2017, a Michigan woman named Katie Fahy, self-described as "just a person living in Michigan raising a family," put a post out on Facebook saying, "Let's go tackle gerrymandering. Who's with me?" Unexpectedly, a bunch of people came out to join her cause and just like that, she built a movement out of nothing. By the 2018 election, that movement had made a ballot initiative for creating a constitutional amendment to enact an independent citizen's commission to take over redistricting in the state of Michigan. They were enabled by the pre-existing Michigan allowance for citizens' ballot initiatives.

Also spurred on by grassroots initiatives, more states are moving to the commission model that California started to use in 2010. Some states are making changes based on similar ballot initiatives while others, like Virginia, go through their state legislature. The latter model, typically not done out of altruism, is occurring out of a recognition that the political power pendulum is about to swing, and the losing party is suddenly very interested in a fair redistricting process.

So, what does the future look like for redistricting efforts like the one in Georgia? The challenge remains clear. As mundane as the subject may seem on the surface, it is at the critical heart of voting rights, especially for the growing minority populations. The representatives we vote into office hold the critical keys to the most pressing issues in our nation. Our ability to vote for representatives who not only look like us in ideology and diversity, but who also have our best interests at heart, is critically tied to the invisible lines of these district maps.

> Lawler: We know the facts are there to prove that we're right. That's why we have to keep fighting the fight and recognize that we are in this for the long haul because if we wait till 2030, it'll be too late. We know that activism works once people are paying attention. When we talk to the people about redistricting and gerrymandering and get them to truly understand, they are immediately on board. They say, "You're right, it's not fair." Fairness is what we want. If you can get people energized enough to get education and take action, we can actually make a difference.

If we want to work to ensure marginalized communities and disaffected voters have a seat at the table, we must follow the example of the Attorney General Holder and the National Democratic Redistricting Committee. Targeted, nuanced advocacy will be the key to combating the unfair legislative levers that have been utilized to maintain positions of power at the expense of everyday

Americans. While the NDRC, ACLU, and similar organizations may not be the sexiest advocacy organizations, these will be the ones that ultimately level the playing field and give the power back to the people.

3

ENVIRONMENTAL JUSTICE

D r. Mona Hanna-Attisha takes a long sip of water from her sink. She knew the city had recently changed the source of water, but she had faith, like most longtime residents in U.S. cities, that the government would do what was best for the health of their citizens.

She thought that until the day she learned the truth.

After months of scouring patient records, she sounded alarm bells with local authorities. The percentage of children with highly elevated lead levels had skyrocketed since the water switch. She insisted there was a connection, but her claims fell first on deaf ears, before eventually being used as a way to discredit her.

Dr. Hanna-Attisha's story is just another example of the lack of equitable environmental justice in America. In her book, *What the Eyes Don't See*,[39] she not only recaps the cost cutting and greed that led to this environmental emergency but also the amplification of toxic stress that those in poverty deal with on a daily basis. She points to recent neurological studies that found that repetitive stress and trauma in children impacts their life trajectory in a very predictable way: put simply, the more trauma experienced during the earliest stages of brain development, the higher the likelihood of chronic physical and mental disease later in life.

The tragic irony of the Flint water atrocity is just how easily it could have been avoided. Hanna estimates the treatment chemical, corrosion control, would have cost the city between $80 to $100 a day.

"That's all it would've cost to properly treat this water," she says.[40]

Instead, 12 people died, at least 80 were severely ill and hospitalized, and thousands were permanently psychologically impacted by the long-term effects of lead poisoning.

Perhaps even more disheartening is that, in the aftermath of the crisis, it became clear just how much effort was spent to cover up, rather than correct, the issue. Nine elected officials or their staff were charged with nearly 42 counts related to the disaster—ranging from perjury to misconduct to involuntary manslaughter. The desire to avoid admittance of wrongdoing and expose the blatant disregard for life sent political figures into a spiral of lies and cover-up attempts.

"This case has nothing whatsoever to do with partisanship," said Kym Worthy, Wayne County's Prosecutor. "It has to do with human decency, resurrecting the complete abandonment of the people of Flint and finally, finally holding people accountable for their alleged unspeakable atrocities that occurred in Flint all these years ago."[41]

The only positive lesson we can attempt to gain from these egregious acts is that of resilience. The community came together to demand action. They stood behind advocates like Dr. Hanna-Attisha and others to fight for their rights to clean water and transparent government. At the time of this writing, nearly ten years later, the community is still rallying to ensure justice is served; picketing outside of courthouses to ensure convictions are secured for those responsible. While over 659 million dollars in settlements have been reached due to the Flint Water Crisis Class Action Litigation, the Flint water crisis is not over. The lead numbers are currently lower than the threshold that would require government action, but residents are fighting until the levels reach zero.

"This is a story of resistance, of activism, of citizen action, of waking up and opening your eyes and making a difference in our community," she says. "I wrote this book to share the terrible lessons that happened in Flint, but more importantly, I wrote this book to share the incredible work that we did, hand in hand with our community, to make our community care about our children."[42]

Environmental inequities in America take many forms. Here, we will look at three key categories: water, food, and general pollution. We will also highlight legislation that is attempting to level the playing field for communities of color and Native Americans.

WATER

Flint, Michigan is one of many underserved neighborhoods with reduced access to safe water and nutritious foods.[43] Flint's communities, primarily Black and low income, have been enduring poisonous lead exposure through their drinking water since 2014, and limited action has been taken to remedy the situation. Tragically, this is more than a one-generation issue. Lead can harm every organ in the body and thousands of Flint children have been exposed to the toxins and are already exhibiting physical and mental impairments, including learning disabilities.[44]

As the case in Flint demonstrates, environmental justice issues extend beyond direct access to food resources, with water and soil as frequent vehicles for contaminants to enter food systems.[45][46] Another example of this is improperly stored fuel above a watershed, which has the potential to leak and contaminate the water reservoir below. A current example of this can be found in Honolulu, Hawaii, where tap water on the Navy base has become so poisoned by leaking fuel that residents in the affected area can't use tap water and schools are forced to serve students pre-made and frozen meals that don't require water to prepare, such as pizzas.[47]

Clean water, which is essential for all aspects of everyday life, is one of the most basic assurances we should have in American communities. Yet, it is one of the most egregious ways environmental discrimination is negatively impacting communities of color. Contaminated water can leave long-lasting health impacts. People of low-income households who are living in metropolitan areas are more likely to have water that fails safe drinking standards while incomplete plumbing, which has the potential for contaminating drinking water with sewage and pollution, more often occurs among people of low income, rural living, older age, and low-educational attainment.[48]

Maintenance of clean, quality water sources and safe drinking water is under the purview of the EPA Office of Water; they perform this through various measures that regulate pollution and restore polluted water sources.[49] There are various laws and programs intended to regulate pollution entering water sources, including the Safe Drinking Water Act (SDWA), the Clean Water Act (CWA), and the National Pollutant Discharge Elimination System (NPDES).

The SDWA originated in 1974 and was then reauthorized in 1996 to ensure public water systems were maintained at a level so as not to endanger human health, including drinking water.[50] The NPDES was also established in 1972 out of the CWA and was intended to improve surface water quality for humans and environments through the regulation of pollution and effluents entering waterways through a permit system.[51] Both the SDWA and NPDES have proven to be insufficient at substantially maintaining standards necessary for human health, with noncompliance and serious violations present across the U.S.[52]

The Federal Water Pollution Control Act was established in 1948 to regulate the discharging of pollution into water sources to ensure the quality of surface waters. It was amended in 1972 when it became the Clean Water

Act.[53] However, the CWA is also inefficient at deterring the pollution of water sources, as it also has frequently occurring violations,[54] many of which are substantial enough to incur millions in fines.[55][56]

Everyone in America shares in the need for drinking water. All people have a right to safe, clean, and healthy water sources. You should not have to live in a wealthy neighborhood to have safe drinking water. It's not just about money, it's also about the vote. Communities that collectively use their right to vote to elect people who care about their issues and their people will have a voice.

FOOD

No person can avoid the impact of policy decisions made on and about food—voters and nonvoters all have to eat! But low income and disadvantaged populations, in particular, lack or have reduced access to the resources to manage the impacts of environmental injustices on their food sources. For example, a low-income resident of a rural community has limited access to retail outlets that offer healthy food options should their local food sources become contaminated by pollution. In places where healthy food options are available, they are often more expensive and labor intensive to make into a meal than low-quality, convenience-oriented meals. The illusion of choice of food quality relies on energy, time, and an ability to access outlets that provide quality food options, which are not always available to low-income and disadvantaged-populations. A person without a car or other convenient transportation may have to use time and energy-intensive methods to access healthy food outlets—for example, a person living in a city may have to walk long distances or take public transport to access healthy food options due to a lack of access to nutritious food in their urban environment. But even this also requires a person to have the health, strength, and resources to carry their groceries on the return journey. The disproportionate access to nutrition-rich foods for low-income and disadvantaged populations exacerbates this situation with low-quality foods that include health risks, and from there, poor health further limits a person's available resources for accessing healthy food options.[57][58]

Food insecurity is higher for low-income, non-White households than it is for higher-income White households,[59] particularly in rural areas.[60][61] As alluded to earlier, these inequities are often due to higher prices of quality foods and increased travel distances required to access these foods. Native Americans who practice subsistence methods of farming and gathering are at an additional disadvantage as there are limited adaptation options for managing climate change impacts on their resource environments.[62]

Wai Ying Chin, who moved to the United States in 1967, is the 84-year-old sole caregiver to her 107-year-old mother in their third-floor walkup on Elizabeth Street in New York City.

"We were worried," Chin said through a translator. "When we heard that the grocery store right below [us] was going to close, we went and lined up and stocked up on food."

Like many, food insecurity is a daily struggle, one made increasingly worse during the pandemic, according to findings from the NYU Center for the Study of Asian American Health. While access to supermarkets is the primary concern, fear of discrimination became a heightened fear as the pandemic drew on.

"During the pandemic, food insecurity was one of the primary [issues] because—not many people realize that—for immigrants, undocumented individuals, they are not eligible for government subsidies," Chi Loek, Executive Director of the United Asian American Alliance said. "If you're unemployed, you don't have enough savings and you are not able to afford fresh vegetables. They are the most expensive, sold-out food items."

Asian Americans in New York City have some of the highest poverty rates of any ethnic group in the city, according to city data. When COVID-19 first hit the city, Asian workers were one of the hardest-hit sectors of the workforce, data shows. Still, the issue of food scarcity in the Asian community was unexpected among researchers.

The disparity in equitable access to quality foods for low-income and minority populations is further complicated by systemic discrimination in programs and policies, while minority communities are often easy targets for environmentally harmful projects (such as dumps, sewerage plants, waste facilities, and factories) due to discriminatory and/or ignorant zoning laws.[63 64 65]

Action has been more successfully taken in regards to improving food security inequities for low-income and disadvantaged populations through the Supplemental Nutrition Assistance Program (SNAP), the Special Supplemental Nutrition Program for Women, Infants, and Children (WIC), the Food Distribution Program on Indian Reservations (FDPIR)[66 67 68], The Emergency Food Assistance Program, [69] and the Commodity Supplemental Food Program.[70] SNAP provides financial assistance for low- income households to buy eligible foods from approved retail stores[71] while the WIC is designed to improve quality food access for low-income pregnant women, low-income women with babies or small children, and children under the age of five who are at nutritional risk.[72] Improvements in food access for low-income households on reservations—or approved areas near reservations—and households in Oklahoma with a federally recognized member of a Native American tribe is provided by FDPIR[73] while

TEFAP provides food and resources for food banks, soup kitchens, and other community-free food providers.[74] Additionally, CSFP is intended to supplement nutritious foods for low-income older adults aged 60 and over.[75]

More recently, President Biden committed to transitioning to climate-friendly energy by 2035. However, the focus has, so far, largely been focused on energy burdens and less on how this relates to food system equity.[76] An important aspect of this energy transition is the disproportionate impact it will have on low-income households in comparison to wealthier households. Should the carbon footprint of food production be passed onto consumers, low-income households will be disproportionately impacted because they have limited ability to absorb this price increase, especially since low-income households spend proportionately more income on food than wealthier households.[77]

POLLUTION

There is a thick layer of snow on the ground as they march; dozens of Chippewa Indians, primarily women, walk alongside allies Honor the Earth, Sierra Club, Earthjustice, and the White Earth Band of Ojibwe. They march in protest to the Canadian Oil giant, Enbridge's, drilling of the Line 3 Pipeline.

"We've been living here for 10,000 years, drinking the same water, tapping sugar from same trees for maple syrup, harvesting our wild rice," said Winona LaDuke, executive director of Honor the Earth and a member of the White Earth Band of Ojibwe. "It's our most sacred place."

Beyond the honor and sanctity of the region, the pipeline construction, which began in December 2020, has removed or destroyed vegetation, mature trees, wetlands, and some of the highest-quality wild rice in Minnesota, all of which are key parts of the ecosystem that Anishinaabe people survive on. An 1855 treaty gave the Anishinaabe people the right to hunt, fish, and harvest wild rice on the territory. That treaty language did not, it turns out, prevent the permitting of the same land for oil company profiteering.[78]

Pollution has generational implications and is often unavoidable for those without a voice of power. From the inclusion of pesticides in low-quality food, to oil pipelines through Native lands, to flooding and natural disasters caused by climate change, the damage to health and quality of life are far reaching but disproportionately isolated to low-income families and communities of color.

Land and water that comes into contact with toxic substances can become contaminated and enter the food system. The Toxic Substances Control Act, Resource Conservation and Recovery Act, and the Food Quality Protection Act, each administered by the EPA are all intended to prevent and restore areas where this has happened. The Toxic Substances Control Act maintains restrictions on toxic substances, including lead, which can enter food systems through soil and water contamination, often through disproportionate allocation of waste sites and insufficient cleanup of toxic substances.[79] The Resource Conservation and Recovery Act (RCRA) has authority over all stages of the life cycles of hazardous materials. This includes the storage and disposal of waste and hazardous substances, including petroleum and metals (such as lead, arsenic, chromium, and mercury)[80], while the previously discussed 1996 Food Quality Protection Act was designed to regulate pesticide use to reduce the risk to consumers of agricultural produce.[81]

The pesticide, chlorpyrifos, is in a class of organophosphates chemically similar to a nerve gas developed by Nazi Germany before World War II. Its heavy use has often left traces in drinking water sources.

Dr. Gina Solomon, a medical professor at the University of California, San Francisco, and former deputy secretary of the California Environmental Protection Agency (CalEPA), said chlorpyrifos is unusual in that it's one of the best-understood pesticides because it's been so extensively studied. In fact, it's been proven, through medical records of rural farmworker communities, to negatively impact brain development in fetuses, which can affect IQ and lead to hyperactivity.

And yet, efforts to curtail its use under the Obama Administration were reversed by the Environmental Protection Agency under the Trump Administration, forcing states like California, New York, and Hawaii to ban it on a state level.[82]

Pesticides pose risks to human health, which has prompted the 1996 Food Quality Protection Act to regulate pesticide use in crops and reduce harm to consumers of crops.[83] However, this seems to have been relatively ineffective due to a much higher "acceptable" level of risk exposure for workers in the field compared to other occupations in the industry. In 2009, the EPA published documents intended to reduce the disparity between the occupation and non-occupational acceptable risk exposure of pesticides, but it has not progressed into a real policy due to strong opposition by the pesticide industry and pesticide lobbyists.[84] The strong opposition means field workers, who are often low-income or of a disadvantaged-population demographic, are exposed to much higher amounts of pesticides than is believed to be healthy—from this, environments and ecosystems are poisoned. On top of this, low-income and disadvantaged populations are more likely to purchase produce grown with excessive pesticide use, due in large part to the fact that organic produce and produce that uses safer pesticide methods costs more—this results in increased exposure and potential harm from pesticides through such food options.

The Dakota Access Pipeline—like the Line 3 Pipeline above—demonstrates a particular form of systemic discrimination, that of "not in my backyard," which is commonly referred to as NIMBY. The potential harm of an oil spill to a majority-White population was deemed unacceptable; however, the same potential harm was dismissed for the less-vocal and less-politically powerful Native American people of the Standing Rock reservation. The pipeline was originally planned to be constructed close to Bismarck, a 92% White city. Instead, the pipeline was moved to border the Standing Rock reservation amid concerns for the water quality of Bismarck residents, clearly prioritizing White health and safety over the Native American and lower-income residents now located close to the pipeline.[85] Concerns mounted over the pipeline's potential to leak oil and cause contamination to culturally significant lands used for fishing, hunting, and other food sources, or places such as the Missouri River that are used for drinking water. Thousands came out to protest, yet construction and the eventual opening moved forward.[86] Concerned individuals were quickly validated, as the pipeline had at least five leaks in the first six months of operation, causing widespread soil contamination as well as unknown future environmental and human danger.[87]

The blatant racism involved in the Dakota Access Pipeline is representative of the historical and ongoing colonization practices and policies that have interrupted Native Americans' land stewardship practices. This interruption has meant restricted or loss of access to cultural food sources and the destruction of native food habitats.[88] In spite of this harm, rural Native American populations continue to be resilient. In fact, the cultural sharing of resources throughout Native rural lands has increased food security for those residents when compared to similar urban populations.[89]

Climate change is causing extreme events related to weather to occur more frequently and with greater severity. This includes fires, storms, hurricanes, tidal surges, flooding, extreme temperatures, and droughts. Another symptom of the warming climate is increases in average seasonal temperatures across the U.S.[90] The impacts of climate change are disproportionately shouldered by disadvantaged populations in the U.S., including those of low-income, low-educational attainment, those of older age, and the Black, Hispanic, and Native American populations.[91][92]

The increasing intensity and frequency of wildfires disproportionately affects disadvantaged populations who have increased vulnerability to wildfires and are more severely affected by wildfires.[93][94] One manifestation of this during the California wildfires of 2020 was how there was reduced access to firefighting services for low-income communities. On top of this, those most exposed to wildfires are often those from disadvantaged communities; a large proportion of public service firefighters are prison inmates working for negligible wages.[95] On the other end of the weather spectrum, floods also disproportionately impact disadvantaged communities, with the most extensive flooding and damage from Hurricanes Harvey, Katrina, and Ida occurring in predominantly Black neighborhoods.[96][97][98]

Increasing average temperatures and more frequent extreme temperatures increase the morbidity and mortality of exposed populations.[99] Low-income and non-White communities are most severely affected by extreme heat events compared to higher-income and White communities.[100] The extreme low temperatures of winter 2021 in Texas demonstrated how disadvantaged communities can be disproportionately affected by such events due to a lack of access to sufficient heating systems.[101] The discrepancy in ability to manage extreme cold and heat by disadvantaged populations comes from a lack of resources to cool or heat their living space or to access climate-controlled locations during such events; for example, a low-income person may be unable to afford an air conditioner and may live too far away from a communal cool location (such as a library) during a summer heatwave. These accessibility difficulties increase their likelihood of overheating and of exacerbating preexisting or underlying health issues.

As climate change progresses, air quality is also decreasing due to increases in harmful levels of surface ozone and airborne particulates.[102] These reductions in air quality disproportionately affect disadvantaged communities and increase incidences of asthma and respiratory diseases.[103] Asthma and respiratory diseases can typically be managed through medication and controlled environments, but disadvantaged populations are more likely to lack consistent access to medication and/or lack the resources to sufficiently manage their environment to suppress breathing difficulties.[104] A low-income person's limited financial resources may force them to live in an area with frequently poor air quality due to pollution from nearby factories. Their financial position may mean that purchasing an air purifier to reduce polluted air in their living space—not to mention the increased power bill from running said air purifier—is prohibitive, which forces them to be exposed to low quality air.

LEGISLATIVE ACTION

So where are the gaps in legislation? Legislative action has been a roller coaster of two steps forward, one step back. Progress has been made primarily, but not exclusively, during Democratically led administrations.

In 1994, President Clinton signed Executive Order 12898, "Federal Actions to Address Environmental Justice in Minority Populations and Low-Income Populations," with the intention of making federal agencies consider the impacts of their activities, programs, and policies on marginalized and disadvantaged populations and to address existing environmental justice issues.[105] Unfortunately, Executive Order 12898 has been criticized for not doing enough in terms of environmental justice for minority and disadvantaged populations,[106] particularly in its responsibility to go beyond just mitigating dietary insufficiencies among disadvantaged populations.[107]

In 2015, President Obama signed Executive Order 13693, "Planning for Federal Sustainability in the Next Decade," which outlined a 10-year goal of cutting the Federal Government greenhouse emissions by 40%. This was then revoked by President Trump in 2018 through Executive Order 13834, "Efficient Federal Operations," which prioritized efficiency and performance optimization over environmental justice and greenhouse emissions.[108]

In 2021, President Biden introduced Executive Order 14008, "Tackling the Climate Crisis at Home and Abroad," aimed at reducing the disproportionate pollution burden of disadvantaged communities.[109] The National Climate Task Force was then established to mobilize implementation of the whole-government approach to climate change and environmental justice as outlined in Executive Order 14008, including the creation of the Coastal Resilience Interagency Working Group.[110][111] This order has strengthened environmental movements that want increased stringency in permitting,[112] but has made little overall legislative progress.[113] Executive Order 13985, "On Advancing Racial Equity and Support for Underserved Communities Through the Federal Government" was also introduced by President Biden to identify systemic barriers within communities and address these through equitable policies.[114]

Formed in 2021 through President Biden, the White House Environmental Justice Advisory Council provides advice and recommendations to the Council on Environmental Quality and the White House Environmental Justice Interagency Council.[115] The White House Environmental Justice Interagency Council in turn develops recommendations and strategies for addressing historical and ongoing environmental injustices.[116] The Justice40 Initiative was introduced in 2021 to actively address needs and inequity in disadvantaged communities. To do this, the Justice40 Initiative states that at least 40% of the Federal investments intended for climate change mitigation and the change to clean energy are to be allocated to disadvantaged communities.[117]

The year 2021 also saw the administration of The American Rescue Plan Act under President Biden. The Act was borne out of the exacerbated food insecurity experienced during the COVID-19 pandemic, with part of the act designating additional funds to food assistance programs for disadvantaged populations. The act addresses environmental injustices indirectly, since many members of the communities that are carrying heavy loads of pollution and other causes and impacts of environmental injustices will qualify for the additional benefits.[118]

The Bipartisan Infrastructure Law was introduced and included a variety of approaches to reducing the disproportionate impacts of climate change on disadvantaged populations. Investments were made in reducing wildfire risk and in improving drought prevention and water resiliency. Flooding in coastal regions was also addressed through investing in estuarine, coastal, and marine habitat restoration.[119 120 121]

Funding for clean water investments, upgrading power infrastructure to clean energy sources, improving climate and extreme weather event resilient infrastructure, and cleaning up polluted and toxic urban areas were also prioritized.[122 123]

Stimulated by the Biden administration's support of environmental justice, multiple federal agencies have developed their own environmental justice initiatives. The Department of Energy established the Energy Storage for Social Equity (ES4SE) to improve energy resilience among a limited number of disadvantaged communities that experience energy-insecurity due to expense or unreliability;[124] in 2022, 14 applications from communities were accepted to proceed to the next stage of assessment.[125] The Department of Health and Human Services established their own Office of Climate Change and Health Equity to address health equity issues that have arisen out of environmental injustice and climate change.[126] The U.S. Department of Agriculture invested in partnerships to develop more climate-appropriate agricultural and forestry methods in 2021[127] and then, in 2022, it initiated the USDA Equity Commission to assess discrimination in USDA policies and provide recommendations for improving equity.[128] The Department of Justice established an Office of Environmental Justice to prioritize environmental justice in underdeveloped and disadvantaged communities.[129]

While a number of Executive Orders and agency initiatives have been developed due to the Biden Administration's efforts to promote environmental justice, in mid-2022, no key environmental justice legislation has been passed by Congress.[130]

In early 2022, about a quarter of U.S. states had environmental justice-related legislation in place,[131] while general food policies were present across all states in one form or another.[132] All of the state-based environmental justice policies address environmental pollution in various forms (e.g., land, water, air) but few are tailored to specifically address food equity as it relates to environmental justice. Notable states pursuing environmental justice and explicitly incorporating food equity issues include: Virginia—who is pursuing increased food security for low-income and disadvantaged populations[133]—Washington, and Michigan—both of which are taking steps to improve food security for their respective Native communities.

Some of the federal grant programs designed to alleviate the disproportionate impacts of climate change on low-income and disadvantaged populations include the Low Income Home Energy Assistance Program (LIHEAP), Low Income Household Water Assistance Program (LIHWAP), Rural Community Development Program (RCD), and the Community Economic Development Program (CED).

LIHEAP assists low-income households with their home energy needs, particularly heating and cooling.[134] This demonstrates the federal government's recognition of increasing extreme heat events. And, with LIHEAP's advice, they've been encouraging the allocation of funding towards increasing access to functioning air conditioners for disadvantaged populations during summers.[135][136]

Together, LIHWAP and RCD are intended to ensure access to clean drinking water and safe wastewater services among disadvantaged populations. LIHWAP is designed to assist low-income households pay for their drinking and wastewater services when in arrears or when they face difficulty paying their bills.[137] The LIHWAP funds can also be used by states, tribes, and territories during household water emergency events to provide households with bottled water.[138] RCD typically provides very small rural communities with training and technical assistance in water systems, including those for drinking water and wastewater.[139]

The CED is designed for business startups and expansions that mostly hire low-income people, but who pay the employees enough to develop economic sufficiency. This program is not explicitly tailored towards climate change impacts or environmental justice but can be used for environmental enterprises and agricultural initiatives for low-income people who relate to climate change impacts and environmental justice.[140]

4

FAIR AND AFFORDABLE HOUSING

Environmental inequities are closely tied to geography. But what happens when you do not have the power to change your geography? How can the average citizen fight the uphill battle of policy changes needed to undo decades of discrimination?

In August 2022, I interviewed Laurie Benner, the Associate Vice President of Housing and Community Development with the National Fair Housing Alliance. As a true housing expert, her career spans the gamut of nonprofit, real estate, and community development. As she describes it, she sits at the intersection of real estate, housing opportunity, and fair housing.

When asked about the most pressing needs in housing, she was quick to point to racial equity, bias, and discrimination, including the decades of policies designed to deny opportunity to people of color. Some biases, like those found in computer algorithms and machine learning, are hidden and are only just beginning to be uncovered and remedied.

However, bias begins and ends at the human level. More and more organizations are beginning to sound the long-overdue alarm around credit and lending policies; these organizations are also taking close looks at the criteria used to determine an individual's ability to pay, including seemingly intuitive actions (e.g., including rental and utility payments in the calculations).

There are distinct barriers to accessible financial inclusion, capital, and credit access in communities of color. Specific policy issues include access to banks and other payment accounts, issues with credit reporting systems, and affordable short-term and small-dollar credit. This issue is especially pertinent for younger consumers, Black entrepreneurs and businesses, new Americans, and other disadvantaged populations who may lack a co-signer, a bank account, or who lack a credit history. Serving these populations is expensive for the lender—and makes the lender less willing to work with them—which increases barriers to entering the credit system.[141]

Owning a home is one of the most foundational ways to begin to build generational wealth. However, for first-time home buyers from a community of color, it can also be the most daunting. Discriminatory practices have been documented in every area of the process: from lending, to appraisal, to contracts, and even to the post-close valuation of the home.

And this does not even begin to address the emotional barriers that include the fear of the unknown. Many first-generation homeowners, regardless of race, do not hold the foundational knowledge about the ins and outs of home ownership. What does it mean to own a home? What are the responsibilities like maintenance, taxes, HOA policies? For many, the mountain of obstacles is simply too high a barrier to cross.

Progress in fair housing has been swinging on a pendulum for the past two decades. Slow, but steady, progress was made under the Obama Administration, but most of that was heavy-handedly reversed under Trump. The Biden Administration is making strides to re-institute much of that reversal; however, policy advocates call for much more sweeping changes. In early 2022, HUD released a year in review, acknowledging the Biden Administration's efforts to increase affordable housing—including the restructuring of home appraisal systems, the prevention of evictions and foreclosures during COVID-19, assisting the most vulnerable populations, providing emergency housing vouchers, removing barriers for students suffering with debt, increasing housing supply and affordable homes, acting on mutual mortgage insurance funds, and encouraging support for racially minoritized and LGBTQ+ communities.[142]

Despite these gains, the issues are, in fact, still present everywhere. The historic origins of residential zoning are steeped in segregation. Real estate agents were actually tasked with surveying and redlining neighborhoods to keep them homogeneous. Confederate flags in real estate listings were not considered a Fair Housing violation by the National Association of Realtors until 2021.

One other obvious challenge of the industry is the lack of diversity of the profession as a whole. Nearly 98% of industry professionals, such as appraisers, are White males. Creating a more diverse industry would go far to move the needle on systemic racism in the industry.

The issues are just as prevalent in the rental housing space. The National Fair Housing Alliance found over 28,700 fair housing complaints nationwide in 2020. More than 67% of these were alleging discrimination in either disability or race. Black renters are more likely to experience an eviction than Whites. Black and Latino women held both the highest percentages of evictions as well as astoundingly high rates of sexual harassment.[143]

Other housing factors contributing to a negative quality of life include housing quality and overcrowding. Households with more members than rooms have been associated with lower-educational attainment and greater health risks. The post-pandemic affordable housing crisis is only amplifying this issue, leaving many families in substandard housing or forcing them to pair with multiple families in one home to make ends meet. More than half of Americans say the availability of affordable housing is a major problem, especially among underserved and underrepresented populations including young and racially minoritized people.[144] The definition of affordable is becoming a moving target, especially as the cost of rent is growing but the area median income (AMI) is not.

The key piece of intertwined importance in this work ties back to where we began this chapter: environmental justice. In short, where you live matters. Your home is the central point of everything in terms of opportunity or lack of opportunity. Where you live dictates your access to financial institutions, employment, transportation, technology, access to healthy food, and so many other day-to-day elements, so everything that someone needs to lead a healthy and successful life all centers around where they live.

In fact, an analysis of Opportunity Atlas—a new data tool from the U.S. Census Bureau and Harvard University's research institute, Opportunity Insights—shows that opportunity and social mobility still elude far too many people in far too many places. In nearly every place in the country, children whose parents were low-income often have poorer-than-average outcomes as adults. However, factors that inhibit mobility are within society's control to influence; schools, violence, incarceration, housing, job access, and quality health care are some of the reasons that zip codes and census tracts matter for life outcomes. These factors can be improved with appropriate investment, human interest, and good policy. [145]

When asked about progress being made in fair housing around the country. Benner was cautiously optimistic.

> *Benner:* Currently, there is a lot of attention on racially explicit solutions and programs. Racial equity has been a priority of the Biden Administration since day one. Additionally, the National Association of Realtors, the Mortgage Bankers Association, and other industry leaders are leaning into issues of racial equity by developing educational resources and communications about the importance of overcoming

long-standing inequities in housing.

In truth, the National Association of Realtors is making up for past sins. It initially opposed the Fair Housing Act of 1968, actively lobbying against stricter regulations. And while some of its more conservative members continue to hold opposition to these initiatives, the association is taking a stronger stance in favor of including a prominent place for fair housing and diversity, equity, and inclusion in its Code of Ethics, at their conferences and events, and in collaboration with state and local associations.

And there are new collaborations being formed between organizations like the National Association of Counties, the National Association of Affordable Housing Lenders, the U.S. HUD, USDA, the National Council of State Housing Agencies (NCSHA), the National Low-Income Housing Coalition (NLIHC), the National Association of Local Housing Finance Agencies (NALHFA), the National Association of Home Builders (NAHB) and the Housing Assistance Council (HAC). The more these organizations share information, resources and coordinate their efforts, the bigger push they have to change the policy discussion.

Benner closes with a nod to other seeds of optimism, such as special-purpose credit programs (SPCPs), which were made allowable by the Equal Credit Opportunity Act of 1974, but have been rarely, if ever, used to date. However, the National Fair Housing Alliance and the Mortgage Bankers Association partnered to create a toolkit intended to walk lenders, step by step, through the process of creating their own programs. SPCPs are an important tool to begin the process of chipping away at the wall standing between communities of color and generational wealth.

> *Benner:* In a country quite literally built on White supremacy, perpetuated through a legacy of racism, the time is long past to dismantle the structural barriers that continue to plague our neighbors and friends. I'm heartened by recent efforts and urge policymakers to do more and hold their fellow elected officials accountable.

While they go hand in hand, fair housing is only a good solution when it is accompanied by affordable housing. Even prior to the 2008 Great Recession, the percentage of Americans paying more than 30% of their gross incomes for housing was increasing. Approximately 75% of renters in the ten highest-cost metropolitan areas are only earning between $30,000 and $45,000, and almost 50% of those earning between $45,000 and $75,000 had high housing costs. In 2015, 75% of the eligible population paid a disproportionate share of income on housing.[146]

Since the Great Depression, affordable housing has been utilized as a public policy tool to reward and offer jobs to returning WWII veterans, alleviate civil unrest in the 1960s, bolster the 1970s economy, and incentivize public private partnerships throughout. However, despite being well intended, even the earliest policies—such as the National Housing Act of 1934 creating the Federal Housing Administration (FHA)—upheld racial and ethnic discrimination through strict loan origination guidelines.

The journey of public housing began with the creation of the Public Housing Authority and continued with the Housing Acts of 1956 and 1961 and the Housing and Urban Development Act of 1965. These acts cumulatively expanded the federal government's role by setting up various incentives and systems for private developers to receive subsidies, first for the elderly and eventually for all low-income individuals.

By 1968 however, these policies were already showing cracks in their sustainability. In a whirlwind of perfect storm conditions, the Public Housing Authority model was quickly a losing proposition. Inflexible inflationary measures, rental rates tied to a resident's annual median income, federal government subsidy reductions, and mandatory priority admittance given to those facing extreme poverty all correlated to vastly reduce PHA's rental revenues. Public Housing Authorities were quickly in the red and public housing became less desirable and more stigmatized due to a lack of proper management and maintenance.

While today's PHAs are embarking on intentional efforts to more progressively target underserved populations—through programs like the New Market Tax Credit, HOPE IV, and the Choice Neighborhood Program—the stigma of public housing, heavily tinted on racial lines, bleeds over into other environmental and health factors such as access to clean water, healthy food, accessible medical care among others. And there is one policy area where stigma and racial bias has proved particularly deadly: transportation policy!

5

TRANSPORTATION

In her book, *There Are No Accidents*, Jessie Singer offers an eye-opening perspective on the misnomer of the concept of "accident." Her premise, that most of what we call "accidental" is actually a systemic issue being compartmentalized into individual incidents, is backed by extensive research and first-hand accounts. Some of the most shocking elements in her book are related to transportation policy issues. Here in this excerpt, we hear her research paint the picture more clearly.

In Jacksonville, Florida, one of the top ten U.S. cities where pedestrians are most likely to be killed by drivers, police disproportionately issue jaywalking citations to Black people. Researchers at ProPublica found that in a five-year period ending in 2016, police issued 55% of the city's jaywalking citations to Black people, who make up only 29% of the population. Black people were three times more likely to be cited for crossing the street than were White people. Similar studies have found evidence of racist enforcement of this violation in cities much safer for pedestrians, such as New York. In 2019, police issued almost 90% of jaywalking summonses to Black and Latino pedestrians, who make up about half of New Yorkers. In the first three months of 2020, New York City police issued 99% of the jaywalking summonses they wrote to Black and Latino people.[147]

Racism is prevalent, too, in sentencing for vehicular homicide. But where being Black means that you are more likely to have to pay a fine for jaywalking, if a driver kills you while you are crossing the street, being Black means that your killer pays less of a debt to society than if the driver had killed a White person. Researchers have found that vehicular homicide, essentially the unintentional but negligent killing of a person with a car, is a crime with a shorter sentence when the victim is Black. In 2000, researchers at Dartmouth and Harvard University cataloged U.S. Bureau of Justice Statistics data on sentence length for vehicular homicide—largely drunk driving accidents—based on the victims' characteristics. They looked at reams of sentencing data from courtrooms across America and found that when prosecutors charged a person with vehicular homicide, the prison sentence was 53% shorter if the victim was Black. If a prison sentence is the measurement of the value of the victim's life, Black life is worth less than White life. The authors of the study concluded that there was something more sinister to sentence length than a measure of justice—they called this "the taste for vengeance."

There is no better way to truly understand how something as seemingly innocuous as transportation can have these inequitable effects, other than hearing from those directly affected. I had the pleasure of interviewing Amy Cohen, the co-founder of Families for Safe Streets, an organization she describes as "the group no one should ever have to join." Founded in 2014 in New York City, they now have chapters across the country. Each advocates for safer city streets and more pedestrian-focused transportation planning.

"My son was killed on October 8th, 2013. And it was an unimaginable loss. I had so much pain and then it just had to go somewhere."

Cohen began speaking out about her son's tragedy and eventually connected with Transportation Alternatives, who later became the parent organization to Families for Safe Streets. In early 2014, two dozen families from across New York City had their first meeting and decided to work together to end this crisis. The group began with an initiative to push to lower New York City's speed limit, something that requires a change in state law.

> *Cohen:* People told us it would take ten years. That first event was in February. The legislative session is only from January to June, and by June we really surprised people by being successfully able to advocate for a lower speed limit in New York City. We realized having a face to the crisis can really make a difference.

Cohen was quick to acknowledge that there is no one solution to this issue, but that, rather, it is a complex set of policy alternatives that have to gain support and be implemented. The group has pivoted much of their efforts to this grander planning mission and have since included advocating for the redesign of existing roads and building new roads with safety as the priority.

Cohen: Most of our roads are big, multi-lane, wide lanes that encourage people to drive really fast. Building roads that are a little narrower, having things such as intersections and traffic circles can make it much safer, especially in urban areas where you have people walking and biking and driving all in a condensed place. Those are the most dangerous and the most important. It's all these highly technical roadway design issues.

Cohen: One of our big successes was successfully transforming what in New York City was called the Boulevard of Death, Queens Boulevard. [This place had] the highest number of people killed on Queens Boulevard each year. It runs seven miles right down the middle of Queens into Manhattan, crossing and bifurcating many, many neighborhoods, mostly low-income. And yet we showed by transforming the Boulevard of Death into the world of art, of life, you're showing what is possible. And almost no one has been killed since it was redesigned.

In many of these bifurcated neighborhoods there is often no other way than to cross these large, dangerous roads, and there's no place to cross safely. Basic road revamping, such as tree barriers in the middle or on the sides of roads or even just greening the roads, makes people naturally slow down. However, these are considered luxuries reserved for socially advantaged neighborhoods. But in truth, they are safety measures.

Cohen: I will give you one tragic example. A woman was trying to cross the street with her four kids on Roosevelt Boulevard in Philadelphia. It's in the lower socioeconomic area of Philly and has six or eight lanes. She had gone to a family barbecue. They'd all had this great time together with family. It was evening and they were crossing Roosevelt, pushing a stroller with four kids. Two cars came hurling down the street, racing. One hit her. The mom and three of the four kids died. Heartbreaking. Tonya Bird, her aunt, has since become a really powerful advocate. She was fighting for speed cameras on Roosevelt and also the redesign of Roosevelt moving forward.

When asked what keeps her up at night, Cohen had this to say:

Cohen: More than 100 people are killed every day like my son. It's just a horrible number. It's the equivalent of a regional plane crashing every single day in silence. No one is talking about this. To me, it's unimaginable, the continuing carnage and the devastation to the family and the community. And I hear from a lot of those people all the time. We get emails. People find us online or on social media. Continuing carnage and the devastation to the family and the community.

It's really about collective responsibility, a safe system approach is really a collective responsibility. Humans are going to make mistakes. This is not about one bad driver. It's about building safe speed, safe roads, safe vehicles. It's about protecting those most vulnerable, supporting those personally impacted as a collective, systematic approach.

In sharp contrast to this idea of collective responsibility is another story from Singer's work, this one out of Georgia:

In the spring of 2010, Raquel Nelson, with her three children, got off a bus and stood at the intersection of Austell Road and Austell Circle in Marietta, waiting to cross the street directly across from her home. Nelson, a single mom, moved her family around by bus, like most people in her apartment complex, because she could not afford a car. Though the bus stop was right across the street from Nelson's home, the nearest crosswalk across the four-lane highway was a twenty-minute walk up and back down the other side of the street. Like most people in her complex, Nelson walked her kids across the busy street instead of going out of her way. This time, on April 10, 2010, it was dark because the family had missed a prior bus, and her four-year-old was carrying a goldfish in a plastic bag—a lot of reasons to not go out of their way. When they crossed the street, a man named Jerry Guy ran over one of Nelson's children with his van. Guy fled the scene. The four-year-old child, A.J., died from his injuries. Nelson and the other two children survived. Guy was partially blind, admitted to drinking and taking pain medication early that day, and had been previously convicted of two hit-and-run accidents on the same day in 1997, one on the same road where he struck Nelson's son. Police charged him with the hit-and-run, cruelty to children, and vehicular homicide. In time, a judge dropped all charges but the hit-and-run. Guy was sentenced to two years in prison and ended up serving six months. A judge also charged Nelson in her son's death: with reckless conduct, with crossing the street somewhere other than the crosswalk, and shockingly, somehow, with vehicular homicide. There's no homicide-level crime for being a pedestrian, but the urge to blame Nelson was powerful enough that the charge for killing someone with your car was applied. An all-White jury convicted Nelson, a Black woman, on the last charge. She faced up to three years in prison until her case attracted national media attention, and a judge offered her a retrial. She ended up with a year's probation and forty hours of community service for the crime of someone else killing her child. She would likely need to run across the four-lane highway where her son died to reach the bus to attend that community service. Bringing criminal charges against Jerry Guy, a partially blind intoxicated repeat-offender hit-and-run driver who killed a child, is a reasonable manifestation of blame. Perhaps this punishment will be enough to keep him off the road. Bringing criminal charges against Raquel Nelson, a single mother with only two hands who needed to cross a highway with three children, is a grotesque manifestation of blame. But blaming either of them does little to prevent the accident from happening again, because blame fails to address the dangerous conditions that produced this accident, namely the absence of a crosswalk at an intersection pedestrians need to navigate.

Raquel Nelson lived in a suburb built for people with cars; she and a growing population couldn't afford one. There was a bus stop but no crosswalk. There was an apartment complex and an intersection but no traffic light. There was a four-lane highway but no easy way across. In an interview with National Public Radio, David Goldberg, a spokesperson for Transportation for America, had a more pointed way to explain metro Atlanta Traffic Operations' decision not to install a crosswalk for Nelson and her neighbors. The agency did not address the safety issue, because addressing it would be tantamount to admitting that there was a problem that the traffic engineers who designed the road and the state and local officials who enabled them needed to solve. Blaming Guy or Nelson made all that disappear. "If they were to go out and fix the problem," he explained, "it would be a tacit acknowledgment that the problem existed." Fixing the problem means there is a problem. Blaming someone means there is no problem at all.[148]

Another organization looking to hold the government accountable for these trends is Smart Growth America. I spoke with Beth Osborne, the Director of Transportation for America, an arm of Smart Growth America. As the former Deputy Assistant Secretary at the U.S. Department of Transportation, she worked on numerous issues related to safety and livability.

In her current role, she focuses on what she calls the "least safe transportation system in the developed world, and not by a little, by far the most."

Osborne: So, it's expensive. It's inefficient. It's inequitable. It's unsafe.

She and the portion of her team called the National Complete Streets Coalition, are responsible for the seminal report in the industry, *Dangerous by Design*, started in 2009.

In the 2022 report, Smart Growth America and The National Complete Streets Coalition, with support from the Centers for Disease Control and

Prevention, reveals the alarming and sustained increase in the number of people being struck and killed by motor vehicles while walking on or near the public streets of our nation. They also offer a number of solutions.

As the title indicates, the report concludes that the high number of pedestrian deaths cannot be attributed to happenstance. To the contrary, given the fact that our nation's streets and roads are built to be used by both motor vehicles and people on foot, the inherent design of many of our roads encourages drivers to travel at relatively high speeds, thus making deadly interactions with pedestrians much more likely.

The numbers of pedestrians killed nationally declined until 2009. In that year, the trend reversed, marking a steady increase from one year to the next, from 4,109 killed in 2009 up to an estimated 7,265 in 2021. During that time, drivers struck and killed a total of 64,073 pedestrians.[149]

However, the authors are careful to point out the limitations on their data. The Fatality Analysis Reporting System (FARS), created by the National Highway Traffic Safety Administration (NHTSA) has numerous limitations. It fails to properly account for fatalities involving people with disabilities. Wheelchair and scooter users are still inappropriately grouped with road users like skateboarders and roller skaters. Local crash reporting that feeds into FARS has major issues too, such as not recording race or ethnicity in a significant share of fatalities. Nevertheless, enough good data exists to see trends in location and income.

DANGEROUS BY DEMOGRAPHIC

The increase in fatalities was distributed unequally across the states. The top 10 most deadly states for pedestrians (2016-2020) were New Mexico, Florida, South Carolina, Arizona, Delaware, Louisiana, Mississippi, Nevada, California, and Georgia. All of the top 20 were clustered from the West to the South. The authors attributed this to low-density sprawling land uses and high-speed, multi-lane arterial highways—that have been the dominant form and most common design for highways—meaning that state and federal transportation funding is poured into street designs that are deadly for pedestrians.

Although people of all ages, races, income levels, and abilities are affected by dangerous street design, certain populations bear the brunt of the burden. People of color, low-income residents, and older adults are much more likely to die while walking. Low-income communities bear a greater share of poorly designed streets that lack even the most basic pedestrian safety features like crosswalks, signals, and refuges, and are frequently divided by wide, high-speed roads that create life-threatening conflicts for people walking.

While 11% of all reported pedestrian fatalities failed to specify race or ethnicity, what data there is paints a disturbing picture. The pedestrian deaths per 100,000 by race and ethnicity (2016-2020) are:

Deaths per 100,000	Race or Ethnicity
1.2	Asian /Pacific Islander
1.5	White, non-Hispanic
1.8	Hispanic
3.0	African American
4.8	American Indian or Alaskan Native

Older adults, people between the ages of 50 and 65, and people over 75 are also more likely to be killed on our streets. And while the federal database of fatalities does not include the household income of people struck and killed while walking, we know that the lower the income of the census tract, the more likely a person is to be struck and killed while walking there.

WHY CERTAIN AREAS ARE MORE DANGEROUS

What is it about these places that make them so dangerous for pedestrians? Why not, say, New York City, which you would expect to be high on the list, but which doesn't even crack the top 20 in pedestrian fatalities?

The reason falls along historical context. In the 1950s, America became consumed by the idea of straight and spacious modern highways. Of course, pedestrians are barred from walking along federal highways. But the urge to create more new streets into the hearts of cities took hold, and engineers simply did not consider pedestrians to be an important concern. They also did not show any respect for traditionally low-income or ethnic neighborhoods. When streets are straight, travel lanes are wide and plentiful, and intersections are infrequent or uncontrolled, drivers operate at higher speeds than is safe. It's also a matter of the designs of the streets and sidewalks themselves. For example, gently rounded corners at intersections (with as much as a 30-foot turning radius) allow drivers to maintain a relatively higher speed while forcing pedestrians to walk further to cross the street; contrast those with the street corners in Manhattan, which have a much sharper 10-foot turning radius that forces drivers to go slow.

Dangerous by Design includes a robust section on recommended alterations including:

· Better and more robust pedestrian accident data, as well as on walking

in general.
- The adoption by the United States Department of Transportation (USDOT) in cities, towns, villages, and anywhere with many conflict points and vulnerable users, or where pedestrian safety and vehicle speed are incompatible goals.
- The assurance by NHTSA that vehicle design does not impede direct vision of people in front of the car and incorporate pedestrian survivability into the safety ratings.
- The Federal Highway Administration (FHWA) should update design standards, like those in the Manual on Uniform Traffic Control Devices (MUTCD) and they should stop prioritizing vehicle speed over safety.
- USDOT should prioritize safety by using the $200 billion in discretionary competitive grants that they control from the Infrastructure Investment and Jobs Act (IIJA).
- States should prioritize safe access to destinations for people walking on streets in developed areas, whether big urban areas or rural villages.
- Use proven street designs that save lives and make urban neighborhoods more vibrant.

The 1956 Highway Act that funded the interstates was created out of a desire to move vehicles, trucks, and personal vehicles over longer distances at high speeds to more-economically connect communities. Unfortunately, the negative consequences of interstates and connected high speed highways unequivocally falls on communities of color, communities that can't afford the property value of a place that isn't built near a highway. However, lower-income communities do not have the time, connections, or power to fight highway expansions that disrupt their communities. And when they do, they're fighting against wealthier communities.

Osbourne: Then you get into another layer of the issue. We are a nation where we provide affordability through deprivation. In these communities, we won't give you sidewalks. We won't give you transit. We won't give you bike lanes. We won't give you parks. All this will keep your property value down. So, what do you do there? Just say, yeah, you're right. We won't give you access to get around safely because that's how we're going to provide you affordability. It's now called equitable to deny people the basic safety amenities of being able to access the things they need in order to keep prices low.

I think a lot of the issue with public transportation is we have to start by saying what are we trying to accomplish with public transportation, which actually might require us to back up and say, what are we trying to accomplish with transportation in general? My organization's mission is to connect people to jobs and essential services. That, to me, is the point of the transportation system. However, that's not actually what we measure in transportation. In transportation, we measure whether vehicles are moving at a speed limit. Nobody needs to drive anywhere to accomplish that. People could just go out for a ride or drive in circles and never get anywhere. Trying to determine whether people can reach essential destinations is a different issue. And when you take it from that perspective, you look at the transportation system very differently. Transit, when it's good, is not just a social service. The nations that do transit well provide great transit to those who need it. But it's not an afterthought. It's a beautiful system everybody wants to use. It includes some rail, some buses of different sizes and some van pools. And it is interconnected with those getting around by bike, scooter and foot.

The latest data continues to show that circumstances get significantly more dangerous for those who move around by foot or by a mobility-assisted device like a wheelchair. However, where the DOT made changes, fatalities went down 34%. Even with this, positive results must be documented, iterated, and shared. The way ahead is clear. All we need is the will to make it a reality.

To gain a broader perspective on infrastructure's inequities, I interviewed Benjamin Dierker, the Executive Director of Alliance for Innovation and Infrastructure (AII), a think tank that studies infrastructure policy and recommends innovative approaches. AII was founded by Brigham McCown, the first administrator of the Pipeline and Hazardous Materials Safety Administration (PHMSA). After his service in the Navy, McCown came to USDOT in the Federal Motor Carrier Safety Administration before taking his role at PHMSA.

I asked Dierker how his organization approaches the most pressing infrastructure needs in America. He had this to say:

Dierker: It's a broad question, so I'll take a couple of different angles. As an organization, we try to look at any given public policy or any challenge and see first, what is causing it, what are the issues leading to it, and try to diagnose root causes. Then we look at what people are proposing as solutions and look to see if those solutions are thinking through the unintended consequences. If you think of public policy like a balloon; if you squeeze it, there's some other part of that balloon that's going to jut out. And so, if people aren't thinking through all of that—both the intended consequences and the unintended—there's very likely some bad outcome that's going to happen.

From there, he offered an example using climate change: while there is a significant amount of alarmism, fear, and emotional language in politics and in public policy generally, that is especially the case around climate change. Without diminishing the absolute need to tackle the issue, at its core, climate change is an energy issue, one that is wrapped around a transportation issue. Therefore, it is critical that advocates of climate policy realize that certain provisions can have negative economic effects (e.g., the increasing price of cars which will, in turn, disproportionately affect lower-income populations and potentially price them out of buying options). Low- or no- emissions vehicles may be a winning climate strategy, but if only the *top one%* can financially access them, it is not truly moving the needle. Similar discussions can be had around improving and implementing higher vehicle safety measures like rear backup cameras. However, these genuinely valuable and proven safety add-ons can raise the cost of cars, meaning lower-income families cannot access the newer, safer cars.

> *Dierker:* These are good things to have, but should it be regulated and required, or is there another way to achieve the outcome we want that might not price people out of vehicles? So, what I would say to a voter is while something might sound like a great idea, try to just think one or two steps ahead. Maybe you enact this policy and maybe it does lead to this desired outcome, but does it also lead to this negative outcome? That can be hard to do, especially if it's a niche area, but simply remain open, willing to engage opposing ideas and potential negative unintended consequences.

AII is a nonpartisan independent group, and has a board of directors and advisory council—from both parties that have been in three or four different presidential administrations—and includes academics and local officials, which are things they are very proud of. Yet, Dierker is quick to point to the current political environment as a cause for concern.

> *Dierker:* We want to be able to say, we are an independent voice that's evaluating issues. But as soon as you say, you know, natural gas is a needed fuel for example, you have one side of the aisle saying you are climate denier, one side saying you aren't going far enough, and a third group asking why nuclear was left out of the conversation. It's just a very difficult environment to speak into and one we know is going to be harder to push rational policy in.

In another example, Dierker discusses the Highway Trust Fund. He points out a simple fact: we all require good roads, even those who don't own a car and who use public transportation. Every vehicle on the roadways must help pay for maintenance and repair. Every gallon of gasoline is federally taxed at $0.18 cents. Diesel is $0.24. And that rate hasn't been raised since 1993, despite substantial changes to both the economic and physical contexts. The average weight of vehicles is heavier. We now have high fuel-economy vehicles, hybrids, and electric vehicles that are going far, far further on the same tank of gas or not paying at all. This leaves the Highway Trust Fund, which was rated to be insolvent by 2022 without an infusion, unable to pay for the roads and maintenance.

The Highway Trust Fund consists of two accounts: highway and mass transit. While the gas tax supports both, mass transit does not *contribute* to the funding replenishment. So, when the majority of elected officials began valuing mass transit, the pull from that account increased without any supplemental replenishment. It was a solution that caused unintended, significant highway infrastructure issues, despite giving us mass transit. It's all a trade-off; eventually you must pay for it.

Whether we increase the gas tax enough to pay for both accounts or determine a separate funding source for mass transit, the current solution is not sustainable. To further complicate the issue, the intended funding model for the Trust Fund was, in essence, "pay as you go" to offset wear and tear from driving. However, it is significantly more complex than that. Building *new* roads and road beautification projects remove resources from this account and are inequitably distributed to higher-income areas. Add to that the increase in hybrid and electric cars that utilize the roads without contributing the same share of the funding. All of this is depleting funds that would otherwise be used for maintaining existing roads.

> *Dierker:* And that's going to lead to actual deaths on the road. People aren't thinking about that politically. No one wants to raise the gas tax. No one wants to eliminate the gas tax to take the money out of the general fund. But the consequence is real life or death issues on the roadways. People are going to die. There's going to be traffic incidents which become these broader ripples. If your concern is climate, that's vehicle tailpipe emissions while sitting and idling in traffic. If your issue is safety, that's deaths due to poor road conditions and potholes. If you are concerned with economics and efficiency, traffic bottlenecks lead to lost productivity. All these consequences stem from that one small thing.

When asked about the best- and worst-case scenarios, Dierker had this to say:

Dierker: One of those true things is our economy, in fact, the world economy, is still reliant on fossil fuels. And we actually do continue to need fossil fuels. I view the energy transition as a relay race and fossil fuels have the baton right now. And before you hand off a baton in a relay, both parties have to be running. They have to be running, approaching their full speed before the hand-off happens. Renewables are moving, but they're not at that speed where you can pass the baton and say, Great, you take it from here. If we move too quickly, we are going to have things like rolling blackouts and the 2021 Texas winter disaster.

So that's not to say we're going in the wrong direction, so long as we maintain robust energy as a goal. Rather, we're going in a good direction too fast. The good news is, out of adversity often comes innovations. We are seeing greater efficiency in a lot of energy production because people are being forced to innovate, create new inventions that are going to make things better and easier in the energy space. A lot of innovation is happening in electric vehicle batteries or solar panels. There are a ton of these innovative technologies being generated because people continue to recognize there's a problem and causing them to make strides in innovation.

I asked Dierker directly about other ways infrastructure issues disproportionately affect lower-income and populations of color. He referenced an article in the *Journal of Environmental Science and Technology* that recently conducted a study showing low-income and communities of color have higher rates of natural gas and methane leaks.[150] While the study simply points to the large disparity, in his view, this is reflective of a "damage prevention" issue. Typically, lower income and communities of color tend to be in older homes built in the forties and fifties—which are more likely to have these leaks—or in more densely populated urban settings where natural gas distribution lines are highly concentrated. This led us to a broader discussion around damage prevention.

Dierker: When I think about damage prevention, I think about pipelines. Not the big oil, 42-inch steel pipelines that are crossing the northern plains. Rather, the one-inch natural gas distribution lines that are under all of our homes and in cities. And that's probably one of the leading public policy issues that people don't talk about.

Every five or ten years, you may see an entire neighborhood explode and grab national headlines. Everyone freaks out. The NTSB gets involved. But the overall issue is a daily occurrence and involves common excavation work. People are digging all around the country all the time, whether they're just in their front yard to plant a tree or a construction crew laying the foundation for a building. But when they dig, they obviously can't see through the dirt. That means they're likely to hit one of the over 20 million miles of pipelines, cables, or electrical lines buried just below the surface across the country. Fortunately, there are effective technological solutions, policy changes, and accepted best practices to avoid digging into these underground facilities, yet many just aren't implemented systemically. And that's frustrating. So that is one of the things that keeps me up at night, because I know there's a solution to a major problem that people just haven't done.

I asked Dierker to dive deeper into the root causes behind this lack of action and his response—economic, as opposed to political—was surprising to me. His explanation surrounds the 811 call system, which is the number everyone must call before digging to have the local utilities come out to the property and mark existing lines. Within the 811 system, there are multiple parties, including homeowners and construction workers who are actively digging, locators who are spray painting the ground to represent facility locations, utility companies who own the lines in question, and the call centers taking and routing the 811 calls. Each of these stakeholders have differing levels of legitimate power based on ownership and economics.

Utilities effectively pay for the whole system, so no changes are made without their buy in. Utilities, or facility owners/operators (to include natural gas companies, telecom companies, and others), are organized, wealthy, and have power. Excavators use the system for free. They call 811, get their site marked, and then do their dig without paying any fees. They tend to be less economically empowered, less sophisticated, unorganized, and have no bargaining power or coordination. These are independent contractors, mom-and-pop businesses, or individual homeowners. They're unrelated to one another.

Every year in the U.S., there are over 500,000 excavation incidents where the person digging hits a pipeline, electrical line, water main, or other buried facility. Logically, all excavation damage is caused by the excavator, but not every incident is their fault. It could have been the locator, the one call center, or the utilities who caused the primary error. So, when new technology or techniques arise or when best practices should be implemented in law or regulation to protect excavators but utilities and the systems they support don't want to pay for it, the excavators are effectively discriminated against because they do not have the money, power, or influence to effectuate change.

Natural gas distribution lines are one of the most struck underground facilities. These are concentrated primarily in urban areas—which also tends to impact lower income and minority communities. Leaks that do occur there can go unnoticed or unremedied for extended periods of time. When they are detected, they can cause evacuations, asphyxiation, or explosions that impact whole communities, all which were innocent in the process, as they didn't do the digging.

> *Dierker:* I think there is a relevant climate and environmental concern as well. When natural gas and other facilities are struck, they release hazards. Every excavation incident is avoidable. The entire 811 system is designed to prevent every incident and the technology and best practices waiting in the wings but not being implemented can further reduce damages by over 80% . The longer these reforms are not made, the more environmental harm, the more deaths and injuries, and the more economic loss there will be—and it costs roughly $100 billion annually. These costs accrue mostly to innocent parties: the neighbors who lose internet or electricity, the community evacuated due to natural gas leaks, the entire city rerouted for traffic to avoid an incident, etc.

Dierker goes on to point to studies linking higher rates of natural gas leaks to lower-income areas and communities of color. And while it is a commonly held belief that such leaks are an economic issue or a social justice issue, they are actually an infrastructure issue that can be solved. It starts with updating our infrastructure to avoid damage and explosions and extends to reforming the processes that protect critical infrastructure.

To conclude our time together, I asked Dierker what he would hope to share with voters.

> *Dierker:* I would say first, don't think about everything nationally. The things that are affecting you are often local. The federal government is not the solution to all your problems. And even if it were, the federal government doesn't know how to solve something on your street. You know who does? The city council. Somebody who lives in that neighborhood. That would be my first thing. Look local, start local, get educated on local officials and you're going to solve a lot of those problems.

6

CRIMINAL JUSTICE

Being Black in modern America means you are likely to have a deeply conflicted attitude toward the police, the courts, and the prisons—collectively known as our system of criminal justice. Or, perhaps more accurately, and as famed Civil Rights Attorney and Author of *Open Season*[151] Ben Crump has said, criminal INJUSTICE!

In a reasonable world, if a Black person is a victim of a crime or needs some sort of emergency assistance, the arrival of a police officer should be a welcome sight. After all, it's the job of the police to come to the aid of citizens in distress, and law-abiding citizens have equal needs in emergencies. We pay taxes, have jobs, and own or rent homes and automobiles, and should be entitled to protection from crime. In fair and just society, that would be the end of the story.

But sadly, reality is very different. Not all, but many, police departments, courts, and prison systems are not impartial arbiters of the law. Instead, they serve as weapons wielded by the entrenched power structure, to maintain three goals: power, control, and money.

Even in the small examples above from transportation, the system is set up to maintain the existing, racist, social structure that favors the privileged and systemically oppresses minorities. Success at these first two goals ensures that those in power and those in control have greater and easier access to wealth and the levers of power, and that this access continues generation after generation.

The third goal is, in many ways, more simplistic: money. In many towns across America, the police and the courts act as an unregulated tax collection agency, one meant to extract wealth from offenders who are forced to pay exorbitant fees and fines for everything from having a broken taillight to filing a motion in court. While these fees and fines are assigned equally by offense, the likelihood of being in an offending position is significantly skewed against people of color.

Money and power go hand in hand, and the police and courts, with their extraordinary constitutional authority to control the lives of citizens, are an effective tool for ensuring that both remain in the hands of the privileged, the well resourced, and power brokers.

America's system of criminal injustice begins on the streets and in the neighborhoods—with the local police. This is the first step: the entrance to the funnel that leads to the courts and then to the prison system. Many White, privileged people can spend their entire lives and never enter this portal. Their encounters with the police are cordial and even positive. In contrast, most Black people can recount frequent interactions with the police—and many are negative.

The problem is significant. There are an estimated 16,000 police departments in the United States, and they employ 450,000 officers. The biggest is the New York City Police Department, with 36,000 officers. The smallest are the countless one-man departments in towns and school districts across rural America. While some are fair and just, the George Floyd, Breanna Taylor, and Elijah McClain murders—and dozens more—illustrate a systemic pattern of police power being used inequitably and forcing victims to pay the ultimate price.

A DEPARTMENT OF DYSFUNCTION

The Kansas City Police Department (KCPD) is the principal law enforcement agency serving Kansas City, Missouri. Founded in 1874, the department consists of about 2,000 employees and has an annual budget of $249 million (2021). Of these, roughly 1,200 are uniformed officers.

The city itself is the largest city in Missouri by population and area. As of the 2020 census, it had a population of 508,090.

Governance of the KCPD rests with the Kansas City Board of Police Commissioners, which coordinates with the Chief of Police, sets policy, makes promotions, and holds both closed and open meetings. Four of the five members of the board are selected by the governor, following approval of the Missouri legislature. The fifth member of the board is the mayor of Kansas City. Commissioners normally serve four-year terms, but can be replaced by the governor, who, from 2018 until 2024, was Republican Mike Parson, himself a former sheriff of Polk County from 1993 to 2004.

Mike Parson, who, as governor, ultimately had more authority over the Kansas City Police Department than any other individual person has been characterized as a right-wing politician who professes to deplore racism while quietly supporting efforts to maintain and even strengthen the White power structure.

In July 2022, the *Kansas City Star* published a series of reports exposing systematic racism within the KCPD itself. Entitled "Racism in the KCPD,"[152] the series, written by Glenn E. Rice, Luke Nozicka, and Katie Moore, featured accounts from twenty-five current and former Black officers of various ranks who told stories of discrimination and racist abuse, backed up by scores of department e-mails, internal police memos, legal documents, lawsuits, and videos. It pointed to a system that forced Black officers out of the department on dubious pretexts while keeping the upper leadership decidedly White.

Some of the most disturbing revelations included:

- During the past two decades, the percentage of Black officers in the KCPD has actually *declined*. In a city that is 28% Black, only 11.6% of officers are Black, down from 12.3% in 1998.
- Over the past 15 years, at least 18 Black officers identified by *The Star* had tendered resignations to the department directly due to racist treatment. The department called this getting "papered out." Resigning officers' cite regular instances of White officers using racist stereotypes such as being lazy and eating fried chicken. Some have stated being called "boy" and the n-word while in the line of duty.
- Since 2009, police leaders have been aware that discipline in the ranks is meted out unequally. An internal assessment never made public by KCPD showed that according to court records, while Black officers made up 11% of the force, they received 18% of the disciplinary actions.
- Homicide detectives hold a coveted position in the KCPD but only about 9% are Black.
- Victims are also treated inequitably. KCPD detectives send cases to Jackson County prosecutors for about 73% of White female victims but only 51% of Black male victims.

The inequities are not simply in what is happening, but also what is not happening. White officers receive minimal consequences for more heinous actions than their Black counterparts. Former KCPD detective Eric DeValkenaere remained on the payroll more than two months after being convicted of second-degree involuntary manslaughter in the 2019 killing of Cameron Lamb, whom DeValkenaere shot while Lamb was backing his pickup into his garage.

Four other officers, including some charged with felonies like assault, continued to work for months while facing prosecution. That quartet included officers Matthew Brummett and Charles Prichard, who, in 2020, were charged with assault for their parts in the brutal arrest of a Black transgender woman whose face was slammed on the pavement.

From 2011 to 2017, under the leadership of Darryl Forte—the city's first and only Black police chief—there was hope for change. He spoke out about racism he faced from coworkers, created a diversity officer position, and implemented de-escalation tactics to address problems of police brutality that fell disproportionately on Black residents. He was chief for six years before being replaced by Rick Smith. Many Black KCPD cops compared it to the change from Barack Obama to Donald Trump. Within the KCPD, it was back to business as usual, and racism in the ranks made a swift return.

In November 2021, Chief Smith announced his retirement. The Black community was not sorry to see him leave. "I want people to know we tried to work with Chief Smith and get him to make the appropriate changes to meet the needs of the community," said Lora McDonald, Executive Director of the social justice agency, More 2. "When that didn't happen, we started maneuvering toward asking for his termination or for him to leave."

On September 19, 2022, the U.S. Department of Justice sent a letter to the Board of Police Commissioners informing the board it was opening an investigation to determine whether the KCPD was engaged in a pattern or practice of discrimination based on race in violation of Title VII of the Civil Rights Act of 1964. The letter stated, "Our investigation is based on information suggesting that KCPD may be engaged in certain employment practices that discriminate against Black officers and applicants, including those that have a disparate impact based on race, in entry-level hiring, promotions, and assignments to Detective, in imposing discipline, and by maintaining a hostile work environment."

As *The New York Times* reported, Mayor Quinton Lucas, a Democrat long critical of the practices of the KCPD, told reporters that the problems have been known for years. The department's Board of Police Commissioners, on which he now sits, should have conducted its own inquiry years ago, he said. "I think it is time—frankly, past time—that we look internally at the department to see what we can do better."[153]

IN PREDATORY POLICE DEPARTMENTS, CASH IS KING

In a trend casually labeled "revenue policing," there is evidence some police departments are targeting Black citizens with onerous fines and fees to swell their budgets.

Consider the small town of Brookside, Alabama. If this sounds like the introduction to an episode of *The Twilight Zone*, you can rest assured that many Black residents of Brookside feel that's exactly where they're living. Nestled along the banks of Five Mile Creek in North-Central Jefferson County, in land area, it's only six square miles. As of the 2020 census, the population of this former mining town was just 1,253. The racial makeup was 79.5% White, 18.5% African American, 0.7% Hispanic or Latino of any race, 0.3% Native American, 0.2% from other races, and 1.4% from two or more races. But what sets Brookside apart is the size of its police force. In 2022, it boasted nine officers, or one for every 144 residents—for relevance, New York City has one officer per 238 residents and, across the nation, the average is one for every 588 residents. In 2018, there was just one officer—Chief of Police Mike Jones. In that year, they towed 50 vehicles. Jones hired more officers and set them loose on the community. In 2020, the number of tows skyrocketed to 789. Traffic tickets cost motorists thousands of dollars and have become the town's largest source of revenue. In 2021, more than half of Brookside's revenues stemmed from fines and forfeitures.[154]

As AL.com revealed, in the entire eight-year period between 2011 and 2018, the tiny town reported to the state just 55 serious crimes—none of them homicide or rape. But in 2018, it began building a police empire, hiring more and more officers to patrol its six miles of roads and mile-and-a-half jurisdiction on Interstate 22. Brookside officers have been accused in lawsuits of fabricating charges, using racist language, and literally "making up laws" to slap fines on innocent passersby. Defendants must pay thousands in fines and fees or pay for costly appeals to state courts, and low-income residents can become caught in a web of debt from which they cannot escape.[155]

"Brookside is a poster child for policing for profit," said Carla Crowder, the director of Alabama Appleseed Center for Law & Justice, a nonprofit devoted to justice and equity. "We are not safer because of it."

Like all systemic trends, there is rarely a single cancer that can be eliminated to solve the issue. Chief Jones had the full support of Mayor Mike Bryan as well as the local judge, who held municipal court just once a month.

On January 25, 2022, Jones resigned under pressure. Leah Nelson, research director at Alabama Appleseed, said the departure of Jones was welcome news, but it didn't solve the deeper issue. Jones "is just a symptom of the problem," she said. "As long as criminal justice policy and tax policy are intertwined, we'll see versions of Brookside pop up. We need policy reform."

Predatory police departments tend to target Black drivers. As Kelsey Shoub and others wrote in "Fines, Fees, Forfeitures, and Disparities: A Link Between Municipal Reliance on Fines and Racial Disparities in Policing,"[156] studies have shown that more municipal revenue is raised through fines, fees, and forfeitures in communities where a greater proportion of the population is Black and where there is no Black representation in local elected offices.

Traffic stop outcomes, including searches, vary by the race of the driver. These disparities are typically attributed to either officer bias or institutional racism. During both traffic and street stops, Black people are stopped and searched disproportionately more than White people. They are also more likely to be arrested, incarcerated, experience longer prison sentences, and even killed.

A large-scale study of racial disparities in police stops across the United States analyzed data on approximately 95 million stops from 21 state patrol agencies and 35 municipal police departments across the country. Curiously, the authors found Black drivers were less likely to be stopped after sunset. Why the anomaly? The best explanation is that, at night, it's more difficult to determine a driver's race.

Revenue policing has its costs too. On August 9, 2014, 18-year-old Michael Brown was shot and killed by police officer Darren Wilson in Ferguson, Missouri, a suburb of St. Louis. The Civil Rights Division of the Department of Justice (DOJ) investigated and found that, while racism was a factor, the bottom line was revenue policing: "Ferguson's law enforcement practices are shaped by the city's focus on revenue rather than by public safety needs." The DOJ found that the disproportionate rate of police stops, searches, and arrests of Black residents resulted from city officials' growing dependence on municipal fees and fines, which police and court officers were exhorted to produce through aggressive enforcement of traffic violations and petty offenses. ArchCity Defenders, authors of an early and influential white paper on the troubled municipal court system, demonstrated that many other St. Louis municipalities have similar or worse practices than Ferguson.

TO SERVE AND PROTECT

The motto of most police departments is "To Serve and Protect," but for many Black citizens, this motto stops short of their communities. Statistics on Black citizens being targeted by racist police forces, not just random racist officers, but by the system itself, are overwhelming. Pew Research on Black and White attitudes towards the police are telling.

- In a 2019 Center survey, 84% of Black adults said that, in dealing with police, Black people are generally treated less fairly than Whites. Perhaps more surprising is 63% of White survey participants agreed, indicating an awareness of the problem.

- Black adults are about five times as likely as Whites to say they've been unfairly stopped by police because of their race or ethnicity. Black men are the prime targets. Even when just walking, 59% of Black participants say they've been unfairly stopped.
- White Democrats and White Republicans have vastly different views of how Black people are treated by police. 88% of White Democrats agree that there is inequitable treatment by race, while only 43% of White Republican participants agree.
- White police officers continue to deny systematic racism. Nearly all White officers (92%) said the U.S. had made the changes needed to assure equal rights for Black people. Only 29% of their Black colleagues agreed.
- White police officers tend to believe that fatal encounters between Black people and police are isolated incidents. A majority of Black officers (57%) said that such incidents were evidence of a broader problem, but only 27% of White officers and 26% of Hispanic officers agreed.[157]

As long as the White majority denies the systemic nature of these instances, efforts to ignite change will continue to stall. We must elect officials who recognize the reality and who authentically vow to weed out the cancers that exist in these systems.

YOUR DAY IN COURT

Police departments don't gauge their success on how many little old ladies their officers escort across the street. They gauge their success on how many crimes they solve, and you solve a crime by making an arrest.

Every day, police officers make decisions based on two questions:

- What constitutes a crime? What transgression warrants placing someone under arrest?
- Who is the suspect in the crime? Does the race of the suspect make a difference?

The answers to those two questions are, "It depends," and "Yes." On the street, police officers have wide discretion when faced with non-violent, misdemeanor offenses such as loitering, driving without a license, or marijuana possession. A person acting erratically could be charged with disorderly conduct or a person without access to a bathroom could be charged with public urination.

For such offenses—or perceived offenses—Black people are more likely to be arrested than White citizens, and these statistics only amplify in more serious offenses. The NAACP reports that while only 5% of illicit drug users are Black, they represent 29% of those arrested and 33% of those incarcerated for drug offenses. Black and White people use drugs at similar rates, but in the third step of the system—incarceration—the imprisonment rate of Black offenders for drug charges is almost six times that of Whites.[158]

In the United States, people who identify as Black comprise 13.6% of the population. According to The Sentencing Project, in 2016, Black Americans comprised 27% of all individuals arrested in the United States—double their share of the total population. That same year, Black youths accounted for 15% of all U.S. children yet made up 35% of juvenile arrests.

A key driver of the disparity is the stubbornly held belief among White law enforcement officers that people of color commit more crimes and therefore require harsher oversight. "One reason minorities are stopped disproportionately is because police see violations where they are," said Louis Dekmar, the president of the International Association of Chiefs of Police, and the chief of LaGrange, Georgia's police department. "Crime is often significantly higher in minority neighborhoods than elsewhere. And that is where we allocate our resources."

In reality, it's more of a case of police working harder to *find* crime in Black neighborhoods. Politicians initiate sweeping programs designed to appeal to White suburban voters, often disproportionately targeting Black and Brown citizens. "The War on Drugs" and policing policies including "Broken Windows," and "Stop and Frisk" sanction higher levels of police contact with Black citizens, resulting in greater opportunities for arresting Black people on charges such as disorderly conduct.

"Stop and Frisk," championed in New York City by disgraced former mayor Rudy Giuliani and continued by Michael Bloomberg, broadly targeted male residents of neighborhoods populated by low-income people of color. However, it was shown to be ineffective, and this assessment was further validated when crime in New York City continued to decline after scaling back the practice.

Nationwide surveys highlight disparities in the outcomes of police stops. Once pulled over, Black and Hispanic drivers are three times as likely as White drivers to be searched and twice as likely as to be arrested. And to underscore the racist foundation for these numbers, searches of Black drivers and their vehicles produce a lower "contraband hit rate" than searches of White drivers. In other words, when White motorists are searched, it's more likely to find a valid law enforcement infraction. But Black drivers are searched gratuitously. More searches and fewer results add up to blatant harassment.

In our court system, judges have great discretion when setting bail or ordering defendants to be incarcerated in the local jail before trial. This is called "pre-trial detention." Being jailed before trial is a significant disruption: it throws a defendant's life into disarray and can result in job losses or children being removed from the home.

In 2016, Black people were subjected to pre-trial detention in local jails at a rate 3.5 times that of non-Hispanic Whites. Young, Black men are about 50% more likely to be detained pretrial than White defendants, and in large urban areas, Black felony defendants are over 25% more likely than White defendants to be held pre-trial.

70% of pre-trial releases require a money bond, a significant burden for low-income defendants, who are disproportionately people of color. Black and Latino people are more likely than Whites to be denied bail, to have a higher money bond set, and to be detained because they cannot pay their bond. Because they are more likely to be low income and to have criminal records, they are often judged to be higher safety and flight risks.

PLEA DEALS AND MANDATORY MINIMUMS

The overwhelming majority of criminal cases in the United States are resolved through plea deals. In the federal system, approximately 97% of convictions are the product of guilty pleas. These deals should be a win-win for all sides: the state gets a conviction, the court gets a case resolved and off the docket, and the accused—who admits guilt—gets a lighter sentence.

But for plea deals to work ethically, the system must be fair and transparent. Plea deals determine what crime the defendant is convicted for, which then triggers the applicable sentencing guidelines, such as range, and statutory minimum and maximum sentences. By deciding which *initial charges* to file, prosecutors can set the starting point for plea negotiations. They have considerable power to reduce charges—such as felony charges—to misdemeanors, drop concurrent charges involving less serious crimes, and drop or reduce charges carrying a possible incarceration sentence so that the defendant serves no jail or prison time.

As researchers Sonja B. Starr and M. M. Rehavi noted in "Racial Disparity in Federal Criminal Sentences,"[159] prosecutors must often subjectively assess the strength of evidence and choose how to characterize facts that are often ambiguous. For instance, if a gun is found in the car that transported a defendant to a burglary, the prosecutor must decide whether to allege that the burglary therefore legally qualified as a "crime of violence," that the gun qualified as a "firearm," and that the defendant "carried" it "during and in relation to" the burglary. These conditions are necessary to trigger a five-year mandatory minimum sentence by federal law, which would run consecutively to the burglary sentence. However, a prosecutor might decide to charge the defendant with every possible crime, then, during the plea deal talks, remove the gun charges that he wasn't interested in anyway. Or he might choose to "swallow the gun" at the outset and just charge burglary.

The prosecutor's decision to bring particularly severe initial charges, such as those carrying mandatory minimums, can adversely affect outcomes for defendants, even when the severe charges are reduced in plea bargaining; the threat of the initial charges may induce the defendant to plead guilty on less favorable terms.

Based on their research, the authors calculated that significant reduction in the number of incarcerated Black men could be achieved by eliminating the disparity in mandatory minimum charges. With 95,400 Black men incarcerated in federal facilities, removing an estimated 9% who were unfairly sentenced would ultimately reduce the steady-state number of Black males in federal incarceration by nearly 8,000. The Bureau of Prisons estimates that it costs $29,027 per year to incarcerate an additional prisoner. The direct federal budgetary savings of reducing the prison stock by just 8,000 men would be approximately $230 million per year.

A study from Carlos Berdejó of Loyola Law School found significant racial disparities in plea deals that suggested some prosecutors use race as a proxy for criminality. When evaluating which defendants are likely to commit crimes in the future, prosecutors may consciously or subconsciously rely on racial stereotypes. After analyzing more than 30,000 Wisconsin cases over a seven-year period, the study found significant racial disparities in the plea-bargaining process. Black defendants were more likely to not be offered a plea deal at all, and to be convicted of their highest initial charge. White defendants were 25% more likely to have their most serious initial charge dropped or reduced to a less severe charge. White defendants with no prior convictions were over 25% more likely to receive a charge reduction than Black defendants with no prior convictions. When compared to similar defendants who faced initial felony charges, White defendants were approximately 15% more likely to be convicted of a misdemeanor instead.[160]

In cases that began as misdemeanors, the disparities were even greater. White defendants facing misdemeanor charges were nearly 75% more likely to have all charges that carried potential imprisonment dropped, dismissed, or reduced to lesser charges. White defendants with no prior criminal history and charged with misdemeanors were 46% more likely than similar Black defendants to have all charges carrying a potential sentence dropped or reduced to charges that carry no potential imprisonment.

SENTENCING

The last opportunity the court system has to exert influence is during sentencing. In sentencing a guilty defendant, every judge has sentencing guidelines. The United States Code sets the minimum mandatory and maximum sentences for offenses. Courts must impose the minimum and never exceed the maximum. During federal sentencing, the judge may consider any information concerning the background, character, and conduct of the client being sentenced, and adjust the sentence accordingly.

A "departure" is a change from the final sentencing range computed by examining the provisions of the sentencing guidelines themselves. For example, it can be initiated by a prosecution request to reward cooperation. A "variance," by contrast, occurs when a judge imposes a sentence above or below the otherwise properly calculated final sentencing range based on application of the other statutory factors of the law.

According to the United States Sentencing Commission, federal prison sentence length is often associated with demographics. After controlling for a wide variety of sentencing factors, the Commission found that Black male offenders receive sentences on average 19.1% longer than similarly situated White male offenders. The Commission reported that non-government sponsored departures and variances appear to contribute significantly to the difference in sentence length between Black male and White male offenders. Black male offenders are 21.2% *less* likely than White male offenders to receive a non-government sponsored downward departure or variance. Even when Black male offenders receive a departure or variance, they get less and end up with sentences 16.8% longer than similar White male offenders. In contrast, there was a 7.9% difference in sentence length between Black male and White male offenders who received sentences within the applicable sentencing.

7

THE PRISON SYSTEM

I n every step in the criminal justice process, police, district attorneys, and judges have opportunities to tilt the application of justice towards either fairness or bias. Police choose whom they stop and detain, using flimsy pretexts at times. They choose whom to arrest or let go. Prosecutors choose the severity of the initial charges. They choose to seek a plea deal or pursue conviction. The judge can let the defendant go on their own recognizance, determine the amount of bail, or choose to confine them in pre-trial detention. Judges have flexibility in how they conduct the trial and significant authority over sentencing. For a defendant, especially one of low economic means, these decisions can have life-altering consequences even before the trial has started.

If the system is biased, it's easy to see how even slight differences in how citizens are treated can, over time, accumulate to a significant disparity. If the defendant is convicted and sentenced to prison, he or she enters the third step of the criminal justice system.

The United States—the "Shining City on the Hill"—has the world's biggest prison system, largest prison population, and the highest per-capita incarceration rate of any nation on Earth. One out of every five people imprisoned across the world is incarcerated in the United States. The U.S. prison system, which includes prison, parole, and probation operations, costs U.S. taxpayers an estimated $81 billion per year. Court costs, bail bond fees, and prison phone fees generate another $38 billion in individual costs.

While our national prison population peaked in 2009 and has declined slightly since then, it's still the world's largest. With a population of 331 million, the U.S. has roughly two million people incarcerated. The NAACP adds the people being held in jails before trial to that count, bringing the number up to 3 million. In contrast, China has a population of 1.4 billion, and only an estimated 1.7 million people behind bars. And Russia has an incarceration rate of about half the United States'.

Ethnically, the U.S. prison population is 40% Black, 39% White (non-Hispanic), 19% Hispanic, 1.5% Asian, and 0.5% everyone else. According to the U.S. Bureau of Justice Statistics, in 2018 the imprisonment rate for Black males (2,272 per 100,000 Black male residents) was 5.8 times as high as for White males (392 per 100,000 White male residents).[161]

The First Step Act, a very modest bipartisan criminal justice reform bill aimed at easing prison sentences for those incarcerated in the federal system, garnered some Republican support while also exposing divisions within the party. Many worried it made the party of "law and order" seem weak on crime. For example, Senator Tom Cotton (R, Arkansas) slammed his colleagues' efforts to pass the bill, saying the United States is actually suffering from an "under-incarceration problem."

Cotton ridiculed what he called "baseless" arguments that there are too many offenders locked up for relatively small crimes, that incarceration is too costly, and that "we should show more empathy toward those caught up in the criminal-justice system." His logic? "Law enforcement is able to arrest or identify a likely perpetrator for only 19% of property crimes and 47% of violent crimes. If anything, we have an under-incarceration problem."

The man who mattered when Republicans controlled the Senate, Majority Leader Mitch McConnell, initially refused to bring the measure up for a vote without enough votes to pass. "It's extremely divisive inside the Senate Republican Conference. In fact, there are more members in my conference that are either against it or undecided than or for it," McConnell told *The Wall Street Journal*.

A TWO-FOLD PROBLEM

The United States has a twofold problem: there are too many people in prison, and too many *Black* people in prison. How did we get here? The United States did not always have a huge prison population. From 1925 to 1974, the total population of U.S. prisons remained at fewer than 20,000 people. There was no particular imbalance between the numbers of White and Black prisoners during this time, either. The rate of incarceration was consistent at about 100 per 100,000 people in state prisons, and far fewer in federal prisons.

Then the number began to steeply increase, especially for Black people and—to a lesser degree—for Hispanics. By the year 2000, the incarceration rate for Black people had soared to 4,000 per 100,000, driven primarily by increases in state prison systems.[162]

Not only did rates of incarceration soar, but the *length* of sentences increased. In 1984, there were 34,000 people serving life sentences in the United States. By 2016, the number of people serving life with parole (LWP) and life without parole (LWOP) had swelled to nearly 162,000 ... and it wasn't by accident.

In the early 1970s, the era of mass incarceration began as a deliberate government policy. It was ignited by political rhetoric that focused on an uptick in crime and was orchestrated by people in power, including legislators who demanded stricter sentencing laws, state and local executives who ordered law enforcement officers to be tougher on crime, and prison administrators who were forced to house a growing population with limited resources.

As Black Americans achieved growing measures of social and political freedom through the Civil Rights movement, politicians on both sides of the aisle took steps to curb those gains. "Blackness" was associated with violence, even though, as anyone who lived through the late 1960s in America knows, White anti-war students were violent, too. Still, few of them ended up in prison.

As Richard Nixon said in 1968, "The first civil right of every American is to be free from domestic violence, and that right must be guaranteed in this country . . . I pledge to you that the new Attorney General will open a new front against the filth peddlers and the narcotics peddlers who are corrupting the lives of the children of this country." The "Silent Majority" knew what he meant, and many in the minority community believed "law and order" meant "lock up more Black people."

To understand why this movement began and grew, we need to step back and see it in context. From the 17th century to the 21st, our use of mass incarceration has changed from a viable system of punishment to a political, elitist power play, one whose effects on the Black community have been devastating.

On the heels of the Second World War—in which many Black soldiers fought—came the Civil Rights Movement of the 1950s and 1960s. Black activists—from Dr. Martin Luther King Jr., to the Black Panthers, to Malcolm X—garnered growing support. Repelled by acts of violence, including the gruesome lynching of Emmett Till in 1955, many condemned the old ways of Klan-style terror.

The last remaining Jim Crow laws were overruled by the Civil Rights Act of 1964 and the Voting Rights Act of 1965. On paper, at least, people of color were given equal rights under the law. However, while the era of state-sanctioned lynching was over, the fight for real equality was just beginning.

Having been deprived of the economic tools of slavery and the subsequent repeal of Jim Crow laws, White elites found a new and potent tool for maintaining the power structure; using the criminal justice system to incarcerate as many people as possible, for as long as possible.

THE PHILOSOPHY BEHIND THE CARCERAL SYSTEM

One of Michel Foucault's most influential works, *Discipline and Punish*,[163] offers a philosophical and historical account of the birth of the carceral system in Western societies. Throughout the piece, Foucault—one of the most renowned thinkers of our time—dissects the relationships between punishment, power, and society.

The book begins with a gloomy description of an 18th century execution in France. It depicts Damiens, a servant who had attempted to assassinate Louis XV, and the barbaric display of violence that ensued.

While many might argue that the institution of punishment simply became more humane over time, Foucault views the concept of power as central to the changes; for starters, punishment ceased being a spectacle. Before, the conventional wisdom held that public executions reconstituted the sovereignty of the monarch, reminding society of the consequences of regicide. In reality, the public often related to those breaking laws, as they were often poor, and thus victims of monarchs' absolute power.

During executions, many gathered in public squares to "hear an individual who had nothing more to lose, curse the judges, the laws, the government and religion". Disturbances were commonplace, which "began with the shouts of encouragement, sometimes the cheering, that accompanied the condemned man to his execution". With the rise of enclosed systems, like prisons, the public no longer had a platform for an anti-elite discourse. On the contrary, an image of a criminal was carefully manufactured, convincing society of the inherent evil in the condemned men and women.

With the rise of industrialization rose the need for discipline, to ensure an uninterrupted production of profit-generating commodities and reduce dissent. Discipline, in this case, was meant to "increase the forces of the body (in economic terms of utility) and diminish these same forces (in political terms of obedience)". Prisons, which seem so natural to us today, were created to warehouse those who failed to conform with the new realities in order to reeducate them. Through "coercion by [constant] observation", prisoners engage in hard labor and are "also rewarded individually as a way of reinserting them morally and materially into the strict world of the economy". And here, too, we see the connection between the systems of punishment and elites. Even today, while petty crimes of the lower classes are strictly punished, there is a continuous growth in "great national or international illegalities directly linked to the political and economic apparatuses".

The very existence of prisons ensures that the rest of society remains disciplined. Convicts serve as reminders to people not to break the law; they are "examples of men who are ever before one's eyes, whom one has deprived of liberty and who are forced to spend the rest of their days repairing the loss they had caused society".

Consider, for example, how courts operate today. Rather than simply judge a crime, the accused person's tendencies are examined in an effort to construct a psychological portrait of a criminal mind. In fact, "judgment is also passed on passions, instincts, anomalies, infirmities, maladjustments—[all] intended to neutralize [a criminal's] dangerous state of mind". As such, courts try to create an image of a wicked man, a personality type that "normal" people need to avoid. These court and prison practices have also become key in other societal activities. Today, "the judges of normality are present everywhere; we are in the society of the teacher-judge, the doctor-judge, the educator-judge". Overall, the criminal justice system, interlinked with the rest of societal apparatus, seeks "the fabrication of the disciplinary individual".

The symbiosis of prisons and society, represented through the prisms of economy, power, and discipline, is what makes the prison abolitionist movement such a hard task. The penitentiary system, rooted "in mechanisms and strategies of power, could meet any attempt to transform it with a great force of inertia". Nevertheless, abolition is possible. The first step is, of course, realizing that the prison system, which has become such a key part of our lives, is not something that has always existed, and thus, is something that can be changed. After all, before prisons became commonplace, some of the biggest intellectuals questioned the system, calling penal imprisonment "useless, even harmful, to society: it is costly, it maintains convicts in idleness, it multiplies their vices".

ARE PRISONS OBSOLETE? THE MOVEMENT TO ABOLISH THEM

Our society views prisons as something natural, solid, and inescapable. The penitentiary system has been in place for so long that it has become hard to see any viable alternatives. When one commits a crime, they should lose their liberty. While nearly everyone is familiar with the campaign to abolish capital punishment, "the prison is considered an inevitable and permanent feature of our social lives". While the prison abolition movement has a history of more than 200 years, "abolitionists are dismissed as utopians and idealists whose ideas are at best unrealistic and impracticable". Angela Davis, in *Are Prisons*

Obsolete,[164] questions those premises, reminding us of other cruel institutions that once seemed permanent.

Those who questioned slavery, for example, were considered utopians too. In fact, "the belief in the permanence of slavery was so widespread that even White abolitionists found it difficult to imagine Black people as equals". The same thing happened in the era of segregation. In Alabama in the 1950s, when the governor "attempted to prevent Arthurine Lucy from enrolling in the University of Alabama, his stance represented the inability to imagine Black and White people ever peaceably living and studying together". The current penal system has overtones of racist systems, too. Thus, Davis believes that, not only is the abolition of prisons possible, she claims that prison abolition is necessary to create a fairer society in the United States. The parallels between the carceral system and the slavery institution are undeniable. In fact, when the prison system, which relied on hard manual labor, first took hold in the United States, "Thomas Jefferson, who supported the sentencing of convicted people to hard labor on road and water projects, also pointed out that he would exclude slaves from this sort of punishment, since slaves already performed hard labor". Moreover, "both institutions subordinated their subjects to the will of others; like Southern slaves, prison inmates followed a daily routine specified by their superiors, both institutions reduced their subjects to dependence on others for the supply of basic human services such as food, both isolated their subjects from the general population, [and] both frequently coerced their subjects to work".

Second, while prisons claim to rehabilitate inmates, in reality, I believe they contribute to recidivism and a general decline in mental health of the convicts. Methods like solitary confinement further aggravate this issue. Charles Dickens wrote extensively about solitude in prisons, claiming that "very few men are capable of estimating the immense amount of torture and agony that this dreadful punishment, prolonged for years, inflicts upon the sufferers". This observation remains true today. One study indicates that "there may be twice as many people suffering from mental illness who are in jails and prisons than there are in all psychiatric hospitals in the United States". Inmates who seek reconciliation, on the other hand, are constantly denied education and reintegration into society. For example, "Congress took up the question of withdrawing college funding for inmates; the 1994 Crime Bill eliminated all Pell Grants for prisoners, thus effectively defunding all higher educational programs".

Furthermore, with the rise of private prisons, many prisoners have become victims of exploitation, and have been denied basic human rights and civil liberties. In the second half of the 20th century, "the number of American medical research programs that relied on prisoners as subjects rapidly expanded as zealous doctors and researchers, grant-making universities, and a burgeoning pharmaceutical industry raced for greater market share". By the time the practice was outlawed in 1974, "numerous cosmetics and skin creams had already been tested; Johnson and Johnson, Ortho Pharmaceutical, and Dow Chemical are only a few of the corporations that reaped great material benefits from these experiments". Corporations and state governments make money on mass incarceration. In 1995, "Dial Soap sold $100,000 worth of its product to the New York City jail system alone". By 2003, the 34 private jails in the state of Texas "generated about 80 million dollars annually for Texas". As such, it is questionable whether state governments would even be interested in resolving the mass incarceration issue. On the contrary, it seems they profit from the existence of a larger number of convicts.

Davis, like Foucault, sees that the penal system is intertwined with the rest of the political apparatus. Thus, the abolition of prisons alone seems implausible. The prison industrial complex "is a set of symbiotic relationships among correctional communities, transnational corporations, media conglomerates, guards' unions, and legislative and court agendas". Therefore, to resolve the issue of mass incarceration, fundamental structural changes are necessary. Any solution that "fails to address racism, male dominance, homophobia, class bias, and other structures of domination will not, in the final analysis, lead to decarceration".

Educational institutions need to change, and "unless schools become places that encourage the joy of learning, these schools will remain the major conduits to prison". The immense wealth inequality in the United States needs to be addressed, "the racial and class disparities in care available to the affluent and the deprived need to be eradicated". Finally, the war on drugs needs to be modified with common sense solutions, like the legalization of marijuana and decriminalization of the same. There are simply too many people in prisons for small dosages of a drug that has health benefits and that is far less dangerous than alcohol and tobacco.

THE NEW JIM CROW?

In 2010, when Michelle Alexander's *The New Jim Crow*[165] was published, the United States was already the nation in the world with the most incarcerated individuals. In terms of people in prisons, the country "dwarfed the rates of nearly every developed country, even surpassing those in highly repressive regimes like Russia, China, and Iran; the rate was nearly eight times that [of Germany], or 750 [people in prison] per 100,000 [adults and children]". Furthermore, "the United States imprisons a larger percentage of its Black population than

South Africa did at the height of apartheid". Thus, Michelle Alexander asks whether the current carceral system in the United States is yet another policy of exclusion for African Americans, a tool reminiscent of the institutions of slavery and segregation.

The idea of White supremacy is tied to the institution of slavery. Having enslaved millions of Black folk through the Transatlantic trade, an idea of White superiority was born. Over time, "faith in the idea that the people of the African race were bestial, that Whites were inherently superior, and that slavery was, in fact, for Blacks' own good, served to alleviate the White conscience and reconcile the tension between slavery and the democratic ideals espoused by Whites". Obviously, when the institution of slavery fell after the American Civil War, people's perception of race did not change overnight. On the contrary, most Southern states immediately adopted laws to disallow the full inclusion of the Black population into society, and to keep the plantation economy alive. For example, "nine Southern states adopted vagrancy laws—which essentially made it a criminal offense not to work and were applied selectively to Blacks—and eight of those states enacted convict laws allowing hiring-out of county prisoners to plantation owners and private companies". What followed, as we know, was a period of lengthy segregation, where White and Black folk were separated in virtually every aspect of economy, housing, and everyday activities.

On the other hand, the fall of segregation during the Civil Rights Era resulted in a massive increase in African American political participation, although only momentarily. The rate of voting Black citizens skyrocketed, "in Alabama the rate leapt from 19.3% to 61.3%; in Georgia, 27.4% to 60.4%; in Louisiana, 31.6% to 60.8%, and in Mississippi, 6.7% to 66.5%". Most importantly, race stopped being a subject of the political discourse, at least on paper. Michelle Alexander argues that, in reality, politicians who were raised with White supremacist ideals and a belief in inherent racial hierarchy sought new ways to exclude African Americans. The solution was soon found. Elites in power "developed instead the racially sanitized rhetoric of cracking down on crime—rhetoric that is now used freely by politicians of every stripe". Moreover, with President Nixon's declaration of the war on drugs, a new "backlash against Blacks was clearly in force". Very soon, "90% of those admitted to prison for drug offenses in many states were Black or Latino, yet the mass incarceration of communities of color was explained in race-neutral terms; the new Jim Crow was born."

THE WAR ON DRUGS

According to Michelle Alexander, the war on drugs is central to the issue of mass incarceration and is the most connected to the warehousing of American citizens in prisons. In fact, "drug offenses alone account for two-thirds of the rise in the federal inmate population between 1985 and 2000; drug arrests have tripled since 1980; more than 31 million people have been arrested for drug offenses since the drug war began". When placed against murder convictions, "homicide offenders account for 0.4 of the past decade's [2000s] growth in the federal prison population, while drug offenders account for nearly 61%% of that expansion". Meanwhile, the war on drugs has done very little to stop the supply and distribution of narcotics. In reality, "in 2005, for example, four out of five drug arrests were for possession, and only one out of five was for sales" (p. 59). Moreover, the drug war has done little to stop the spread of hard and dangerous drugs. Marijuana, "a drug less harmful than tobacco and alcohol—accounted for nearly 80% of the growth in drug arrests in the 1990s".[166]

Yet, especially in the Reagan era police, funding in the United States skyrocketed. Between "1980 and 1984, FBI anti-drug funding increased from $8 million to $95 million; Department of Defense anti-drug allocations increased from $33 million in 1981 to $142 million in 1991; DEA anti-drug spending grew from $38 million to $181 million". The membership of SWAT teams increased dramatically—"in 1972, there were just a few hundred paramilitary drug raids per year in the United States; by the early 1980s, there were three thousand annual SWAT deployments, by 1996 there were thirty thousand, and by 2001 there were forty thousand".

On numerous occasions, the establishment has displayed its full support of random police searches, despite their unconstitutional nature. Despite the Fourth Amendment's prohibition of searches without a warrant, a rule known as the "Terry Decision stands for the proposition that, so long as a police officer has reasonable articulable suspicion that someone is engaged in criminal activity and [is] dangerous, it is constitutionally permissible to stop, question, and frisk him or her" The Supreme Court has ruled that "the police are free to use minor traffic violations as a pretext to conduct drug investigations, even when there is no evidence of illegal drug activity". In another case, "the Supreme Court has ruled that "walking a drug-sniffing dog around someone's vehicle (or someone's luggage) does not constitute a search".

At the time of the declaration of the war on drugs, the American media was filled with images of Black criminals and drug users. This "media bonanza inspired by the administration's campaign solidified in the public imagination the image of the Black drug criminal". In a 1995 survey, when asked what comes to mind when picturing a drug criminal, "95% of respondents pictured a Black drug user". This bias, combined with a new set of police rights when it came to random searches, resulted in astonishing racial disparities in drug arrests. In 2000, a Human Rights Watch Report found that "in seven states, African Americans constitute 80 to 90% of all drug offenders sent to prison". In Florida, "a reporter obtained 148 hours of video footage documenting more than 1,000 highway stops conducted by state troopers; only 5% of the drivers on the road were African American or Latino, but more than 80 of the people stopped and searched were minorities". This bias, obviously, has no statistical or logical backing. On the contrary, one study in 2000 reported that "White students use cocaine at seven times the rate of Black students, use crack cocaine at eight times the rate of Black students, and use heroin at seven times the rate of Black students; nearly identical percentages of White and Black high school senior use marijuana; White youth are more than a third more likely to have sold illegal drugs".

PRIVATE, FOR-PROFIT PRISON CORPORATIONS

The Corrections Corporation of America launched the era of private prisons in 1983 when it opened an immigration detention center in a former motel in Houston, Texas. Now known as CoreCivic, today this Nashville-based company owns, leases, and operates prisons, immigration detention centers, and residential reentry centers. It owns or manages 74 prisons and jails in the U.S. with a total capacity of 74,957 beds, which represent more than half of all privately owned prison beds. This makes CoreCivic the largest owner of private prisons in America.

As reported by *Mother Jones*, CCA and other prison companies have written "occupancy guarantees" into their contracts, requiring states to pay a fee if they cannot provide a certain number of inmates. For example, Winn Correctional Center, a state prison for men and part of the Louisiana Department of Corrections prison system, was guaranteed by the state to be 96% full. This means the state has an *incentive* to convict and sentence people to that facility.[167]

The American Friends Service Committee reports that CoreCivic's prisons have long faced a laundry list of abuses: prolonged use of solitary confinement, medical negligence, physical and sexual abuse, forced prison labor, overcrowding, allegations of inhumane living conditions, excessive use of force, spying and voyeurism, understaffing, and other problems.

In Tennessee, a 2020 audit revealed that CoreCivic often fails to investigate sexual abuse and harassment allegations, keeps inadequate medical and mental health records, and frequently closes down prison programming and services, including recreation time and transportation to and from medical appointments due to understaffing.

AFSC also noted that CoreCivic and other private prison companies are incentivized to increase their profits through the continuous growth of the criminal punishment system. To do that, you need to influence politicians. Since 1998, CoreCivic has used federal and state lobbying, campaign contributions, and participation in associations that draft policy to influence lawmakers. In 2021, the company employed 15 lobbyists, ten of whom previously held government positions. Through its political action committee (PAC), from 1990 to 2020, the company spent $3.5 million on political candidates, with the vast majority of funds donated to Republican candidates.[168]

In January 2021, President Joe Biden issued an executive order ending federal use of private prisons. Unfortunately, this order has no effect on the states.

PERMANENT RIPPLE EFFECTS

The prison system is incredibly effective at disrupting not only individual lives but families and communities. As a result of the mass incarceration of Black individuals, millions have been deprived of basic human rights and civil liberties. The 'Whites only' signs of the segregation area may be long gone, "but new signs have gone up—notices placed in job applications, rental agreements, loan applications, forms for welfare benefits, school applications, etc."[169] Some offenders may "lose the right to vote [and] will not be permitted to enlist in the military, possess a firearm, or obtain a federal security clearance". As a result, as of today, "more African Americans are under correctional control—in prison or jail, on probation or parole—than were enslaved in 1850, a decade before the Civil War began".

Incarceration can be damaging to the health of the inmate. Incarcerated persons—both Black and White—are five times more likely to be infected by HIV than the general population. Across America, arrest and incarceration have effectively replaced emergency mental-health care, particularly in low-income communities of color. In many prisons, the percentage of people with mental illness has continued to go up even as the prison population has declined. Today, nearly 50% of the people in U.S. jails and more than 30% of those in U.S. prisons have been diagnosed with a mental illness, compared to about 20% in the general population.

Incarceration is linked to mood disorders, including major depressive disorder and bipolar disorder. The prison environment can be damaging to mental health, as it removes people from society and strips all meaning and purpose from their lives. And as clinical psychiatrist Dr. Seymour L. Halleck has observed, "The prison environment is almost diabolically conceived to force the offender to experience the pangs of what many psychiatrists would describe as mental illness."

A prison sentence is a major life-altering event that impedes the building of stable lives in a community, including gaining employment and finding secure housing after release. Incarceration reduces lifetime earnings, as many companies will not hire convicted felons, and even a marijuana conviction can blight a resume. High levels of imprisonment in communities feed a vicious cycle of high crime rates and neighborhood deterioration, thus fueling greater disparities. The incarceration of a loved one or breadwinner can cause families and friends significant emotional distress, residential instability, and loss of income and property.

More than one out of every six Black men who, today, should be between 25 and 54 years old have vanished from their communities due to incarceration and early deaths. Their absence from the community removes voters, workers, taxpayers, and more. A history of incarceration has been linked to vulnerability to disease, a greater likelihood of cigarette smoking, and even premature death. Many of the formerly incarcerated also suffer from a loss of their rights. In 12 states, a felony conviction means being forbidden to vote. In 34 states, people who are on parole or probation cannot vote. As of 2020, 5.2 million Americans were prohibited from voting due to laws that disenfranchise citizens convicted of felony offenses. For many, confusion about the law is a potent weapon.

In 2018, Ex-felon Desmond Meade lead a movement leading to voters in Florida approving a ballot measure to automatically restore the right to vote to people with prior felony convictions—except for those who had committed murder or a felony sex offense. But during the following legislative session, the state legislature passed legislation requiring these newly enfranchised citizens to fulfill every part of their sentence—including paying any outstanding fees or fines—in order to regain their voting rights.

As NPR reported, Nicholas Warren, a staff attorney with the ACLU of Florida, noted that state lawmakers essentially created a "pay to vote" system, but never created a way for former felons to figure out how much they owed or if they owed anything at all. "There is no simple way for a person who is coming out of their felony sentence to check whether they are eligible to vote," he told NPR. "And the rules are very complicated in Florida."

As I mentioned earlier, in August 2022, the new "Elections Crime Unit" of Governor Ron DeSantis's election police arrested 20 people on charges of voter fraud. But some of the 20 individuals told law enforcement officials that they sincerely believed they were able to vote when they cast their ballots. Florida voting rights advocates asserted the prosecutions were the product of the state's failure to create a system where individuals and election officials could easily verify whether a person had the right to vote after serving time for a felony conviction.

WHEN A TRAFFIC TICKET BECOMES MUCH MORE

In 2016, Leslie Turner was arrested for failing to pay a traffic ticket. In Nevada—as in 12 other states—traffic violations are treated as a criminal infraction. If you miss a payment on your ticket, it's just like failing to appear in court, and the judge can issue a bench warrant for your arrest.

As the *Nevada Current* reported, she missed her payment because she had a child born with a medical condition and wanted to stay home to care for him. With the help of her mother and Clark County Social Services, she was able to postpone her return to work for a few months while managing to keep up her rent payments. But she just couldn't afford the ticket. "I just didn't pay it because I didn't have the money," Turner said.[170]

After missing a payment, Turner called the court to explain her situation but was told she would either have to attend court or surrender to authorities. Fearing arrest, and despite her son's condition, Turner returned to work to generate some income to get back on her payment plan. One day, after dropping her child off with a babysitter, she was pulled over and taken to jail. This happened on a Wednesday evening, and she was kept behind bars until Monday the following week.

Judges are encouraged to consider the defendant's ability to pay when setting bail, but doing so often isn't the case. Turner's bail was set at $1,500, more than she earned in a month. People who can't afford bail remain stuck in jail, kept away from their children, and can lose their jobs, all before even being convicted of a crime.

In 2017, North Las Vegas paid about $6 million for its judicial system, which suggests the municipal court is entirely self-funded by the fines, fees, and assessments it imposes. Sadly—or perhaps by design—Nevada courts are not required to collect demographic information on those who pass through the system, nor does law enforcement keep records on those who have a bench warrant (due to an inability to pay, for example), who is being stopped, and for what violations. This failure to keep records makes it nearly impossible to monitor impact based on race, color, disability, or other federally protected categories.

Turner now works for PLAN Action's mass liberation campaign, which works to end mass incarceration and holds fundraising events to help make bail for those who cannot pay it themselves.

Culture Wars

Culture Wars in America have been raging since the abolition of slavery, at least in the view of University of Washington, Seattle political science professor Christopher Parker. Any time Americans most deeply held values are in conflict with their neighbors the ground is ripe for disagreements and heated political debates.

In fact, author Andrew Hartman believes the modernity of culture wars is simply a reboot from decades ago.

> "The things that we now associate with the Republicans in terms of their anti-trans, anti-critical race theory – the culture wars they're fighting right now – you see all of this even during the Reagan years."

Whether you agree these are old wine in new bottles or completely new vintage, the modern iteration of these culture conflicts has manifested in three key areas affecting millions of Americans; Education, Sexuality, Women's Rights. Fueled by unrepressed racism and emboldened by the MAGA movement, this all-out assault of discriminatory policies is shadowed only by the tidal wave of disinformation that is giving it power.

The human toll of many of these politically charged conservative agendas are not inconsequential. Just another illustration of the power a vote can have on the realities of everyday life.

8

EDUCATION

With the rise of voucher and school choice programs and cultural flashpoints, the American education system has been thrust into the spotlight of our political discourse. As we speak, public schools are on the verge of shutting down due to lack of funding and depressed attendance, as public dollars flow to private institutions. In Florida for example, during the late 1990's, Florida Governor Jeb Bush made education reform a central tenet of his administration. The two-term governor touted adding good old-fashioned competition to motivate public schools to perform better and alternatively using tax dollars as a way to help families and students who were trapped in failing public schools without the financial means to seek private school options. Fast forward to today, and Governor Bush's policies have evolved into a robust state funded voucher system regardless of the public school performance or the financial status of the family. Through voucher programs and eligibility expansions to nearly the entire population, private and charter school vouchers are receiving record amounts of state tax dollars at the expense of public schools statewide. It's clear that some political leaders have decided that state assisted private system is a better solution to failing public schools rather than trying to fix our current public education apparatus. This philosophy is a political one and carries with it other policies that may further disadvantage students in the public school system. If this bothers you, it's important to choose your lawmakers wisely and make sure your votes reflect your interest.

Education in the United States has always been another complex political and policy area. It sits at the intersection of child, workforce, social-cultural, community, and democratic development. The task of equipping our children with a safe, affordable education to understand today's issues and prepare for tomorrow's problems is not an easy one. There are no straightforward answers.

There are countless individuals, of all backgrounds and influence levels, who are invested in education outcomes, however, their investments in these outcomes are often with conflicting interests. Prospective voters need to know their position and power as participants and vital stakeholders in the public education system.

Within towns, municipalities, and cities, the voter has the direct power of electing the school board of their local public school district. Voters can participate in state- and federal-level elections that elect legislators who have the power to change or maintain funding structures and resource allocation, negotiate labor conditions with education unions, incentivized school choice initiatives, and more. Local, state, and federal policymakers have historically reacted to political education movements with fast-acting legislation. We have seen this exemplified through the contentious controversy surrounding Critical Race Theory.

CRITICAL RACE THEORY; A BRIEF HISTORY

In the late 20th century, Critical Race Theory began as an academic and legal concept created by legal scholars and professors such as Kimberlé Crenshaw, Richard Delgado, Alan Freeman, Derrick Bell, and many more. The central tenet of Critical Race Theory is that race is a social construct, and this social construct has been ingrained within the legal, institutional, legislative, and judicial systems within the United States. Other tenets include racism as ordinary behavior and not a departure in the United States: material determinism, intersectionality, and counter-narratives. These tenets require critical challenging of the constitutional law principles, equality theory, and liberal order amongst others to understand the intersection between race and power. In early scholarship, Critical Race Theorists often critiqued Critical Legal Studies, an earlier postmodernist, and Marxist legal analysis for failing to consider racial oppression and race in their deconstruction of legal systems. Today, Critical Race Theory remains largely an analysis that is taught in law schools and graduate programs. Scholars and practitioners in educational spaces apply Critical Race Theory to observe educational policies and practices which reproduce racial inequity, reject the dominant racial hierarchy narrative, connect historical racism with systematic education inequity, and advocate for sustainable and equitable educational opportunity.

Following the *1619 Project*'s publishing in the New York Times in 2019[171] and the national protests from the murders of George Floyd, Breonna Taylor, and Ahmaud Arbery in 2020, there was a widespread wave of political retaliation by right-wing policymakers on local and state levels. Amid a national backlash against anti-Black racism and police brutality, Manhattan Institute Senior Fellow, Christopher Rufo, developed and designed a method to convert the complex discourse of Critical Race Theory into a divisive political phrase. The twisted notion of Critical Race Theory that Rufo presented went as far as influencing then-President Donald Trump to order federally-funded agencies to remove training or initiatives that included White privilege or Critical Race Theory concepts. Right-wing voters became increasingly hostile to the concept of Critical Race Theory while being misled about its use in K-12 classrooms. Shortly after Rufo's Critical Race Theory messaging became widespread through Fox News and other right-wing media, there was a significant increase in local school board officials receiving hundreds of violent threats and hostile messages in more than a dozen states.

Numerous states across the country sponsored and/or enacted bills and laws which targeted educational materials that directly spoke about racism, gender identity, and sexual identity. To defend these proposed changes, these policymakers have used the rationale that these materials teach White children to feel shame or guilt and are age-inappropriate or pornographic. Public libraries and schools across the United States are embattled in controversy and conflict over this targeted censorship. The abrupt, heightened societal awareness of systematic racism has led to book banning measures as a calming effort. However, the aggressive political divisiveness has placed a heavy strain on education workers on all levels.

While there are conflicting perspectives on whether there is a present-day national teacher shortage, it is evident that these rampant attacks on academic freedom have led teachers to become the most burned-out labor group in the United States. A recent survey by the State of the American Teacher and State of the American Principal Surveys discovered that 33% of teachers were instructed to reduce gender studies and racism discussions while nearly 25% of English and Social Studies teachers have reported being harassed about bias and instructional content. A public school district in Oklahoma, Tulsa Public School, was downgraded to "accredited with warning" for the district's training materials which "shame White people".[172] It is evident that this divide between book bans and critical race theory is being entrenched along political lines:

> *"According to a poll by The Economist and YouGov in February [2022], most people do not think [Critical Race Theory] is being taught in their*

local schools. Among those asked, 45% claim to know what [Critical Race Theory] is, and 25% of total respondents have a negative opinion of it. But only 21% think children in their community are being taught it: 14% of Democrats thought so, and 35% of Republicans."[173]

What started as a political weaponization of a legal analysis discipline has grown into a contentious battlefield with few boundaries for professional, legal, or personal safety. A federal judge applied for a temporary injunction on Florida's "Stop Woke Act" to partially stop its enforcement due to first amendment violations; the policy prevents private organizations from conducting mandatory workplace training that includes 'woke indoctrination' and personal shame or guilt for historic wrongs. Florida's anti-Critical Race Theory policy is just one of many being pushed on local and state levels.

If the debate over CRT and other pointed policies that undermine teacher's capabilities were not enough, teachers of color face even greater obstacles to their development and success. The systematic racism that operates in school environments includes poorer labor conditions compared to White teachers, more stressful and hostile school environments, higher turnover rates, and more.

In her work *Teachers of Color*, Rita Kolhi applies Critical Race Theory—a now very familiar and household term—to the hidden struggles and conditions that inhibit the retention, development, recruitment, and success of teachers of color. Institutional transformation, such as improving the racial climate within schools, is required to better prepare and develop teachers of color.[174]

"To understand and address the diversity crisis of the teaching force, it is necessary to move beyond discussions of racial representation".

In a similar data-driven analysis, *Despite the Best Intentions* by Amanda Lewis and John Diamond, examines five years of mixed methods data gathering from a case study of Riverview High School's racial-achievement gap. The authors present their rich data, along with meaningful stories from Riverview, classroom practices, and rigorous analysis from the research literature that may alter the development of students along race lines. The book offers a thorough analysis of the many contributing cultural, academic, self-efficacy, and institutional factors that produce racial achievement gaps.

"Race still operates on multiple levels—shaping how we think about and interact with one another, shaping the resources we have available as we move through the world, and shaping how institutions like schools reward those resources".

"While it might seem obvious that some of these resources pay off for students (of course, having wealth helps; of course, knowing the superintendent or principal helps), the ways, in practice, that resources such as relationships, cultural knowledge, and skin color translate into advantages in schools need to be understood as mechanisms of inequality."[175]

Their narrative regarding racial achievement gaps in the midst of modern-day education segregation is shocking. Segregation in schools due to residential and income patterns are influencing shifts in education quality as well, even in diverse schools and districts. We, as voters, must remain aware of how these achievement gaps are developing, what potential gaps might exist, and which candidates are prepared to do something about it.

As it stands, Millennials may be the last generation to be taught America's racial history. This is a very serious issue for our children and for our future. Critical Race Theory is an academic and legal framework that examines the impact of systemic racism on American society, but it has become a political football weaponizing advancement toward a true multiracial democracy. If laws continue to be passed around this country banning the teaching of our history, the next generation will not be prepared to navigate this life without repeating it. Millions of dollars of political power are being used to erase our ability to adequately educate, teach, and inform the next generation. If we lose this battle, we've lost the future.

CHANGES TO EDUCATION LEGISLATION

As a recent political phenomenon, anti-Critical Race Theory and book ban legislations have increased tremendously over the last two to three years. The University of California, Los Angeles's School of Law's CRT Forward Tracking Project is a robust database that attempts to track and analyze anti-Critical Race Theory bills, legislation, resolutions, and other government levers. The CRT Forward Tracking Project's database displayed a rapid increase of anti-CRT bills targeting K-12 and higher education when introduced on state and local levels; between September 2020 and January 2021, there were zero bills introduced or adopted, between January 2021 and April 2021, 10 states had introduced or adopted resolutions and legislation, between April 2021 and August 2021, 22 states had introduced or adopted resolutions and legislation, and between August 2021 and February 2022, 18 states continued to introduce or adopt Anti-CRT legislation. In total, the CRT Forward Tracking Project has tracked over 500 anti-CRT efforts across 38 states and on local and federal levels—endangering K-20 education, private organizations, contractors, and state and federal agencies.

In the collaborative work, *Invisible Children*[176], authors offer a detailed breakdown of several societal factors that prohibit student engagement and well-being and that foster a culture of neglect where students are invisible to the policies needed to support them.

"Michael is not yet nine years old, yet his story of despair, terror, and desperation as his young life and fragile supports [from homelessness] crumbled around him is not unusual. Garbarino (1992) argues that, "in America being poor is deadly", and if you are living in one of the housing projects designed for those who live in the other America, there is no sense of daily stability".

"For our homeless children, who have become postmodern "street rats," the lifelong consequences are deep and scarring . . . Invisibility, concealment, and the savage act of "looking through"—all require confrontation of the growing "stench" in our society and a clear recognition that the human rights of homeless families have long been signed away".

Invisible Children offers an eye-opening account of those underserved in educational spaces due to their conditions being unvalued by society. These spaces are detrimental to student health and learning: school-to-prison pipeline, climate crises, homelessness, religious prejudice, systematic neglect, LGBTQIA+ identities, and more. The authors illustrate the institutional failure of the education system, including historical neglect through policy and advocacy.

These sentiments are further explored in *It's Not About Grit* by Steven Goodman: ". . .conditions that could be avoided by better-quality housing and access to affordable healthcare—such as the overcrowding, lack of waste disposal, rodent infestation, dampness, that Millie and her neighbors experienced . . . There may have been several causes for Millie's illnesses and absences from school, her feeling distracted, and dropping out of her high school and enrolling [in] alternative school. But surely, we can see how the appalling condition of her unhealthy home environment was clearly an important factor".[177]

"Far from being accidental or the natural result of the free market, the fact that so many of our students now live in such stressful, densely populated, segregated areas with high rates of violence and unemployment is one outcome of a history of government-sponsored race-based policies, [and] a caste system of institutional housing discrimination".

Goodman details the systematic methods that educational institutions use to otherize and stigmatize low-income, urban students of color and their surrounding communities. Goodman applies his decades of experience working with curriculum and student development to provide pragmatic pathways for school staff to incorporate a genuinely culturally responsive method of teaching and school climate.

Jonathan Kozol spent years working in inner-city schools before writing *The Shame of the Nation*. During his time in the classroom, he observed how administrators and educators navigate the harmful accountability-based curriculum and behavior-controlling discipline practices to support their urban students against challenging odds. Kozol paints a clear image of the damaging education policies placed on inner-city students who are often Black and Brown students: "Anxiety, for the children, was intensified, according to a fifth-grade teacher, by the ever-present danger of humiliation when their reading levels or their scores on state examinations were announced. "There must be penalties for failure," as the architects and advocates of programs such as these increasingly demand, and penalties for children in this instance were dispensed not only individually and privately but also in the view of others".[178]

"The insult to aesthetics, the affront to cleanliness and harmony and sweetness, are continuing realities as well for children who must go each morning into morbid-looking buildings in which few adults other than their teachers would agree to work day after day".

"Of the 21 children in his kindergarten classroom, four were White. That was three more than I'd ever seen in kindergarten classes in the Bronx; but 99% of children in the school were poor and, despite the modest benefactions of its corporate big brother, the overcrowding of the building and the squalor of the barracks classrooms struck me as a throwback to another era in our history."

Kozol's intention is to uplift children's and school staff's voices around conditions that may be largely unknown to the general public. There is much harm being done in schools that urban communities often pass by and never think twice about.

While much of the discussion around changes in the education policy environment revolve around the K-12, higher education is certainly not immune to equity challenges, especially within the most elite of institutions. "Diversity should not be celebrated the day a college publishes its admissions statistics only to be put on the back burner once the next crop of students arrives on campus. The four years that follow their arrival matter just as much. Diversity must be continuously cultivated. The elite college must change, adapt, and grow right along with its changing student body".[179]

The Privileged Poor points to the difficulty of low-income students persisting at elite colleges and universities. Author Anthony Jack makes poignant revelations about elite college culture and about the disadvantaged student experience using real student stories and insightful analysis. Jack prompts elite colleges and universities to transform their admissions, campus climate, and institutional support practices to better host low-income or disadvantaged students. "It is the responsibility of scholars, professors, and administrators to understand not only how poverty and inequality shape how students move through college, but also how colleges amplify differences between students on a daily basis." "When lower-income students have access to resources similar to those of their wealthier peers, they can and do acquire—and later use—the skills needed to succeed in college and other mainstream institutions."

In order for higher education to be increasingly accessible, voters should show up to the ballot box and elect candidates who understand the barriers high-achieving, low-income students face that prohibit their student engagement, belongingness, and academic success at major colleges and universities.

STATE-BY-STATE LEGISLATION

Despite the ambitions of education-policy czars like Betsy Devos, education will always be a local issue. The heart of the on-the-ground impact happens at the state and local level. To that end, the following list of state-by-state legislation shows a disturbing pattern of targeted attacks on K-12 systems and higher education institutions.

Alabama
Alabama's State Board of Education adopted a resolution targeting K-12, higher education, and contractors. It prohibits curricular content, classroom teachings, and training on anti-CRT content: if any individual bears responsibility for past actions due to their race, if any individual feels discomfort, guilt, distress, or shame based on their sex or race, and if the meritocracy is sexist or racist.

Alaska
Alaska adopted an Attorney General resolution aimed at denouncing Critical Race Theory and prohibits curricular content and classroom teaching of systematic racism in the United States and the *1619 Project.*

Arizona
Arizona adopted two Senate bills (SB 2898 and SB 2439) aimed at regulating K-12 educational content: SB 2898 restricts classroom teaching and curriculum from an individual feeling shame or guilt based on their race, responsibility for past members of the same identity, and presenting the meritocracy as oppressive or racist.

Arkansas
Arkansas adopted Senate Bill 627/Act 1100 aimed at prohibiting higher education, K-12, contractors, and private organizations from classroom instruction

and training about an individual feeling shame or guilt based on their race, responsibility for past members of the same identity, presenting the meritocracy as oppressive or racist, and other divisive issues.

Florida
Florida adopted four House bills (HB 7, HB 233, HB 241, HB 1467) and Senate Bill 1557. Senate Bill 1557 is aimed at K-12 schools and districts and reinforces parental rights and restricts classroom instruction of gender identity and sexual orientations from kindergarten to third grade. House bills were aimed at establishing an annual assessment of "intellectual freedom and viewpoint diversity" within higher education institutions by: expanding legal discrimination to include classroom instruction and employee training that includes Critical Race Theory content, restricting curricular content by banning educational materials with divisive content in K-12 schools and establishing a method of curricular surveillance that includes parent objections, and allowing student education opt-out.

Georgia
Georgia adopted House Bill 1084 and House Bill 1178. House Bill 1084 aimed to restrict training, classroom instruction, and curricular content from discussing divisive topics—such as, if the United States is inherently racist, anything triggering shame or guilt based on individual race or sex, and whether the meritocracy is racist or oppressive. House Bill 1178 regulates classroom instruction and curricular content and requires student education opt-out and curricular surveillance processes to be developed by school boards and districts.

Idaho
Idaho enacted House Bill 377. It's aimed at K-12 and higher education institutions to restrict curricular content on Critical Race Theory and individuals feeling guilt or shame from past actions of people who share their identity.

Iowa
Iowa adopted House File 802, which targeted private organizations, contractors, higher education, and K-12. House File 802 prohibits classroom instruction, training, and curricular content about fundamental racism in the United States, individual discomfort or guilt from past members of the same identity, and the meritocracy being oppressive or racist.

Kentucky

Kentucky adopted Senate Bill 1 to prohibit content that triggers individual feelings of shame or guilt about sharing the responsibility for past actions from a member of the same identity. This legislation targets K-12 schools and employees.

Mississippi

Mississippi adopted Senate Bill 2113. This legislation will withhold funding as a compliance violation if higher education and K-12 entities direct or compel students to affirm any race, sex, national origin, religion, or ethnicity is superior or inferior to another; individuals should be adversely treated because of their race, sex, national origin, religion, or ethnicity.

New Hampshire

New Hampshire adopted House Bill 2, and this legislation aimed to restrict violations of New Hampshire's Right to Freedom from Discrimination in Public Workplaces and Education. The legislation prevents K-12, higher education, and private organizations from classroom teachings and training that promotes discrimination based on age, sex, gender identity, sexual orientation, race, creed, color, marital status, familial status, mental or physical disability, religion, or national origin.

North Dakota

North Dakota adopted House Bill 1508 which directly prohibits Critical Race Theory from curricular content and classroom instruction in K-12 entities.

Oklahoma

Oklahoma adopted House Bill 1775 and House Bill 3092. House Bill 3092 prohibits schools and school libraries from maintaining or producing anything whose subject is the study of sex, sexual preferences, sexual activity, sexual perversion, sex-based classifications, sexual identity or gender identity, or books that are sexual. House Bill 1775 prohibits K-12 and higher education entities from compelling students or employees, through mandatory training, curricular content, and classroom instruction from specific content, regarding if the meritocracy is oppressive or racist in nature, divisive content that triggers individual feelings of shame or guilt about sharing the responsibility for past actions from a member of the same identity, and shared responsibility and guilt from past actions of members with the same race or sexual identity.

South Carolina

South Carolina adopted House Bill 4100 which targets K-12 entities; classroom teachings, curriculum, and K-12 employee training are prohibited from subjects about the United States being inherently racist, shared responsibility and guilt for past actions of individuals with the same identity, discomfort because of one's race or sex, and the meritocracy being oppressive or racially oppressive. This legislation allows South Carolina to withhold funding from K-12 entities that violate this legislation's provisions.

South Dakota

South Dakota adopted House Bill 1012. This legislation was aimed at prohibiting Critical Race Theory and similar content from classroom instruction and curriculums in K-12 and higher education settings. Funding for K-12 and higher education can be withheld by South Dakota if these provisions are violated.

Tennessee

Tennessee adopted House Bill 580 and Senate Bill 2290. House Bill 580 targeted K-12 entities and prohibits curriculum and instructional material that promotes superiority or inferiority of any race or sex, inherently racist meritocracy, the United States as inherently racist, or assigning character traits, values, moral or ethical codes, privileges, or beliefs to a race or sex. Senate Bill 2290 targeted higher education entities by prohibiting divisive concepts, race or sex scapegoating, and race or sex stereotyping in employee or student training. Higher education entities must also conduct a biennial survey on campus climate and diversity of thought.

Texas

Texas adopted House Bill 2497, House Bill 3979, and Senate Bill 3. House Bill 2497 established the "1863 Project" advisory committee to promote patriotic education and Texas' role in the United States history and adhere to foundational Texas principles. House Bill 3979 legislated the social studies curriculum in Texas public schools. This bill defines what social studies topics are essential to developing students' civic knowledge. It prohibits any teacher, school district, or public charter from awarding students with grades or course credit for participating in the following: political activism, racial superiority or inferiority, inherent racism or sexism based on race or sex, *1619 Project*, meritocracy is racist or sexist in nature. Senate Bill 3 established a civics training program for public school principals and teachers to facilitate the teaching of social studies curriculum consistent with Texas law.

Virginia

Virginia adopted House Bill 127. This legislation prohibits any academic year governor's school or administrator, director, employee, or board member from discriminating against any individual race, sex, color, ethnicity, or national origin in the school admissions process.

This is not a fully comprehensive list, but it is designed to provide a snapshot of legislatures' actions from September 2020 to February 2022 in response to a highly polarized political movement.

But there are still lights of hope to draw from. In his book, *Hope and Healing in Urban Education*, Shawn Ginwright tells the story of how powerful restorative and healing justice can be when applied by teacher activists for students in urban communities. Ginwright details the various different methods and concepts of healing justice through ethnographic case studies, using real-life stories of students impacted by this practice. Ginwright articulates a unique perspective on how healing justice practices impact communities and high-stress school environments to create a foundation for sustainable, impactful, and hope-filled social change in impoverished communities. The themes and lessons from this book include the interconnectivity of maintaining human wellness, oppression as a barrier to opportunity and the hope/potential for social change, courageous students' support solutions, and the connectedness of the individual and society.

In one story, a young man's reflections hearken back precisely to realizations I had as a young boy: "When you are young like us, seeing someone shot and killed is a lot different than seeing someone die of cancer. It caused me to reflect on the distinction between dying versus being killed. As an adult, I can point to several family members and friends who have died. Poignantly, however, I realized that the people I knew who had been killed were all young people under 20 years old."

In another, an inner city school was transformed by the introduction of meditation: "To be honest, after she explained to me that the entire school meditated twice every day, I was a bit suspicious. She explained, "We hear the morning meditation bell at 8:35 in the morning and sit for 20 minutes in silence. That gets us ready for the day. Then at precisely 3:05, the afternoon meditation bell [rings, and] we meditate before going home." I might have believed her if she was working at a small private school in Mill Valley where privileged kids get exposed to all sorts of innovative learning opportunities. But she was working at Visitacion Valley Middle School, where the homicide rate had soared, and fights were not uncommon at the school".[180]

This book highlights the critical dissection of urban education issues and the effort educators are investing to make a difference. When we think of education and how it affects our votes on election day, writers and advocates like Ginwright help to educate voters who may not understand the extent to which schools in under-resourced communities are detrimentally affected by the surrounding violence and poverty. And this education, especially in contrast to the disparaging remarks regularly hurled by media hosts and faceless social media trolls, is critical to bring about enlightened change at the ballot box.

9

REPRODUCTIVE RIGHTS

Okay, one medium hot latte with almond milk, no sugar, spinach and feta cheese egg bites, and oatmeal to go. That will be $12.97." Natasha, a young African American college student, rang up the fancy-looking businessman before her. He was talking on the phone and not paying attention to her like most customers she sees daily. The businessman pulled out a shiny, silver American Express credit card and inserted the chip into the feeder. The machine quickly rang, approving the transaction, and the man in the nice business suit put away his card and walked away while still talking on his phone. He had not even bothered to thank her for taking his order.

Unsurprised but still disappointed, Natasha sighed and smiled at the next customer, a young mother with two small and rowdy children. Unsurprisingly, the children ordered sugar-loaded frappuccinos and the mother a coffee with two espresso shots. Natasha admitted that the frantic look in the mother's eyes suggested she needed the extra espresso. At least this time, the customer thanked her before walking to the pickup station with her children.

Later that evening, she found herself exhausted as she went home after her shift. It was the third nine-hour shift of the week and it had her craving a hot bath and a glass of wine to unwind. Her feet ached as she kicked off her cheap sneakers by her bedroom door. She shared an apartment with two roommates.

It was the mid-semester of 2019, and she was a student at the local Georgia university. With the right luck and passing grades, she would graduate sometime in the next two years with her undergrad degree in Statistics. Her family would be so proud of her. Considering that she grew up below the poverty line, her parents struggled to make enough to provide for the family's basic needs. There were many nights when she could hear her parents arguing and worrying that they would not have enough money to pay for rent at the end of the month. She vowed to herself to never have to go through that again. Learning from that experience, once she had the money and the right job, she would do whatever it took to provide for herself and bridge the gap to meet her parents' needs. They would never have to worry about money ever again.

Smiling at herself and contemplating a bubble bath and a glass of her favorite red wine, she concluded it was best to have a quick, hot shower instead. She had a pile of reading and homework to push through, and it was already 7 pm. She wished that she had more time to herself. She felt like she was always playing catch-up with her assignments and personal needs. Taking a deep breath and forcing her stress levels to go down, she grabbed her towel and went to the adjoining bathroom.

Thinking of all the hard work she put in for $9 an hour today, she felt relief that luck had really been in her favor. She had the opportunity to study at a state university with partial scholarships, good part-time job opportunities, and that allowed her to live right by the campus, which was within walking distance from her classes and work. However, things could have been so different—and not necessarily in a positive way—had she made different choices.

Natasha tries to keep the thoughts of the dark times in her life at bay. It was never worth thinking of the past, as it only brought her pain. She had been in a domestically abusive relationship for two years.

Initially, despite what others would say, she did not think her relationship with her ex was abusive. *He didn't hit me*, she would say. But now that she was older and had found the courage to leave him, she realized that not all punches come through a fist. First is psychological abuse, then physical, then sexual. At least, that was the order in which it happened to her. Natasha tolerated his behavior because she would tell herself that he loved her and that she loved him, too. But the physical violence began after she built the courage to stand up to him. It was slightly pushing her around at first, then outright shoves where she would lose her balance and fall. Yet, even when these things happened, she always managed to stay with him. She was not sure if it was out of fear or pure naivety. Hopefully, one day, she will be able to explain to herself *why* she stayed.

Her breaking point was the night after a house party, where she drank to the point of utter belligerence. She had no recollection of having relations with her abuser, but two months later, it became abundantly clear that her pregnancy symptoms were not that of food poisoning.

When she confronted him about having relations the night of the party, he agreed that they had been together and that they'd used no contraception.

Shocked by his confession and knowing it was date rape, she refused to tell him of the pregnancy for fear of being coerced into getting back together.

Although there was a recent movement in State politics to present an abortion ban affecting all people capable of pregnancy, the governor was able to successfully veto the bill to keep a women's right to choose.

At least for now, she thought. It was only a matter of time before someone would come after Roe v. Wade. But at least at the State level, she knew that she had some politicians on her side to keep her in school and continue her journey towards a bright future.

Natasha went to her local Planned Parenthood, where she and her doctor discussed her options. She considered the facts: she was from a low-income family and she had no financial means to care for the child. She was barely able to afford to care for herself. She was medically uninsured. At first, she considered adoption; however, when she thought of her abuser claiming parental rights, she knew the best decision was for her to get an abortion. Even worse, if the baby stayed with her, she would have to see him, and it would be impossible to get him out of her life. Her safety was at risk around this man. She would never expose a child to abuse, especially by the same person who dared to abuse her and who she'd worked so hard to get away from.

It was a hard decision that she mulled over and over, but in the end, an abortion made the most sense given her circumstances. It saved her future and her life, but in a way, it also saved her baby from what would be a traumatic and difficult life.

Natasha's story is heartbreaking at any point in history. But after the monumental overturning of Roe v. Wade, her story takes on an even more ominous quality.

There are few topics of more importance than reproductive rights. Even as early as the 1700s, there was common law that abortion was legal prior to "quickening" (when fetal movements begin). This era witnessed the use of herbal remedies of varying safety and unknown efficacy to terminate pregnancies. Surgical methods with immense risks were employed as well. This changed in 1856 when the American Medical Association commenced a legal drive to put a halt to abortion. Inevitably, by the turn of the century, abortion was outlawed across the United States. It could be argued that, during this century, the main concern of the advocates of the abortion ban was decreased marital fertility because the main demanders of abortion in this era were married women who already had children.

THE COMSTOCK LAWS (1873)

Anthony Comstock, a New York elite, masterminded the original anti-birth control statutes. Born in 1844 and raised in Connecticut as a devout Christian, he would later relocate to New York. Comstock was not particularly pleased with the increasing number of prostitutes and pornography in New York. Thus, in collaboration with the police, he led an anti-obscenity crusade. He would later target the contraceptive industry and paint it something that fostered lewdness and lust.

In 1872, Comstock drafted a bill banning contraceptives along with his anti-obscenity bill and went to Washington to press for its passing into law. Congress passed the bill on March 3, 1873, and subsequently named it the Comstock Act. The statute criminalized dissemination of contraceptives, making doing so a federal crime. Subsequently, twenty-four states domesticated the Comstock laws, prohibiting the sale and distribution of contraceptives at the state level. In Massachusetts, fines and imprisonment were imposed for dissemination of contraceptives or information about contraceptives. Perhaps, because Anthony Comstock hailed from Connecticut, the laws there were more restrictive and included up to one-year imprisonment for married couples who violated this.

Despite the ban of abortion in the 19th century, abortion continued in the underground world. A perusal of the newspapers in this era revealed gruesome stories of women undergoing dangerous abortion procedures. For instance, a December 14, 1877, Vermont newspaper gives an account of the Godett abortion case. Mrs. Herriet Goddett, who lived in Winooski, went to Rutland Vermont, received an abortion, and died of sepsis 11 days later.

Legends of these sorts of stories fill the 19th century, and are evidence of abortion's prevalence. Interestingly, similar to the "camping" that flooded social media after the Roe reversal, 19th-century newspapers ran coded advertisements for women to terminate unwanted pregnancies. One such story, exemplifying the danger, promoted the use of Lysol for the dual function of contraceptive douse and inducements of abortions. Another haunting photo in the July 16, 1933 *Sunday News* showed the face of a fear-haunted housewife, pointing to the clandestine manner with which abortions were carried out.

THE MOTHER OF REPRODUCTIVE ACTIVISM

Margaret Sanger's mother had 11 childbirths and seven miscarriages before dying an untimely, early death. This tragedy fueled Sanger's commitment to devise a means to promote healthy birth control. She moved from Corning to

Catskills to attend a nursing school and subsequently became a nurse in New York, catering to the needs of traumatized women who'd undergone botched abortions.

Sanger coined the term "birth control," and in 1914, she began disseminating information about contraceptives and opened the first birth control clinic in the United States. In 1915, she was indicted and arrested in line with the Comstock laws but was not deterred. In 1921, she launched the American Birth Control League and spent three decades promoting and advocating for effective and safe birth control to America.

By 1950, Sanger's impact was universally celebrated by supporters. However, Sanger was heavily criticized as a supporter of eugenics and a racist agenda that hoped to eliminate an unfit race via the Planned Parenthood organization.

Despite her critics, she was determined to find additional options to innovate from the 1842 diaphragm and 1869 rubber condoms. In 1951, she met a willing medical expert in human reproduction named Gregory Pincus who took on the project. Alongside them, an International Harvester named Katharine McCormick sponsored the research. This syndicate produced a magic pill in 1960 called Enovid; it was subsequently approved by the FDA as the first oral contraceptive. Sanger's dream of providing the masses a safe and effective contraceptive had finally come to fruition.

Sanger's contraceptive pill paved the way for the undoing of the Comstock laws in 1965 Griswold v. Connecticut. The court opined that the private use of contraceptives was a constitutional right. Sanger died a year after the judgment in Griswold's case. It is safe to conclude that she died having realized her dream of finding a means for women to control their own fertility—she won the battle.

THE FREEING OF WOMEN

The late 1960s and early 1970s witnessed massive reform and the repeal of abortion bans across the United States. Between 1967 to 1972, thirteen states reformed their abortion laws to make abortion legal under limited circumstances. California, New York, Washington D.C., Alaska, and Hawaii were the trailblazers in this regard, as they completely repealed abortion bans. These trailblazers set the stage for the eventual 1973 case of Roe v. Wade that would change the trajectory of reproductive rights in the United States for nearly five decades.

Jane Roe, et al. v. Henry Wade, District Attorney of Dallas County (1973)[181]

Even before its 2022 overturn, Roe v. Wade is a case that nearly every American knows by heart. Most Supreme court decisions are granular—little noticed and not allowing for much interpretation of the law. Just a few are landmarks and Roe v. Wade is one of them. It effectively legalized abortion across the United States. It was a case that gave women the right to regulate their own reproductive system. The case reinforced a long-held belief that the United States is founded on principles of liberty, freedom, and self-determination and that those values should extend to women's rights on their own bodies.

The brief history of the case is that Jane Roe, also known as Norma McCorvey, was a Texan in her early 20s who wanted to terminate an unwanted pregnancy in 1969. Abortion was legal in Texas at the time but only for the purpose of saving a woman's life. McCorvey's life was not at risk, thus Henry Wade—the then district attorney of Dallas County—tried to enforce the Texas abortion law. Wade's claim failed on the grounds that the right to privacy is a constitutional right that extended to the right to abortion. It therefore followed that abortion cannot be banned, and a strict scrutiny standard was enforced.

When reading the entirety of Roe's judgment, one very important fact stands out. The case rarely mentions women and, in particular, it never offers reasons why women would want an abortion. For a case that is about abortion, women almost never appear. What one might notice is that the medical framework is set out; for instance, when Roe rules that the right to privacy extends to the right to choose an abortion, it is more about the medical doctor's privacy and not the privacy of the woman. Interestingly, Blackmun, who was the author of the court's opinion in Roe, was the General counsel at the Mayo clinic and wrote the opinion of Roe sitting in the clinic library.

Planned Parenthood of Southeastern Pennsylvania v. Casey (1992)[182]

In the years since Roe, the United States witnessed a vast shift of women's participation in the economic and social life of the nation. This was facilitated, in part, by their ability to control their reproductive rights.

However, 20 years later, under the leadership of Governor Robert Casey, the Commonwealth of Pennsylvania forged the first crack in the foundation that would eventually overturn Roe. In 1992, Pennsylvania enacted new abortion laws, mandating the woman seeking abortion give informed consent. This led to the court case of Planned Parenthood v. Casey where the "undue burden standard" began its debate.

The Casey case led to a swift uptick in abortion regulations, such as mandatory waiting periods and parental involvement laws for minors. Abortion opponents also began a shift in strategy from regulating demanders of abortion to suppliers of abortion, i.e., targeting doctors and facilities.

Dobbs v. Jackson Women's Health Organization (June 2022)[183]

With Trump's appointment of three supreme court justices, the writing was on the wall for Roe's demise. Multiple states began quietly enacting their own individual abortion bans in blatant conflict with the Roe and Casey decisions. Jackson Women's Health Organization challenged this unconstitutionality, and the case made its way to the supreme court to serve as a watershed in the reproductive rights journey in the United States.

In Dobbs's case, a 15-week abortion ban enacted in Mississippi was in clear violation of Roe. Thus, the only remaining abortion provider in Mississippi, Jackson's Women's Health Organization, sued Dobbs, who was a state health officer with the Mississippi State Department of Health. The Jackson's Women's Health Organization argued that the Mississippi law prohibiting abortion after 15 weeks of gestation is unconstitutional, as it infringes on the woman's right to an abortion as established in both Roe and Casey. The supreme court held that the constitution of the United States does not confer the right to abortion and Justice Alito opined that Roe was, in fact, "egregiously wrong."

REPRODUCTIVE INJUSTICE

The supreme court's decision of Dobbs v. Jackson shocked not just the United States, but the world. The decision attacks both the right to privacy guaranteed in the United States constitution, but also targets the right to bodily autonomy. More importantly, this singular act underscores the politicization of the courts and their institutional legitimacy as a judiciary independence.

The inherent danger in the decision of Dobbs is that it strips away a constitutional right equal to the status of half the nation, a move unprecedented in American history. But the effect was not equally felt.

In 1989, Kimberle Crenshaw identified that inequalities, particularly gender inequalities, could be multifaceted. Hence, she coined the term "intersectionality." Intersectionality is a theory and a prism for understanding certain kinds of problems; for instance, an African American girl is six times more likely to be suspended from school than a White girl. This is both a race and a gender problem, as they compound to form complexities that some girls and women face.

Similarly, reproductive justice, coined by twelve Black women in 1994, comprises reproductive rights and social justice. This phrase reflected the lives and experiences of Black women in the United States who have been denied a full range of services and protection. Black women have multiple identities like ability, age, immigration status, nationality, religion, sexual orientation, etc. Black women experience the highest rate of poverty and only make $0.63 for every dollar a White man makes. Nearly 20% of Black women have no health insurance and die four times as often as White women from pregnancy-related causes, regardless of their income or educational status; this is intersectionality at play. Reproductive justice is, thus, the human right that can be achieved when all women and girls have the complete social, political, and economic power and resources to make healthy decisions about their bodies, communities, and families.

The outcome of the Dobbs case will further exacerbate racial and economic inequalities across the United States. Statistics illuminate that the bulk of abortion seekers are women in their 20s and that 85% of them are unmarried. As a population in the United States, Black women are having abortions at higher rates than White women, and a majority of women of all races live below the poverty level. Couple these forced birth scenarios with a lack of mental health, childcare, and foster care funding, and we are looking at an economic welfare crisis of grand proportions within the next two decades.

Hillary Clinton won the popular vote by almost 3 million votes. Donald Trump won more Electoral College votes and won the presidency. As I indicated earlier, Trump appointed three judges to the Supreme Court who eventually overturned a woman's right to make a choice about her body and childbirth. But, in truth, polls indicate that most of America supports a woman's right to choose.[184] In fact, the most recent Pew Research Center study finds 63% of Americans believe abortion should be legal in most, if not all, cases.

Polls don't vote, people do. Your vote counts whether you decide to use it or not!

10

LGBTQIA+

M s. Gonzalez was a third-grade teacher at the local elementary school
in South Florida. Teaching had been her dream ever since she was a
child, and she truly loved what she did. However, lately, society had
created a lot of back and forth on what subjects are appropriate for children
at her grade level to discuss. One of the main conversations was handling the
curious questions of students with parents of the same gender. Additionally, a
student in the fifth grade had a transsexual parent, and that child was horribly
bullied by his classmates. Teachers had spent the whole school year protecting
this child from his peers. Every solution that they came up with provided a
temporary pause to the bullying, only for it to begin again a few weeks later.

During the staff meeting on Wednesday afternoon, the principal led with
the topic of Gender Identity and Sexual Orientation after many teachers found
themselves dodging questions from their students or stopping bullies from
harming children with homosexual or transsexual parents. One of the things that
the principal wanted to make clear was how they were to handle the questions
and to try to keep them as universal as possible—working within the capacity
of understanding that the students had at their age. It was believed that these
conversations at a young age could help students understand that students
with same-sex parents were just like them. While the teachers knew they could
not use the words "sexual orientation" without giggles from the students and
heated letters from parents, they needed to teach the children that orthodox
nuclear family structures were not the *only* type of right family. They knew that
having these conversations not only provided answers to innocent questions but
could protect children from bullying and being ostracized by the student body.

"We should handle this situation as such," the principal began. "If they ask about having two parents of the same gender, we explain that families come in all different shapes and sizes. Just like some can have a mother and a father, they can have a grandma living with them or be raised by their aunt. Therefore, every family is unique on its own, and nothing is considered *wrong*."

"What if they ask about homosexual parents acting like heterosexual parents?" one of the teachers asked.

"Well, they are young children, so if they suggest going further into that conversation, try to get back to the point that we expect them to treat everyone with the same [level of] respect. You may always talk to this child after class with the instruction that they need to discuss that subject with their parents."

That is where Ms. Gonzalez had the idea that it would make the most sense to discuss the subject with the whole class at once to address any questions. While it was all right to wait for the students to come forward with questions, sometimes they were uncomfortable doing so. They often found themselves being bullied and scared to ask for help.

"Would you be opposed to the idea of a light conversation with the class on this subject?" she asked. "I am concerned that not all students are forthcoming with their questions or have instilled some sort of embarrassment because of other students who may have teased them."

After pondering her question, the principal said, "You bring up a good point. I do not mind the conversation, but best to keep it light and be clear that making fun of someone because of this or hurting them in any way will not be tolerated."

Satisfied with the teachers' questions and the approach they needed to take to handle questions of this nature, the principal concluded the meeting and dismissed the staff back to their classrooms.

A few days later, while standing before her class by the whiteboard, Ms. Gonzalez was ready to open the doors to questions regarding sexual orientation and gender identity. This was a delicate subject, but more so, it was important to her that she taught the children that it is okay to have a family that is structured differently.

She wrote on the board with her favorite blue marker in big letters: "Family Types." She began her lesson with a simple question. "Can someone tell me what they think this means?"

The class stared at her perplexed, and she thought maybe she needed to approach it differently. She was talking to eight- to nine-year-olds at the end of the day.

"Let me start with an example. So, a kid named Billy lives in a house." She proceeds to draw a house and a stick figure in the middle. "Who else do you think lives with Billy inside his house?"

Hands immediately went up.

She pointed at the girl sitting in the front of the class. "Amy?"

"Mommy and Daddy," she said quickly.

"Yes, Mommy and Daddy." She drew two taller stick figures on the board. "This is one of many types of families that you can see in your neighborhood. In every house, you can find a different group of family members and more than one under the same name." She proceeded to draw two more houses. "In this house, we can have Aunt Milly as the grown-up, and in this one, we have two daddies as the adults."

Some students giggled.

Taking this as the cue to educate, she continued, "There are many types of families. Some we are used to seeing, and some we are not. And that is okay." She watched as the children nodded collectively. "At the end of the day, we need to make sure that we are treating everyone with respect and equality. Even if they are different than we are."

"I have two daddies," Jasmine chimed in.

"See, perfect example." Ms. Gonzalez said. "Anyone else?"

"I live with just my mom," another student said.

"My grandma lives with us," chimed a Latin student in the back.

And just like that, children with nuclear families and those that did not follow a traditional family structure chimed in, and the giggles turned into awe. It was "cool" to have a non-traditional household by the end of the lesson.

That afternoon, Wesley rushed to the elementary school his two children attended in South Florida. Unfortunately, his meeting in the office had run late today, and he found himself rushing to make it to the school in time for pickup. He hurried, as they were surprising the kids with a Disney trip to celebrate his anniversary with his husband, Tony, and they had a strict departure time. They would be leaving tonight right after dinner. They loved Disney, and Wesley had personally interned for them while he was a college student. And to further show how it ran in their blood, their kids both loved Disney as well. Disney Karaoke was a weekly occurrence in their household and dominated most birthday party themes. In addition, they made an effort to vacation there for a couple of days a year. It was such a tradition at this point, it made perfect sense to celebrate their 10th wedding anniversary with their children at the place they loved most.

He got out of his car and walked toward where Jasmine would be with her third-grade teacher and classmates. Seeing his baby girl, he waved and made his way towards them. His son was already walking towards them from across the schoolyard.

"Ms. Gonzalez, how are you?" He smiled as they approached him. "Did she behave today?"

"She is the gem of the class, and you know it, Wesley."

Ms. Gonzalez laughed as Jasmine made her way to him. She routinely handed him her backpack and went to say goodbye to her friends.

Ms. Gonzalez began, "I wanted to let you know that the class discussed the different types of families we can see in society today, and surprisingly, it went very well. We have a couple of students with unique households, and we taught them that not everyone lives with a mother and a father."

"I see," Wesley said, unsure of how to respond to her.

He had never experienced this while he was in school. Being gay was something that he kept to himself until college when it felt safe to be who he really was. He felt fortunate that he had had the chance to be a father at all, as some Conservative states were pushing back on the notion of homosexual couples adopting children. Jasmine and their son, Samuel, had been taken by Child Protective Services after their mother could not recover from a heroin addiction. Both children had been living in unspeakable conditions and were drastically malnourished and dirty. So, when the opportunity came to take them in, he and Tony jumped at the chance.

"Jasmine was more than happy to talk about how she has two fathers who are into Disney and sports." She smiled. "It is part of our curriculum to teach kids now of unorthodox nuclear families. Not everyone or every family dynamic is the same. Some have divorced parents, gay parents, and even parents who are trans. We have a student whose sister is raising them. It is an essential conversation to have with them. Talking about these subjects teaches the children empathy and compassion, and to be mindful of their surroundings and who they are talking to. We also hope to promote a safe environment for when students identify their gender and sexuality and find that it may not align with what they expected. We want them to know that if this happens, they will be treated with respect and without reproach."

"I wish that I had that growing up. Even though I began my journey as a teen, it would have been nice to know that raising children with another man would not question the quality of their upbringing. If anything, it makes them more accepting and socially aware," he remarks a bit wistfully.

"We have had a few parents complain about the new policy, but despite the governer signing the latest bill to prevent conversations about gender identity and sexual orientation, we have been moving forward to talk about it. It is very hard sometimes to say that I live and am from Florida."

"Tell me about it. I'm gay in 2022 and somehow still fighting for my basic human rights."

"One day, we will hopefully get to a place where we can acknowledge that we are all human at the end of the day and that we should be treated with respect and compassion."

Idealist, aspirational, and enlightened. These are the words to describe the scene above. And yet, it represents the best in the core foundations of education, which literally translates to "an enlightening experience."

Unfortunately, this scenario has become a distinct exception, far from current norm in the American education system.

GAY IN AMERICA

If you identify as lesbian, gay, bisexual, trans, queer, intersex, ally, or any other gender descriptor not listed—that is, LGBTQIA+—conservatives in general, with their perceived tendency toward White, straight, Christian values, don't appear to easily display understanding or a compassion for this way of life. Some people thrive in the simplicity of duality—black or white, right or wrong, capitalist or socialist, gay or straight—preferring a simple-minded view of the world that eliminates complexity and advocates for conformity. These people crave a simple past, a time when "men were men and women knew their place." They further demand sound-bite answers to complicated problems.

By contrast, the modern world—with its myriad of glorious and inspiring subtleties—is frightening, and therefore off-brand. Anything that violates their view of the world as binary and unchanging—carved in stone, if you will, like the Ten Commandments—is dangerous and must be either forced to conform or stamped out.

Ronald Reagan brought condemnation to the national stage while he was president. While there were likely many before him who held personal beliefs of condemnation, Reagan, who occupied the White House from 1980 to 1988, was oddly silent on his personal beliefs about gay rights. However, his shocking and delayed response to the AIDS crisis would not only cost thousands of lives and weaken gay rights overall, but it would also hurt his reputation and have a negative impact on the National Republican Party for decades. Many cynical politicians believed that, as the AIDS epidemic ravaged the gay population, Reagan kept silent on the issue because he didn't want to offend his conservative base. The anti-gay, religious right included Jerry Falwell and his so-called "Moral Majority." Falwell himself said, "AIDS is the wrath of God upon homosexuals." Bureaucrats in the Reagan administration included notorious homophobes such as Pat Buchanan and Gary Bauer. Many of Reagan's new and very right-wing supporters had raised millions of dollars campaigning against LGBTQIA+ people.

Finally, in 1987, after over 20,000 people had died—and near the end of his eight years in office—Reagan belatedly made a presidential address, famously declaring AIDS public enemy number one.

"In the history of the AIDS epidemic, President Reagan's legacy is one of silence," said Michael Cover, former Associate Executive Director for Public Affairs at Whitman-Walker Clinic, the groundbreaking AIDS health-care organization in Washington. "It is the silence of tens of thousands who died alone and unacknowledged, stigmatized by our government under his administration."

Reagan's successor, George H.W. Bush was a moderate Republican who, in 1990, signed the Ryan White CARE Act into law. It was designed to provide federal funding for community-based organizations that serve people with HIV or AIDS. President Clinton was deemed by the ACLU as a mixed-success presidency in relation to gay rights. In a paper published in 1999, they hailed his leadership as advancing lesbian and gay rights further than all of his predecessors combined. Efforts included boldly using his office to help legitimize the lesbian and gay rights movement as an integral part of the broader civil rights movement and routinely including gay issues in his public speeches on civil rights. On the contrary, they also condemn his support of the Defense of Marriage Act and his *Don't Ask, Don't Tell* military policy.

George W. Bush, like Reagan, came down hard against same-sex marriage. On February 24, 2004, as his presidential campaign for re-election was heating up amid his dismal approval ratings, Bush proclaimed, "Today, I call upon the Congress to promptly pass and to send to the states for ratification an amendment to our Constitution defining and protecting marriage as a union of a man and woman as husband and wife."

Under President Barack Obama, the movement made significant gains. When the 1996 Defense of Marriage Act was challenged and the case made it to the U.S. Supreme Court, the Obama administration and Attorney General Eric Holder refused to defend it, and it was struck down, thereby legalizing same-sex marriage. Obama also appointed more openly LGBTQIA+ people to the federal judiciary than any other president in history.

HYPOCRISY ON DISPLAY

On January 20, 2017, the nation entered the Presidency of Donald J. Trump. While proclaiming himself the most pro-gay president in history, he earned just 14% of the LGBTQIA+ vote, the lowest percentage any Republican candidate had received since the gay vote has been tallied.

The Log Cabin Republicans (LCR), an organization claiming to be the nation's original and largest organization representing LGBT conservatives and straight allies who support fairness, freedom, and equality for all Americans, were thrilled with his election, saying in a press release on November 9, 2016 that, "Tonight, America chose change over the status quo, the future over the past, and conservative solutions over empty liberal promises—America chose Donald J. Trump. Log Cabin Republicans extend our hearty congratulations to the President-Elect of the United States!"

In August 2020, before Trump's re-election contest against Democrat Joe Biden, Robert Kabel, chair of the LCR, enthused, "Today, thanks in large part to the leadership of President Donald Trump, the party has delivered meaningful policy victories for gays and lesbians."

But as usual, in the Orwellian "Newspeak" world of Trump and his MAGA supporters, the truth was very different. As *The Washington Post* detailed in that same month, Trump's first-term record on LGBTQIA+ issues was dismal. The common theme? If Obama supported an issue, Trump opposed it.

Trump revoked Obama's executive order, known as the "Fair Pay and Safe Workplaces" rule, which included anti-discriminatory protections for lesbian, gay, bisexual, transgender, and queer contractors. The Trump Justice Department argued that Title VII of the 1964 Civil Rights Act did not protect employees from discrimination based on sexual orientation, again opposing a decision reached under Obama. In July 2017, in a series of surprise Twitter posts, Trump announced that "the United States Government will not accept or allow transgender individuals to serve in any capacity in the U.S. Military." In November 2019, Trump's Health and Human Services secretary, Alex Azar, proposed a new rule that would effectively eliminate discrimination protections for LGBTQIA+ individuals in all its grant programs. In June 2020, the Trump administration finalized a regulation that defined gender as a person's biological sex, reversing an Obama-era rule aimed at protecting transgender people against sex discrimination in health care.

Lucas Acosta, national press secretary for the Human Rights Campaign, said in a statement, "It's unconscionable, insidious, and offensive for anyone to call this administration 'pro-LGBTQ' when the president, vice president, and those who work for them have endeavored to systematically roll back our rights and deny us our dignity."

In August 2022, Victor Madrigal-Borloz, the UN Independent Expert on protection against violence and discrimination based on sexual orientation and gender identity, completed a tour of four U.S. cities. He reported the human rights of LGBTQIA+ people are being deliberately undermined by many Republican-controlled state governments and urged the administration of President Joe Biden to strengthen measures to protect them. "Despite five decades of progress, equality is not within reach, and often not even within sight for all persons impacted by violence and discrimination based on sexual orientation and gender identity in the United States," he said. "I am deeply alarmed by a widespread, profoundly negative riptide created by deliberate actions to roll back the human rights of LGBT people at state level . . . The evidence shows that, without exception, these actions rely on prejudiced and stigmatizing views of LGBT persons, in particular transgender children and youth, and seek to leverage their lives as props for political profit."

According to the 2022 "LGBTQ Travel Safety Index" compiled by Asher and Lyric Fergusson, on a list of 203 nations of the world ranked according to their relative safety for LGBTQ travelers, the United States lands at number 24, behind nations including Ireland, Uruguay, Chile, Iceland, Spain, and our northern neighbor, Canada—which topped the list at number one.

THE RISE OF DON'T SAY GAY

In their zealous attempts to limit the rights of LGBTQIA+ people, conservative-leaning legislators across the country have been blocked by sensible laws affirming the rights of gay adults to live their lives in peace. Once stymied, they pivoted to a new line of attack, one more insidious than any before: claiming the need to shield children from the influence of gay people. The corruption of innocent children is a reliable hot-button issue guaranteed to inflame voters of all walks of life and persuasion.

In 2016, North Carolina's Republican governor, Pat McCrory, signed into law House Bill 2, the "Public Facilities Privacy & Security Act," which is also known as the "Bathroom Bill." The law barred cities, counties, and municipalities from enacting any anti-discrimination policies not already covered by North Carolina state law. Basically, the law prevented transgender people from using public bathrooms that aligned with their gender identity. This was a direct response to a measure adopted by the city of Charlotte, which had enacted a pro-LGBTQIA+ ordinance that explicitly allowed trans people to use public facilities that matched their gender identity, as opposed to their sex assigned at birth.

The passage of the Bathroom Bill led to a flood of similar measures ostensibly designed to "protect children." Dozens of states have introduced bills curbing gay rights, including limiting transgender students' participation on school sports teams that match their gender identity. Democrats say these kinds of measures are all part of the Republican Party's focus on "culture wars," instead of kitchen-table issues of employment, family income, inflation, energy prices, the environment, and taxes. Republicans claim that these issues protect children, and the integrity of girl sports in particular. In North Carolina, the backlash to the Bathroom Bill from the business, sports, and entertainment communities was fierce. Eight months after signing the bill, McCrory lost his re-election bid to then-attorney general Roy Cooper, a Democrat who had strongly opposed HB 2.

But the battle was far from over. The Republican-controlled General Assembly then passed House Bill 142, which was supposed to be a compromise, but which human rights advocates saw as a tepid response. At the time, even Governor Cooper admitted that it was "not a perfect deal" and "not my preferred solution."

Allison Scott, a trans woman who is the policy director at the Campaign for Southern Equality, told NBC News, "I call HB 2 and 142 'bills of trauma.' They were very specifically targeting a group without naming us. It meant more than ambivalence; it was outright hate."

Further south, Florida's governor, Ron DeSantis, has been widely criticized for his policies impacting the gay community under the mantra of "protecting children." In June 2021, he signed into law House Bill 241, dubbed the "Parents' Bill of Rights." It stated that state and public schools cannot infringe on the "fundamental rights" of parents to direct the upbringing of their child—extending to decisions about education, health care, and mental health.

Gay rights advocates saw it as a thinly veiled broadside against them. "This is a direct attack," said Lakey Love of the Florida Coalition for Trans Liberation, "on transgender and gender-nonconforming Floridians, and the LGBTQ youth in particular."

In April 2022, DeSantis signed into law the "Parental Rights in Education" bill, which critics, including Democrats, immediately labeled the "Don't Say Gay" law. They argued that House Bill 1557 attacked gay rights on three fronts:

First, it banned instruction or classroom discussions about LGBTQIA+ issues for kindergarten through third grade. For older students, discussion about gay and transgender issues had to be "age appropriate or developmentally appropriate." This part was largely a symbolic nod to Trump's radical right base. As in many states, sex education was already banned in Florida until the fifth grade. Critics pointed out the law claimed to solve a problem that didn't exist for the state's youngest students.

Second, the "Don't Say Gay" law empowered parents to sue their school district over teachings they didn't like—and the district would be required to foot the bill. This was designed to have a chilling effect and prompt schools to preemptively forbid *any* teachings or conversations about LGBTQIA+ issues.

Finally, the law required schools to tell parents when their child received mental health services. Often, gender-diverse children are uncomfortable expressing their feelings at home and may choose to do so to a school counselor. This provision was a clear warning to school mental health officials to steer clear of "gay talk" but, if it happened, they needed to inform potentially clueless parents.

Republicans argued that nowhere in the bills does it state that you can't say the word gay. That is technically correct, but the wording of the law is vague, perhaps deliberately so. The preamble of the bill prohibits not only "instruction" around gender identity and sexual orientation, but also "classroom discussion" of these topics. And while the law seemingly targets grades kindergarten through third, all grades are affected by the provision requiring gender and sexuality to be discussed in ways that are "age appropriate or developmentally appropriate." These terms are highly subjective, and it would be easy for an uptight parent to object—and to sue the school—over a perfectly innocuous discussion.

Governor DeSantis, who was actively positioning himself for a presidential bid in 2024 as an ultra-Trumpian alternative to Trump himself, made the subtext of the law clear: "I think the last couple of years really reveal to parents that they are being ignored increasingly across education. We have seen curriculum embedded for very, very young children, classroom materials about sexuality and woke gender ideology. We've seen libraries that have clearly inappropriate pornographic materials for very young kids. These leftist politicians, corporate media outlets, some of these activist groups, support sexualizing kids in kindergarten."

Now, let's be real. Most reasonably minded people—Democrats as well as Republicans—don't believe politicians, media outlets, and activist groups in general support such a horrible thing. Such exaggerations and generalizations have their roots deep in the dark corners of partisan politics; remember the infamous shooting incident at Comet Ping Pong Pizzeria in December 2016. Dubbed "Pizzagate," it erupted in November 2016 when Wikileaks published the personal email account of John Podesta, Hillary Clinton's campaign chair, which had been hacked in a spear-phishing attack. Shadowy conspiracy theorists falsely claimed the emails contained coded messages connecting several high-ranking Democratic Party officials and U.S. restaurants with an alleged human trafficking and child sex ring. One of the centers of this fictional ring was the entirely innocent Comet Ping Pong Pizzeria in Washington, D.C. Some extreme right-wingers metastasized the conspiracy into a broader government conspiracy dubbed "Pedogate," in which a "satanic cabal of elites" of the New World Order operated international child sex trafficking rings.

As the wave of threatening calls and messages against Comet Ping Pong and other businesses mounted, the nightmare came to a head. On December 4th,

Edgar Maddison Welch, a 28-year-old man from Salisbury, North Carolina, walked into Comet Ping Pong and fired three shots from an AR-15 style rifle, striking the restaurant's walls, a desk, and a door. No one was injured and Welch was arrested, but the damage remained. The Comet Ping-Pong attack served to enshrine the lie that liberals—and especially LGBTQIA+ Americans—were remorseless corrupters of defenseless children.

The Disney Company is among Florida's largest employers, employing more than 70,000 local workers. However, when they objected to "Don't Say Gay," right-wing pundits and politicians went on the attack. On March 20, 2022, Fox News correspondent, Laura Ingraham, said, "Well now, it's all about pushing a sexual agenda on little children across their entertainment platforms. Now this isn't programming, this is propaganda for grooming. There's nothing these activists hate more, by the way, than a parent who protects her son or daughter's innocence. Oh, wait, daughter, I can't say that because Disney doesn't like such gendered terms."

"Grooming", quickly became the new political buzzword along with "protecting their innocence." Both terms served to deflect and heighten fear.

Following Florida's lead, other Republican states rushed to pass their own anti-gay legislation. On In 2022, Alabama governor Kay Ivey signed a sweeping package of anti-transgender legislation, stripping transgender youth of life-saving resources and further isolating them from their peers and communities. One measure, SB 184, made it a felony, one punishable by up to ten years in prison, to provide gender-affirming care. It also required educators to "out" children to their parents.

Another Alabama law, HB 322, banned K-12 students from using bathrooms and school facilities consistent with their gender identity. The law also prohibited conversations about sexual orientation and gender identity in kindergarten through fifth grade classrooms. South Dakota and Oklahoma have also passed restrictive laws in these areas.

Such laws are expected to have a devastating impact on the mental health of LGBTQIA+ students, who already experience higher rates of depression and suicide. These laws could also amplify the existing culture of fear and suspicion among students and school staffers.

It's not just schools that are being targeted, however. On June 28, 2022, South Carolina Governor Henry McMaster signed into law H4776, the cynically named "Medical Ethics and Diversity Act." This bill would allow healthcare professionals to deny service on the basis of their personal beliefs. It authorized what's known as "medical rights of conscience," a fancy phrase that essentially protects doctors, nurses, and medical students from being fired or punished for opting out of services based on their "religious, moral, or ethical beliefs or principles."

In 2015, Republican representatives introduced the First Amendment Defense Act (FADA). This measure rolled back many Obama-era protections for LGBTQIA+ people. Matt McTighe, Executive Director of Freedom for All Americans, said of this bill, "It's stunning that some lawmakers in Congress continue to prioritize legislation that promotes discrimination against the LGBT community. This out-of-touch legislation does nothing to strengthen the existing protections for religious freedom. All this bill does is make it even easier to discriminate against LGBT people. Americans overwhelmingly support treating LGBT people fairly and equally under the law, and this bill intentionally undermines that very value." Fortunately, the measure died.

Nearly 400 anti-LGBTQIA+ bills were introduced across the country in 2021, which is an unprecedented number of legislative assaults on the LGBTQIA+ community. This list includes more than 100 bills to ban transgender youth from participating in sports consistent with their gender identity, some of which would require children to undergo unnecessary and invasive medical examinations. Another 64 bills would deny transgender youths access to best-practice medical care. 66% of LGBTQ youths, including 85% of transgender or non-binary youths, reported to the Trevor Project that recent debates about state laws meant to restrict the rights of transgender people have negatively affected their mental health. In a similar vein, crisis contacts for LGBTQ youths in Texas saw a 150% increase in those seeking support compared to the same time period in 2020. Many advocates are urging the U.S. Senate to pass the Equality Act, which would provide a national solution to LGBTQIA discrimination and expanding federal reach into schools across all states. Even if the Senate were to try, however, it is unlikely to pass.

But, numbers and laws are high level and may not give us the ground level perspective. In order to do so, I interviewed Liss Smith, the Advocacy and Communications Director at Inside Out Youth Services, and G.E. Loveless, the Community Advisor at Hearts2gether for Equitable Change Project.

Inside Out was founded in 1990 in Colorado Springs, Colorado in collaboration with the El Paso County Public Health Department. It originally served as a support group for queer youths who were experiencing substance abuse issues. Their mission is to build access, equity, and power with LGBTQIA2+ young people through leadership, advocacy, community-building, education, and peer support. But not long after its inception, the founder realized these young people faced so many interconnected issues. In 1992, Inside Out became a nonprofit that worked five days a week through a community center and that used evidence-based programming for youth and their parents or other custodial adults.

"There are a lot of parents who want to do the right thing and want to advocate for their kid and want to love them no matter what they're experiencing. But they just don't have the tools. They just don't know." Smith laments the organization's most requested training is simply LGBTQ 101, which is the basics of acronyms and associated identities. Simply having a baseline understanding helps soften stereotypes and open doors to conversation.

> *Loveless:* "Anyone who has ever met a teenager knows that they see right through you. You cannot be inauthentic with a young person. So, they're going to see if your intention is loving and affirming and supportive, even if you say the wrong thing. They're also going to see if you're coming at them from a malicious angle. And so, just be authentic with them. 'Hey, I don't know if this is a good question to ask. Can I ask you anyway?'"

When asked about the state of the world from her perspective, Smith describes it as "disturbing."

> *Loveless:* "A lot of the rhetoric we're hearing and a lot of the tactics being used are the same ones that have been in use since Stonewall, you know, since the 1960s. But now we have social media that amplifies these messages and tactics in these echo chambers and makes them seem louder and more pervasive than they are. And two, it really affects the way people vote, which affects our actual human rights and experience."

She goes on to illuminate the myriad of new challenges faced by young people navigating the internet social media age. They are connected and paying attention, meaning they see and hear and read all of the negativity and hate thrust upon them; constant voices tell them they are disgusting, they are an abomination, and they are reviled.

> *Loveless:* "If the primary message they're receiving is, 'Your identity is fake or invalid or an abomination,' then that really affects their self-esteem and their mental health. Queer adults are being re-traumatized daily, trying to protect young folks from being traumatized while they are being traumatized."

Smith goes on to tell a story of a young person who came to Inside Out as a transgender person. As ranking members of the New Life Church, their parents would never support transgender people and they felt lost and alone. Rather than focus on the pain, Inside Out worked with this person to really focus on the joy that they could grasp and touch, to let them know that there were other ways of living, being, and thinking, and to shift the focus to one of community and love. The hope was to help them see that, even though their world seemed really small, it was bigger than that.

As a 501c3 organization, Inside Out cannot and does not advocate for specific legislation, parties, or people, but they do work on policy by offering others—outside the organization—educational materials on policy issues and encouraging them to speak up for what they believe is right. They also open forums of conversation for members to share what they are seeing on a local level, such as at school board meetings. While all helpful, Smith believes the most important thing their organization can do is keep promoting the positive messages and hope that those reach the right people; luckily, being a trusted voice for that makes a tangible difference to how people think and feel.

When asked about the organization's successes, Smith was quick to point to education, particularly at the local level and specifically with school boards.

> *Loveless:* "I believe our greatest success has probably come from recognizing our allies on the school board and having direct conversations with them and offering conversations to the other members of the school board."

I also inquired about what keeps her up at night and/or what her greatest current concern is. She was quick to get personal, citing the overturning of Roe v. Wade as a door opener to other freedoms being removed.

> *Loveless:* "The idea that my marriage to my wife would just go away, that scares the daylights out of me. More than that, the idea that as soon as that conversation begins to happen, it's going to be so disgusting and hurt so much because I know how beautiful our love is. And the idea that people would disregard it just because we were both born women is unfathomable to me. That keeps me up at night."

G.E. Loveless was born and raised in East Austin, Texas. He moved to Manor, Texas, when he was about 11 and credits this move to helping him find his spark for activism. As early as high school, he was planting seeds of activism by starting an LGBTQ club and hosting inclusion events. After high school, he founded Austin Justice Coalition before becoming a student ambassador for Austin Community College. In that role, he began working with students across all 11 of their campuses, and shifted from being a very small community activist to a huge community activist in less than a year. He has been working in that space ever since.

As a self-proclaimed African American creative and storyteller, he prides himself on creating more seats at the table for everybody—including for BIPOC, LGBTQ individuals, or simply underserved people—and cares even more about not only creating seats at the table but creating spaces for people to create their own tables.

However, I was interested in more than just his work on behalf of the community; instead, I invited him to an interview to share his unique personal story. G.E. is not only African American and a member of the LGBTQ community, but he is also the son of a bishop and evangelist and an educator. He also considers himself a devout Christian.

During the interview, he said:

> *Loveless:* "I always was reminded of who I was, racially speaking, because my mother, she is from Trinidad and Tobago. My father, he's from Alabama. I grew up in a house where we took pride in multiculturalism. We took pride in who we were as Afro-Caribbeans. And in the area of religion, I knew I was Christian before I really knew my racial identity as a Black man. And when I came into understanding my Blackness, then I started learning about my queerness and who I am in the LGBTQ space. And finally, I learned about intersectionality and who I am within my own space as a middle class being at a young age. And so, looking at all of that, it overlaps in the sense of that there are sometimes spaces where I feel like I can't be every checkbox of my identity.

> "For example, I once attended a men's conference and, for me, I don't go to like a lot of men's events because it's always been an uncomfortable space for me as an LGBTQ person, even though I check the box as a Black man. I simply don't show up in my LGBTQ self in those rooms, in that space.

> "And I feel like that's an issue with a lot of people when it comes to seeking community and representation. Sometimes you don't check all the boxes of your identity when entering a space. You have to raise one or dilute the other. And then you have to think about, like, the vocabulary you use and your mannerisms. It's an entire learned behavior where you just learn to switch. But it's still a process."

I asked Loveless about his experience coming out in light of his religious upbringing, and he said:

Loveless: "I've been blessed with the supportive family I've been given, especially when it comes to being a queer, Black, and Christian. For me, my father has always been my best friend. And I remember when I came out, I was in like middle school or high school and I was talking to this boy and I brought him to my house and my dad had not met him and my mom was observing me, like, who is this boy? After he left, my dad called me upstairs and he was upset simply because I didn't tell him I had a boyfriend. And right then my father and I had a deep conversation about my sexuality. I didn't know what it meant to be gay. I didn't understand what queerness was. I mean, I wasn't familiar with the LGBTQ community at all, and I just knew that I had this attraction to the same gender. And from talking to my father, he was like, Do you feel like this is who you are?

"And the following week, my dad went to the congregation at church. And during one of his sermons, he said, This is a safe space. This open church, anyone is welcome. And right there, he made it known that it was a safe space for anybody. And it just showed me how to be really intentional about creating new safe spaces to be in.

"It still took a little adjustment because, once again, it's a culture adjustment. Now they have vocabulary that we can't use in the house. There are ways of discussing socio-political issues in our religious communities, even in the BIPOC (Black, indigenous, and people of color) communities, that can be sensitive to me because I am LGBTQ. I'm always going to have sensitivity or a lot of passion behind my voice in these communities. But coming out, my parents were really, really supportive in who I was and who I was becoming and gave me that space."

When asked about the additional challenge of being Afro queer in Texas, a state not known for its openness to inclusivity, he expressed fears of being able to live and thrive here long term:

Loveless: "Anxious and fearful. Ultimately, I want to be able to get married and have children and be able to create, like, a stable family life. It comes down to a lack of security and safety. Am I a priority when it comes to politicians at any level, even at the city level? Am I being seen? Am I being heard? Are there policies that not only advocate for me but also benefit me as an African American or as a LGBTQ individual? I think about my other BIPOC LGBTQ friends and their futures in Texas. Are we secure politically? Are we secure financially or economically? Are we secure socially in a sense of having a community?

There are so many socio-political challenges in the kind of inequities that we see in marginalized communities. A lot of people are becoming discouraged from even starting a business. There is a lack of LGBTQ startup founders and not enough BIPOC business owners in some spaces. And even more who are leaving and migrating to other spaces or cities. And so, a lot of youth who had an idea, who want to create something and want to see something grow in their community, are not able to get the access to resources. They have a lack of capital, and they're unable to grow that team because now when you have a lack of resources."

Loveless goes on to describe his personal mission for this chapter of life. His work is focused on creating safe spaces that offer LGBTQ and BIPOC communities physical and psychological safety and equity. Places where youth can find peers. Places where people can feel validated by their own existence. Spaces where ideas can be shared, and different views can be explored without negativity or violence. He is doing this by focusing on events like youth summits and town halls.

Loveless: "We want to ensure that they're comfortable in the space because once they're comfortable, they'll be able to be vulnerable, be able to share their story, be able to network and talk about their story and be able to grow themselves. Because too often we are not heard, or worse, we are not being seen."

I closed out our conversation by offering him space to share his advice to others.

Loveless: "I always tell people that it's about the building blocks toward your ultimate purpose. What are your passions? What do you like to do? Do you like to surf? Do you like to volunteer? Do you like to create? Do you like to design? Do you like to strategize? Write it down. I am. Who are you? And for me, it's like, I am African. I am genderfluid. I am . . . Figure out who you are, [who] that being [is]t. And then figure out what your purpose is or what your passions are. Second, just start. Start doing. And third of all, make friends, connect, build your network, build your community."

The culture wars waged in America today are not only a threat to our democracy and freedom but they also negatively impact our economic stability as well. The tides of repression are rising and, whether or not you have children, are BIPOC or a log-cabin Republican, are a woman or belong to the LGBTQIA+ community, we are all at risk.

VOTE FOR YOUR FAMILY VALUES

These issues are complicated, and I can personally see valid beliefs on both sides. But it is simply one more reason that everyone's vote matters. What I believe is right for my family and what you believe is right for yours may differ, but we have the right to select individuals who represent whatever beliefs we hold. We exercise that right by voting. To combat the discriminatory culture crisis while also honoring their own individual views issue by issue, it is important for allies to stay grounded in the support of home-grown organizations in the trenches of the chaos.

SECTION

4

—

A Way Forward

The Democratic Party is a large, complex, and diverse organization. In that regard, it's not unlike Wal-Mart, Apple, Google, General Motors, or any other industrial corporation. Like them, the Democratic Party has leaders and followers (or employees), and a set of goals to attain. Both Democratic and Republican parties have some similarities to organizations such as the U.S. Army, which is also large, complex—and in the case of Democrats—diverse, but unlike a for-profit company, they are not intent on selling a product but on providing a service—namely, the defense of the nation. Now, they both have different ideas of how to defend our nation, but therein lies the major distinction between the parties. There are also large, charitable organizations, such as the YMCA and the Red Cross, whose non-profit missions are to help people live better lives.

All of these organizations must live within, and serve, a large and diverse population, and their internal composition—the people who work there or support the organization—should reflect that same diversity. There are also many smaller organizations whose very existence is defined by their *rejection* of diversity and insistence upon a self-defined standard of purity. But we'll talk more about them later.

Given the commonalities of large size, complexity, and diversity, there are two important distinctions that set any political party apart from any other type of organization:

First, there is a distinction in the mission. All political parties have one goal—*to win elections.* If a political party doesn't win elections, nothing else it does will matter.

Second, in comparison to industrial corporations, political parties have very few paid employees. The vast majority of party members are volunteers or friends. They identify with the political party because they believe in its mission and think that if they help members of the party get elected, their lives will improve. Anyone can "join" a political party at any time or leave at any time. The only actions that matter are *if you vote and for whom you cast your vote.*

Elections are contests. During an election, voters can become extremely emotionally invested in the success of their party and in its candidates. Or, they can be indifferent and take no interest. They can choose to vote for their own candidate or one from a competing party. There are no rules.

11

THE TWO MAJOR POLITICAL PARTIES

On the surface, political parties seem highly decentralized. The mission of the party—that is, how it wants to affect the community and the nation—is determined by consensus. However, the reality is that they hold sophisticated power vacuums that trickle down influence from a centralized circle of party influencers. In America, our two main political parties share the same goal: to win elections and shape the direction of the nation and the states according to the beliefs and aspirations of their members . . . at least on paper. In truth, over the last decade we have seen political power split between those generally fighting against too much change (the Republican base), and those fighting for revolutionary change (the Democratic base).

Let's begin by looking at some numbers. Estimates vary, but roughly 36 million people in the United States identify as Republicans, 49 million as Democrats, and there are about 30 million independents. Common political knowledge estimates most independents vote with Democrats on most issues, which gives the Democratic party a sizable edge. And yet, even with approximately 252 million people of voting age, we still have more than 130 million adults not affiliated with any party; in truth, most are not registered at all. According to the Council on Foreign Relations, as many as 45 million unenrolled or unaffiliated voters went to the polls in the 2020 presidential election. The question is, who were they and how can we capture their interests in future elections?

While each party has a set of foundational values that their members support, at the end of the day, voting is about *emotion*. It's about how voters *feel* about a particular candidate. It's true that some people vote a "straight ticket"—that is, they check the candidates in their party regardless of "candidate quality" (to use a recent expression from Senate Minority Leader, Mitch McConnell). But many voters pick and choose and will cross party lines for a candidate they like. As examples, take the Commonwealth of Massachusetts. It is overwhelmingly Democratic, but they've regularly elected Republican governors, with the most recent being two-term Governor Charlie Baker, first elected in 2014. In 2010, Bay State voters elected Republican Scott Brown to the U.S. Senate. Despite his appeal to pre-election voters, he was incapable of holding their interest once he was elected and as such, he failed to win re-election. Even historically if we look back to 1967, Massachusetts voters sent Republican Edward William Brooke III to the U.S. Senate, making him the third Black U.S. senator (he went on to serve two terms).

If there are any generalizations to be held about this entire complicated system, it would be this: most elections illuminate two things that matter to voters—issues and emotions.

Issues are considered a voter's rational assessment of the future actions of a candidate based on his or her record and campaign promises. Will the candidate support affirmative action? What is the candidate's position on abortion, police reform, bank redlining, school choice, separation of church and state, taxation, etc.? Will the candidate enact laws that I agree with and will they help me and my family live a better life? It isn't just about the issues as they are written in a party platform and on paper. It's truthfully about how well the party and its candidates can articulate those issues to the public. If they cannot be articulated to the target audience, they might as well not exist.

Second is emotions, or how the party's candidate makes the voter *feel* about themselves. Does this candidate make me happy? Am I proud to be associated with them? Is the candidate going to aggressively defend my interests against my enemies? In a culture that I view as inherently tribal, is the candidate "one of us," or does he or she represent "the others?"

The election junkyard is full of perfectly rational, sensible candidates who were right on the issues and would have served their constituents well, but they lost their election because they failed to make *the emotional connection* with the voters. This list includes Democrats Al Gore in 2000, John Kerry in 2004, and Hillary Clinton in 2016. All of them were highly qualified, and all of them lost to Republicans less qualified. This is an issue of voter *motivation*, which is critically important.

Ask yourself—which would any candidate rather have: 100 supporters, of whom 30 will actually get out and vote; or only 50 supporters, of whom 40 will go to the polls and cast their ballot? The latter scenario will win every time. It's a number's game.

Forging a winning emotional bond with constituents has *no relationship* to how a candidate will perform in office. Campaigning and governing are two separate things. They require two different skill sets. Repeatedly throughout history—and most notably with the rise of Donald Trump—we see the rise of charismatic personalities who forge a powerful emotional bond with their constituents, while their actions in office do *nothing* to directly benefit those constituents. This emotional component leaves rational observers on the sidelines scratching their heads and asking, "Why are those people voting for this guy? Don't they see he's unqualified?" They vote for the guy—and eagerly send him their hard-earned money—because he makes them *feel* good. They vote for him because he provides answers they can easily understand and embrace. They vote for him because he gives them someone to blame for their misfortunes.

PARTY EVOLUTION

For any party to grow and to win elections, its leaders and members must understand the opposition—In the United States that means understanding the other party.

From the 1968 presidential election of Richard Nixon to the ascendance of Donald Trump in 2016—a span of 48 years—the Republican Party was generally one of smaller federal government, lower taxes, strong military, strong local law enforcement, the destruction of unions, "states' rights," and policies that favored big business as opposed to employees. And since 1973, when the U.S. Supreme Court ruled in Roe v. Wade, the Republican Party has dedicated itself to its repeal, as well. The party accomplished its goal in 2022 when the conservative-majority court ruled in Dobbs v. Jackson Women's Health Organization that laws governing abortion must be left for individual states to decide.

In contrast, the traditional Democratic Party values support a robust federal government, a broad and fair tax base, social welfare programs for those left behind, trade unions, an end to discrimination in all its forms, the protection of the environment, and police accountability for officer misconduct.

The ascendancy of Donald Trump in 2016 disrupted the traditional Republican Party. Suddenly, rather than adhering to carefully crafted principles espoused by the likes of William F. Buckley Jr. (and like the values listed above), the party seemed to surrender to the will and whims of one man. While Trump amplified many traditional Republican positions—including generally opposing the prioritization of diversity, equity, and inclusion programs and positions, low taxes for the wealthy, and denial of environmental concerns—he made several abrupt reversals, most notably his overt embracing of Russian dictator Vladimir Putin and his admiration for various other anti-Democratic leaders. In choosing his advisors and nominating judges, Trump displayed little regard for professional qualifications, and instead—ominously—showed a preference for those who expressed a personal loyalty to him.

This replacement of an agreed-upon set of conservative values and ideas—however distasteful to many Americans—with the fealty to one man was highlighted in the presidential nominating convention of 2020 when the Republican Party didn't bother to update or review its official party platform from 2016. This reliable party ritual was abandoned, and the party's official website carried the message, "Resolution Regarding the Republican Party Platform," which stated, "RESOLVED, [and] that the Republican National Convention [would] adjourn without adopting a new platform until the 2024 Republican National Convention."

Except for a minority of outliers—including U.S. Representative Liz Cheney (who lost her Republican primary in August 2022, thereby ending her term in office) and Senate Minority Leader Mitch McConnell—the Republican Party of the 2020s belongs to Donald Trump himself or to Trump-diehard supporters like Congresspersons Matt Gaetz, Marjorie Taylor Greene, Byron Donalds, and Texas Governor Gregg Abbott. This is not taking into account former Trump allies such as Florida governor, Ron DeSantis. And now that Donald Trump is the party nominee for the 2024 Presidential election, the positions of the party are whatever Trump expresses at any particular moment. With the exceptions of "Never Trumpers" like former Rep. Liz Cheney and Lincoln Project supporters, anything that Trump supports, the party supports, even if it flies in the face of the old-school Republican playbook. Even as a Democrat, I miss the old-school ideals of the traditional Republican party like so many others in America.

For the Democratic Party to grow, we need to first understand our own party as it stands today and then fully grasp what we are up against. Remember, voters always have a choice. In a presidential election, the choice is, largely, binary: either Republican or Democrat. While voters will choose the candidate they *love the most*, it also matters whom they *hate the least*. Whether a voter chooses the Democratic Party candidate is influenced by what the Republican Party is offering. If the Republican candidate is personally attractive and the Democrat is weak or flawed, a normally Democratic voter may choose the Republican and vice versa.

This begs the question: can we define the typical Democratic and Republican voter? In fact, yes, we can. And the truth is today's voter has not strayed as far from the traditional voters of years past. According to the Data Analysis and Social Inquiry Lab at Grinnell College, when the two groups are compared, some general attributes can be seen. While both parties draw from all demographics, the Republican voter is most likely to be White, male, rural, strong gravitation of those with only a high school education, but also high income. The Republican is more likely to be "nativist," meaning the Republican is more likely to agree with four conditions of citizenship: being born in the United States, living in the United States for most of one's life, the ability to speak English, and to follow the Christian religion. The Democratic voter is most likely to be either White or Black, female, urban or suburban, with a college degree, and lower income. The Democrat is less likely to be nativist and will not agree with some—or all—of the four conditions.

For the past several decades, it's been widely accepted that the Republican Party is more monolithic while the Democratic party is more of a "big tent." Lincoln Mitchell, in the *Huffington Post*, opined in 2012 (admittedly, a lifetime ago in politics) that, "American politics is increasingly defined by a two-party system where one party, albeit imperfectly and generally not easily, reflects the racial, ethnic, and other diversity tensions and strength that is central to 21st century America, while the other is increasingly simply a party of White, heavily Christian Americans. Today, Americans who are non-White, non-Christian, or non-straight are far more likely to be Democrats than Republicans. This is true at the level of ordinary voters, grassroots activists, and elected officials." Lincoln was obviously speaking in general terms, but the perceptions are accurate to his point.

According to conventional wisdom, the Democratic party looks much more like today's America, while the Republican Party continues to look more like yesterday's America—or an America its followers would like to imagine and are willing to show up continuously and fight for. Remember, having the greater number of people in your party is not what is most important; it's more about which party has the greater percentage of people showing up to vote.

HISPANIC VOTERS AND THE WHITE MINORITY

In the United States, the traditional demographic of a White majority with various smaller minority groups (primarily Black, Asian, Hispanic) is changing. New census statistics project that, in 2045, the nation will become "minority White." During that year, Whites will comprise 49.7% of the population, with all minority groups *combined* equaling 50.3%. The ratio is projected to be 24.6% for Hispanics, 13.1% for Blacks, 7.9% for Asians, and 3.8% for multiracial populations.[185]

Numerically, the greatest change will be in the number of Hispanics. They are a growing force in American politics, and the Census Bureau estimates that in 2022, about 19% of the U.S. population is Hispanic. And they are a racial group who shows up to vote; as Gallup reported, exit polls after the 2020 presidential election showed that about 13% of voters were Hispanic, up from 7% in the 2000 election.

Hispanic voters have traditionally leaned Democratic, but that's changing. In Texas, Hispanic Americans represent 39% of the population, but they are shifting to the right, as exemplified by such headlines as "GOP Eyes Latinos in South Texas in Effort to Regain Congress"[186] and "Why Democrats Are Losing Texas Latinos."[187]

Many Democrats hoped that Donald Trump's controversial statements and policies directed at immigrants from Mexico and his pledge to "Build the Wall" would drive Hispanic voters to their party, but that hasn't happened. The assumption that Hispanic voters would automatically embrace the Democratic Party has been misguided. Hispanic men in particular are socially conservative and many hold anti-abortion views. A majority (55%) are Catholic. They tend to support gun rights and strict immigration policies. Unlike Black Americans, Hispanics have little collective memory of institutional racism directed toward them. While experiencing mistreatment—as many immigrant groups have been—Hispanics have never felt the full brunt of the racist machine and thus, want less government involvement in their lives.

Democrats have lots of real reasons they should be worried," said Joshua Ulibarri, a Democratic strategist who has researched Hispanic men for years, to *The New York Times.* "We haven't figured out a way to speak to them, to say that we have something for them, that we understand them. They look at us and say, 'We believe we work harder; we want the opportunity to build something of our own, and why should we punish people who do well?'"

THE IMPORTANCE OF SMALL BALL ELECTIONS

Republicans have been extremely strategic with creating election laws that result in voter suppression and gerrymandering to build their strength in elections. They have energized their base by not shying away from culture wars. Smartly, over a period of years, they've stacked the U.S. Supreme Court with conservative ideologues who, most notoriously, recently overturned Roe v. Wade and ushered in a new era of state-sponsored forced-birth laws, a few of which force victims of rape and incest to bear children. As of the time of this writing, 14 states forbid abortion bans at all stages of pregnancy, only six have exceptions in cases of rape, and five have exceptions for incest.[188]

During the COVID-19 years, Republicans turned their attention toward the most local elections of all—the ones for the local school boards. This focus helped them gain big strides in their pursuit to impose state and church control over what is taught and what books are read in schools. Here's just one example—when California Republicans convened in Anaheim in the spring of 2022, in addition to the usual candidate speeches and endorsement battles at the Marriott Hotel, they held an hour-long session in a small conference room, which could be massively consequential for the state GOP in November.

As reported by *Desert Sun*, the meeting, led by Shawn Steel, a former party chairperson, focused on running for local school board seats. He's one of the biggest proponents for strengthening the GOP by recruiting new candidates and voters in what are traditionally nonpartisan races. "When you're a minority party, like Republicans in California," Steel told CalMatters, "You have to think, 'Well, what can we do as a party to make a big difference?' You see the schools are just in great free fall and chaos. Parents don't want to send their kids there. So, this is the time to get people that are otherwise angst-ridden, upset, [and] powerless."

Their goal was to capitalize on COVID-19 pandemic frustrations and concerns over so-called "Critical Race Theory" and other issues they whip up among parents of school-aged children to win school board seats—and then leverage those platforms for legislative and congressional races by inciting core Republican voters and attracting frustrated independents. The numbers are substantial. According to the California School Boards Association, about half of the 5,000 total local school board seats in California were up for election in November 2022.

"We recognized early that education is going to be a major motivating issue for many Californians this year," said Ellie Hockenbury, spokesperson for the state GOP. "Whereas it is often the case that top-of-the-ticket races help turnout for down-ballot races, we also believe that local races could be just as big a motivator for many to drive turnout. Having strong candidates in school board races could help our slate of candidates at every level."

Shawn Steel added, "I'm just trying—and the party is trying—to get the word out: There's a whole lot of stuff going on in your backyard. Don't worry about Ukraine, don't worry about D.C. You can do something socially useful and start showing up to your school board meetings."

But when Steel says, "Do something useful," in his own words he exclaims, "Do something to help spread the Republican Party clampdown on secular freedoms. Do something to brainwash more kids into being Republican robots. Do something to codify forced birth. Do something to suppress voices of Black and underrepresented peoples." These comments and sentiments are offensive to reasonable Americans everywhere, including the Republican ones.

Leon County School Board Member Darryl Jones, alarmed by Steel's comments stated, "As Chairman of a school district with over 30,000 Students during the COVID-19 pandemic, I saw firsthand how partisan games can be a literal matter of life and death. While me and my colleagues were working to save lives and protect our most vulnerable, ultra-right wing detractors were deployed and used as political props to earn accolades from folks who did not even live in the state of Florida. Ultimately, we were able to rise above and keep our kids and teachers safe while moving our district positively beyond the challenges of COVID-19."

Democrats and Independents across the nation are allowing Republicans across the nation to turn traditionally non-partisan school board positions into breeding grounds for the Marjorie Taylor Greenes of the future. But it's not their fault. They are simply showing up to fight and elect people who believe what they believe. I can't fault them for that. I fault others for not fighting as hard and for not showing up to do the same. Without additional voices being expressed at the ballot box, this is our new reality and we need to recognize it and face it head-on.

As Tip O'Neill, the legendary Speaker of the U.S. House of Representatives, said, "All politics is local." To that we must add, "All voting is local." In every election—from your neighborhood school board to President of the United States—every vote counts.

THE ELECTORAL COLLEGE SYSTEM

The electoral college system, enacted by the 1787 Constitutional Convention served as a compromise with Southern states who wanted each non-voting enslaved person to count as ¾ of a person, which would give greater power and advantage to low-population rural states that currently vote strongly Republican. In today's political landscape, a candidate for president can capture more electoral college votes with fewer popular votes. The last two Republicans to win a majority of the popular vote in a presidential contest were father and son: George H.W. Bush in 1988 and George W. Bush in 2004. George W. Bush didn't win a majority of the popular vote in 2000, nor did Donald Trump in 2016—but both captured the White House.

For Democrats seeking to capture the White House, the electoral college is a major problem. Disadvantage in the system forces key races in battleground states to take center stage. But even more importantly, combating this will require a re-framing of how we see, and interact with, the election process.

When the average voter looks at a presidential election, he or she sees that millions of votes are cast. In the 2016 election, 139 million Americans voted—at the time, it was a record number. Four years later, the total turnout was 156 million—another record. It's easy to see why someone might think, "If 156 million people are voting, then obviously my one vote doesn't matter."

But when we begin to think of national elections as decentralized and local, it is easier to see how the state, county, district, and even the ward or precinct all play into the strategy. Your local election may include only a few thousand voters—or even just a hundred, but at that level, every vote matters.

How the states award Electoral College votes to candidates is important. Every state is allocated a number of electoral college votes equal to the number of senators and representatives in its U.S. Congressional delegation. That means two votes for its senators in the U.S. Senate plus the number of votes equal to the number of its Congressional districts. For example, Idaho has 4 votes—two senators and two representatives. Texas has 38 votes—two senators and 36 representatives.

When awarding votes to the candidates, each state can decide whether it follows a winner-takes-all system or an apportioned Congressional district system. From 2016 to present, all states—except for Maine and Nebraska—have a winner-take-all policy that is based on the statewide vote. Maine and Nebraska, however, apportion one individual elector based on the winner of the popular vote for each Congressional district—two in Maine, three in Nebraska. The other two electors for each state are based on the winner of the overall statewide popular vote.

States have the authority to make changes in this system. In 2017, the Virginia General Assembly introduced HB 1425, which would have changed Virginia's winner-take-all system to one based on apportioned Congressional districts. The bill was sponsored by Republican Delegate Mark Cole, who claimed the bill would increase voter turnout because it would make people feel more like their vote mattered. He said Northern Virginia (which was majority Democratic) was so populous that it always carried the state, which made people in rural Virginia (who were majority Republican) feel their vote didn't count.

In 2016, the overall statewide winner, Hillary Clinton, was awarded all 13 of Virginia's electoral college votes. Had the HB 1425 system been in effect in 2016, Republican presidential nominee Donald Trump would have received six of those votes and Clinton only seven—with the exact same popular vote. While this would not have changed the outcome of this election, it is easy to understand how it could under other circumstances.

Regarding HB 1425, the measure died in committee. Neither then-Governor

Terry McAuliffe nor his successor, Ralph Northam, both Democrats, would have signed it. Under new governor, Republican Glenn Youngkin, only time will tell if he encourages the legislature to revisit the measure.

Historically, and a topic of controversy since the nation's inception, the Electoral College was enshrined in our Constitution as a compromise between the election of the President by a vote in Congress and the election of the President by a popular vote of qualified citizens. The Electoral College consists of 538 electors. A majority of 270 electoral votes is required to elect the President. Each state has the same number of electors as it does Members in its Congressional delegation: one for each Member in the House of Representatives plus two Senators. In many states, the candidate who wins the popular vote receives all of the state's electoral votes.

One of the most significant criticisms of the Electoral College system is its potential to give states disproportionate power in electing the President compared to their population. This is best illustrated by the example of Wyoming, which receives three electoral votes (or 1 per 193,000 people), while California receives fifty-five electoral votes (1 per 727,000 people). If you were to live in Wyoming, your vote would carry nearly four times the weight of a California voter, highlighting the system's individual impact. As you can imagine, this reality starkly contrasts the idea of an equal democracy, which so many of us associate with the United States.

There are political consequences to this disproportionality in votes' significance. Smaller, more rural states tend to vote Republican. Giving these states' voters more power via the electoral college generally benefits Republicans on the presidential stage. Furthermore, this system also makes swing states, where the votes between the two major parties are very close, very important. From a political operations standpoint, this forces presidential campaigns to focus on several key states, such as Michigan, South Carolina, and Wisconsin, at the expense of states that are solidly in the camp of one particular political party.

When given this information, the natural question is if the Electoral College has elected a president who did not win the popular vote in a given election. For many of us, the most recent example was one of our most consequential political moments: the 2016 presidential election. In 2016, then-candidate Donald Trump defeated Secretary Hillary Clinton by a margin of 304 to 227 electoral votes, even though Secretary Clinton won the popular vote by over 2.5 million votes. Along with the 2016 election, the Electoral College has produced four other presidential outcomes (1824, 1876, 1888, and 2000) where the candidate who was elected president did not win the national popular vote in the election.

While proponents of the system say that the Electoral College is a mechanism that prevents the silencing of the majority party, the reality of the process is that it's simply undemocratic. The Electoral College unfairly empowers small and competitive states at the expense of population centers and states that generally go for one specific party affiliation.

The product of this inequality? Disaffected voters.

12

THE FEAR OF AN UNCERTAIN FUTURE

I f you put aside specific policy issues, the core differences between Republicans and Democrats lie in how they view the past and, by extension, the future. If a person believes the past was a golden age of peace and plenty, he or she will want it to return, and—in comparison—the future will look scary and unattractive. For example, many White voters have a rosy-eyed view of the 1950s, seeing it as the time of American global dominance and the growth of "Leave It to Beaver" suburbia.

If a person believes the past was painful, he or she will not be interested in going back there. In contrast, the future will look more attractive. For example, most Black voters do not look back upon the 1950s as a pleasant time in our history. To them, it means Jim Crow, oppression, displacement through urban renewal programs, and even lynching, such as the murder of Emmett Till in 1955.

The deep spiritual core of the Republican party is a *fear of change and disruption*, combined with a yearning for a past that was more noble, more ordered, and more respectful of traditional White Christian values. It has an emotional pull whose power cannot be underestimated. It's no mistake that, suddenly, in the summer of 2020, Republican politicians were talking about the United States as an explicitly Christian nation, and some were openly using the phrase "Christian nationalism." Rep. Marjorie Taylor Greene, Rep. Lauren Boebert, and Pennsylvania gubernatorial candidate Doug Mastriano have said it, and—tellingly—very few of their Republican colleagues have denounced them.

For many, this is shocking, because Christian nationalism has historically been identified with Nazi Germany, *but* that term was much too provocative to use in public. Christian nationalism is the belief that the American nation is defined by Christianity, and that the federal and state governments should enshrine it into law. These believers think that traditional belief in separation of church and state was a misinterpretation of the true intent of the White, Christian founding fathers. Today's extremists assert that America is and must remain a "Christian nation"—not only in the past but in the future. If we lose our "Anglo-Protestant" roots, we will lose our identity and our freedom. Obviously under these terms, if you're Muslim, Jewish, or anything else, then you're on the wrong side of Lady Liberty.

The seeds for the yearning for a golden past were planted by Ronald Reagan in 1980, when he used the phrase "Make America great again" in a Labor Day speech. "This country needs a new administration with a renewed dedication to the dream of America, an administration that will give that dream new life, and make America great again." Later that year, he used the line in his convention address: "For those who've abandoned hope, we'll restore hope, and we'll welcome them into a great national crusade to make America great again." He was also famous for his cynical stance on the role of the federal government, when he said in a 1986 news conference, "The nine most terrifying words in the English language are: I'm from the Government, and I'm here to help."

This theme was repeated by George W. Bush in 2000 and then amplified to gargantuan proportions by Donald Trump in 2016. But what do these seemingly innocuous phrases really mean? It depends on the listener. For White voters suffering from anxiety about their declining share of the national population, the words mean, "I hear you. We're going to roll back the clock to a time when the Black people and immigrants knew their place, and Americans ruled the world." But to most Black voters, the words mean, "If you think you're making progress toward a more equitable society, and movements like affirmative action or DEI focused programs will help counteract institutional racism, you'd better scale back your expectations."

At the core is the tension between the federal government and "states' rights." To fearful White voters, the federal government was—and still is—the bad guy, the enforcer of civil rights, and the champion of destabilizing social progress. To Black voters, especially in the South, the federal government was their savior. It was the federal government that ended cruel Jim Crow discrimination endorsed by the states. The Civil Rights Act of 1964 narrowly won victory despite fierce opposition from Southern states. As Georgia Democratic Senator Richard Russell proclaimed, "We will resist to the bitter end any measure or any movement which would tend to bring about social equality and intermingling and amalgamation of the races in our [Southern] states."

DEMOCRATS WIN BY BUILDING A CONSENSUS

In his book, *Flipped; How Georgia Turned Purple and Broke the Monopoly on Republican Power*, Greg Bluestein looked at the events of the past two decades that contributed to Georgia emerging as a powerful swing state in a sea of red.

For much of the twentieth century, Georgia had been a stronghold of the Democratic Party . . . but not the Democratic Party we think of today. Promoting White supremacist measures, Democrats in Georgia were able to garner the support of the local population in nearly every race. They mobilized "the unwavering support of rural White workers, stoked by crowd-pleasing populism, who backed segregationist and racist measures that disenfranchised Black residents; it was a monopoly built on a revulsion toward Reconstructionist policies promoted by Abraham Lincoln's Republican successors". [189]

By the end of the twentieth century, however, demographic changes in Georgia drove a switch in political opinion. In Atlanta, the growing suburbs "[filled] in with newcomers with no allegiance to the Democratic Party, [and] tilted increasingly toward the GOP; the revolution really took wing, though, when an irascible party-switching state senator named Sonny Perdue won an upset victory in 2002 to become the first Republican governor in Georgia since Reconstruction". Since then, Georgia has become a sure win for the GOP in every election. The party even chose the state as the site of its victory party in the presidential election of 2020, as "Republicans had shut out Democrats in every presidential election in Georgia since 1996 and hadn't lost a statewide seat since 2006. The Georgia GOP was so dominant that for much of the decade, Democrats struggled to recruit even fringe candidates for some top-tier races or, worse, didn't bother running anyone at all". When Republicans lost the 2020 election, it came as a shock to many. Nevertheless, the change in Georgia's political allegiance did not switch overnight.

Traditionally, throughout the 21st century, those Democrats who ran for office in Georgia relied on a mixture of conservative and liberal policies to appeal to the state's White, rural population. These 'Republican-lite' candidates "campaigned as moderate versions of Republicans, heralding support for gun rights and opposition to abortion while running, screaming, from national party figures". After Donald Trump won the state in 2016 "by about five percentage points without so much as a campaign rally in the state during the closing months of the race", however, the situation changed. And no one was as pivotal to this change as Stacey Abrams, a Democrat minority leader in the Georgia House of Representatives. In January 2017, during a meeting in downtown Atlanta, "over the course of about fifteen minutes, she spoke of mobilizing liberals by promising expanded access to health care, promoting a more equitable economy, and a push to register, and then engage, overlooked Georgia voters. Above all, she made the case that Democrats could win back Republican-held territory if they embraced authenticity rather than [setting] aside their priorities to try to win over wavering moderates".

Rather than appeal to conservative Georgians, "she embraced liberal issues that Democrats competing statewide in earlier elections would have avoided: she backed a hike in the minimum wage, supported gun control measures, opposed abortion restrictions, railed against new crackdowns on illegal immigrants, and endorsed the removal of the enormous carving of Confederate war leaders from the face of the state-owned Stone Mountain". Most importantly, she realized the need to engage the disenfranchised voters in Georgia. After all, the racial outlook of the state had changed during the recent decades. While "in 1970, Georgia had been roughly three-quarters White, by 2018, White Georgians scarcely made-up half of the state's population". One of her most famous accomplishments, the New Georgia Project, sought to "engage hundreds of thousands of voters of color disconnected from state politics". While Stacey Abrams was instrumental in turning Georgia into a "purple" state—one that swings between Republican and Democrat candidates—she was not alone. From Lucy McBath to Jon Ossoff to Raphael Warnock, the Democratic playbook in Georgia was one of community building and true community-focused messaging.[190]

Lucy McBath's story was a tragic one: her son had become the victim of gun violence. Specifically, young Jordan had been fatally shot during an incident with a White man, after refusing to reduce the volume of music in the car. The man "unloaded ten bullets at the careening vehicle; three sliced through Jordan's door, striking him in the groin, heart, and lungs" The trial which followed "attracted attention from a nation already shaken by the shooting death of another Black teen from Florida; in early 2012, the killing of Trayvon Martin led to a cultural reckoning".

After an initial period of grief, McBath clenched her teeth and decided to tackle the injustice. Soon she became a national spokesperson for Moms Demand Action, where "she made her case for new firearms restrictions to the predominantly White suburban moms who seemed ready to embrace the issue; but she also spoke with faith leaders, communities of color, and others she felt were often left out of the discussion. As she grew in the role, so did her platform". When offered to run for the United States House in 2018, she agreed, although reluctantly. After all, "it meant a much more difficult campaign than a state House race, with all the fundraising pressure, media scrutiny, and political attacks that go along with competing for a district that a year ago was at the center of suffocating attention". Nevertheless, "the mass shooting in Parkland, Florida, refocused her attention".

At the center of McBath's campaign was the gun control issue. Nevertheless, "McBath was careful not to become a single-issue candidate. She tied Handel to Trump's more unpopular plans, such as an attempt to repeal the Affordable Care Act's pre-existing conditions protections, and immigration crackdowns that resulted in family separations. Above all, though, McBath's demand for stronger gun restrictions remained the North Star of her campaign". Eventually, the tactic of authenticity worked, and "McBath won the election by about three thousand votes, and her narrow victory was the biggest success story for Georgia Democrats after another round of statewide losses". Winning a district which had been lost by Ossoff just a year earlier was a big signal to the Democrats about the switching political opinion in Georgia.

Jon Ossoff, while coming to power under less tragic circumstances, had his fair share of roller coaster political moments before securing his place in the U.S. Senate. After surprising even his closest friends by entering the Sixth District race in 2017, he ran a smart and savvy campaign. He appealed to the worst fears of liberal voters, as well as to the youth. For example, "one early ad he ran featured a clock ticking down from thirty seconds as it insisted that the president is not only embarrassing us on the world stage, he could start an unnecessary war".[191] Apart from taking hits at Trump, however, he tried to avoid controversial issues so as not to polarize his more moderate voters. He believed that a strong anti-Trump demographic existed in the district, but that they also had to be dealt with cautiously. Specifically, "his working theory was that he had a grassroots army at the ready, eager to be mobilized to fight back against Trump; he just needed to keep them energized without doing anything to interfere with their commitment".

As the campaign neared, he focused solely on noncontroversial issues, such as railing against spending excesses by both political parties and promising to work with Republicans on a health-care overhaul or immigration reforms rather than hammering GOP policies. The tactic worked, but only partially. He secured endorsement from the parties' top brass and fundraising spoils to match, but his less-than-energizing bipartisan message failed to ignite the fire in voters he needed to win. Inevitably, Ossoff lost the runoff election, although the narrow margins became a sign of the weakening Republican stronghold in Georgia. Not to mention that it was an important illustration of the country's widening division. Voters were no longer looking for the bipartisanship that once reigned supreme. It was a lesson Ossoff would not forget in his next run.

And that next run came just two years later. With Stacy Abrams giving a hard "no" to a potential run, Ossoff formally announced his Senate campaign in September 2019 and that he planned to run on a platform of combating corruption in Washington and the mustering of a grassroots army.

During the campaign, no one did more to engage voters than Ossoff himself. Despite already having a large base of support, he instructed his staff "to build an unprecedented network of field staffers they called community mobilizers. [Through them], text messages were sent to tens of thousands of young unlikely voters, largely from minority communities, inviting them to apply, though many learned about the program through old-fashioned ways: flyers posted on telephone poles or word-of-mouth chatter. His twenty-five-person team raced through the more than twenty thousand applications that came pouring into the campaign and wound up interviewing roughly three to four hundred people a day.

Moreover, Ossoff tried to appeal to young voters through social media. Notably, "Ossoff emerged as a superstar to many in the Generation Z crowd with TikTok videos that began airing in early December and quickly collected millions of likes". Furthermore, Ossoff was engaged in every part of his own campaign, even helping design the ads. He "played a hands-on role in developing his runoff ads, co-authoring in some form or fashion every one of them. Each was directly aimed at winning over Black voters, with emotional spots featuring young men voicing concerns about police brutality, business owners struggling with the economic slowdown during the pandemic, and women excited by the prospect of dramatic change in Washington". Finally, Ossoff recognized the need for direct engagement with voters. Nearing the election day, "he went out on his own for a four-day, seven-stop tour of Georgia that featured prominent local figures". When Perdue failed to appear in the last public debate with Ossoff, the contrast was striking.

Georgia Republican Johnny Isakson had occupied Georgia's second Senate seat since 2005. Earning bipartisan praise throughout his 45 year career, he was seen as an icon of finding common ground. However, by 2020, Isakson's Parkinson's would force him to step down and open the seat for the first time in over a decade.

Raphael Warnock quickly emerged as the top candidate, and he formally announced his candidacy in January 2020. A pastor from Atlanta, he was seen as a "preternaturally gifted candidate who could have invigorated Georgia's Black electorate and embraced liberal policies long neglected by the state's mainstream Democrats".

Warnock sought to maintain authenticity to connect with Georgian voters. His advisors urged him to remain the reverend; that meant sharing his life story, explaining to voters what guides his moral compass, detailing his background as an activist, and promoting his personality to make Georgians feel as if they knew him.

Warnock's ads were mainly defensive, countering his opponents' misinformation. Overall, "Warnock's campaign aired 64 ads during the runoff, many of them featuring the pastor speaking directly to the camera and many with defense in mind. When Republican commercials brought up Warnock's past remarks about the Reverend Jeremiah Wright—whose sermons became a flash point in Barack Obama's 2008 presidential bid—his campaign responded with an ad highlighting his work against hate crimes". He followed the same strategy during a public debate, defending against any criticism that came his way while maintaining honesty and authenticity.

The timing of this election cycle was dominated by two issues: COVID-19 and Black Lives Matter. During this time period, several developments in Georgia put the Republicans in a compromising position. First, during the COVID-19 pandemic, despite more than ten thousand deaths and hundreds of thousands who fell severely ill in Georgia from the virus, Governor Kemp made a decision to reopen businesses, earning strong criticism from Atlanta Mayor Keisha Lance Bottoms and even from President Trump himself. Second, the murder of George Floyd, and later the death of Ahmaud Arbery, ignited the Black Lives Matter movement in Georgia and galvanized the liberal masses.

Warnock's opponent, Kelly Loeffler, had already earned a lot of criticism for her White, elitist background and conflicts of interest due to her extraordinary wealth. Most damning, as the co-owner of a WNBA franchise, her support of Trump on his anti-BLM remarks drew backlash from the league. As a result, Warnock—who was little known to anyone outside Atlanta before—garnered a public image after social media exploded with images of players across the WNBA wearing the pro-Warnock T-shirts ahead of nationally televised games.

These were not the only challenges faced by the GOP. First, the party was deeply divided. Each faction had a different opinion on how to run the campaigns. Second, while Trump had lost the election, candidates still relied on his support to win, which would only disillusion more moderate voters.

Democrats made use of the situation and welcomed what many deemed the "Republican Civil War." Some amplified the chatter from pro-Trump figures promising to skip the vote or write in the president's name (which would automatically disqualify their vote), liberal groups financed billboards in conservative parts of the state that read PERDUE/LOEFFLER DIDN'T DELIVER FOR TRUMP—DON'T DELIVER FOR THEM". Even Trump's visit to Georgia wasn't helpful, as he only "briefly praised the two Senate Republicans before spinning lies about votes in Georgia coming out of ceilings and leather bags".

The Democratic candidates, on the other hand, recognized the power of unity. They understood that the party needed to introduce Warnock and Ossoff as a joint ticket, and to counter the misinformation that continued to permeate the media. Most importantly, everyone in the party understood the need to flip both seats. Ossoff and Warnock synchronized their policy themes around three issues to energize liberals: health, jobs, and justice. Moreover, both realized the need to mobilize disenfranchised voters.

Eventually, both Ossoff and Warnock won their fights. The Democrats' victory in Georgia was a landmark event. The turnout numbers were unprecedented, as "a record three million people voted before Election Day, smashing the previous record for total turnout in a Georgia runoff set in 2008, when 2.1 million cast ballots in the overtime match-up between Republican senator Saxby Chambliss and Jim Martin". Moreover, "exit polls revealed that the Democratic candidates had neared a vaunted 30-30 target that had long eluded them: capturing 30% of Georgia's White vote while achieving a Black participation rate of 30% of the overall turnout".

As the 2024 election looms, the lessons from the Georgia swing offer an increasingly important roadmap for the Democratic Party moving forward. Democrats must find a way to connect with voters and build authentic communities—ones built on real engagement, real connection and most importantly, real trust. We also need to heed the success of the Warnock/Ossoff strategy of collaboration.

While the Republican party remains under the control of Donald Trump or his mentees, the Republican tent is very small, but very focused, in its energy. The litmus test for Republican candidates is simple: if you pay fealty to Trump, you're in. If you defy Trump, you're out. Trump voters are highly motivated and seem willing to win by any means necessary or at any cost.

TRUMP AND ACCEPTED COGNITIVE DISSONANCE

The 2016 and 2020 U.S. presidential elections saw significant support for Donald Trump among some of the poorest voters in the country—a seeming contradiction given his background and policies. Trump, a billionaire from New York, embodied the elite financial interests many of his supporters felt had marginalized them from "The American Dream." Yet somehow, his populist rhetoric and promises to dismantle the very system he was a part of resonated with these voters. Trump's ability to present himself as an outsider fighting against a corrupt establishment allowed him to connect with those who felt left behind, despite his policies often favoring the wealthy and big business.

This apparent contradiction is glaringly evident in Trump's tax policies and regulatory rollbacks, which mainly benefited large corporations and the richest Americans, while the working class was left to foot the bill. For instance, the 2017 Tax Cuts and Jobs Act significantly reduced corporate tax rates and adjusted individual income tax in ways that disproportionately favored higher-income brackets. These actions were taken even as Trump promised relief and attention to poor folks. The dissonance between his platform of economic populism and the actual implementation of policies that favored the upper echelons of society showcases a stark hypocrisy.

Additionally, Trump's narrative and policies around health care and social services further exposed these contradictions. He repeatedly attempted to repeal the Affordable Care Act without a clear replacement, which would have left millions without insurance—many of whom were from the lower-income brackets that formed part of his electoral base. The persistent advocacy for cuts to social programs essential for many poor Americans, made under the guise of reducing government spending, starkly contrasts with the increase in military and border security expenditures. This prioritization reflects a misalignment between his poorer supporters' actual needs and their expressed desires, which further illustrates the hypocrisy of the relationship between Trump's political strategies and the interests of those who got him elected.

So, why do they vote for him?

As mentioned earlier, the economically challenged Trump followers supported the former president largely due to his stances on immigration and globalism. Voters who support Trump often feel left behind by the rapid economic and demographic changes in the country, and Trump's rhetoric and policies on curbing immigration and opposing global trade agreements resonate with their sense of economic insecurity and cultural displacement. This allegiance occurs despite studies suggesting that Trump's economic policies, such as those listed above, may not benefit these voters. For these people, the appeal of restoring a perceived loss of national identity and regaining control over domestic affairs overrides immediate economic concerns—this leads these voters to support Trump as a champion of their values against globalist trends.

In contrast to the Republican small tent, the Democratic party is a big tent—maybe too big. As Daniel A. Cox wrote in *The Democratic Party's Transformation More Diverse, Educated, and Liberal but Less Religious*, in 2022, 56% of Democrats were White, roughly one in five (21%) were Black, 18% were Hispanic, and 4% were Asian or Pacific Islander. 50% identified as liberal, a significant increase from only 28% in 1998. In addition, he says Democrats are far less religious today than they were a generation ago, with only 43% saying religion is a very important part of their lives.[192]

These changes mirror that of the nation as a whole, but they don't guarantee Democratic wins at the ballot box. The increased diversity of the electorate has primarily come not from Black voters but Hispanic, Asian-American, and multiracial voters. Those groups generally support Democrats, but not always by margins large enough to carry an election. In order to win contested elections, Democrats need to forge alliances among three diverse ethnic groups—Black, Hispanic, and White—and between centrists and progressives.

MILLENNIALS ARE THE NEW BOOMERS

Millennials, born between 1981 and 1996, can take control of our political process if they so choose. Their influence is increasingly significant given their sheer numbers and distinctive preferences, which diverge from those of previous generations. However, millennials also show lower voter turnout rates compared to older generations. While they have the potential to influence elections decisively, their actual impact is often mitigated by lower electoral participation.

According to Pew Research Center data, millennials are the largest adult generation, surpassing Baby Boomers. They are the most ethnically and racially diverse generation in American history, and they hold an overall greater lean towards liberal social policies, environmental concerns, and progressive economic measures. Millennials have lived through recessions, the first Black president, a global pandemic, and one of the most politically divisive periods in our nation's history.

Millennials exhibit distinct voting patterns that have the potential to reshape the political landscape. As mentioned earlier, they tend to lean liberal and support Democratic candidates more consistently than older generations. In the 2020 Presidential Election for example, data indicated a significant preference for Democratic candidate Joe Biden among younger voters.

The policy preferences of millennials are noticeably progressive and focus on issues like healthcare, climate change, and income inequality. They are more likely than older voters to support policies such as universal healthcare, aggressive climate action, and higher minimum wages. This generation also values social justice movements, including Black Lives Matter and LGBTQ+ rights, reflecting broader and more inclusive social values.

Millennials pursued education abundantly, as they were told to. They went to college, and once they graduated, many of them walked away with a degree(s) without an economy to serve it. Those who did not receive scholarships or Pell grants throughout their college experience often became so far in debt they were forced into careers that did not align with their actual education or interest. They frequently took jobs that offered hourly rates—salary if lucky—yet such wages were rarely an amount large enough to support the cost of living . . . unless of course an individual came from an upper class home where their parents had the ability to transfer generational wealth and soften life's realities.

So, why haven't millennials taken over our political process?

History proves that the world has never been without some sort of event, disaster, or some sort of chaos. We've learned to live with the possibility of these types of occurrences. However, hate-filled divisiveness extorted by mainstream politics and class structure has exacerbated a continuum of emotional upheaval, especially in millennials. This has influenced a generation of adults and their trust in its governing systems, including political outcomes that have led to ramped disaffection.

Despite their numbers and potential power, several other factors limit millennials' influence in the political process. First is the issue of turnout and political engagement. There is no skirting around the fact that, while the numbers are fuzzy, Baby Boomers vote at about a 20% higher rate than Millennials. With Millennials only recently taking over Baby Boomers as the largest electorate, this engagement gap is huge. Secondly, there is the issue of political representation. Older generations still hold the majority of significant political offices, and they are foremost in influencing policy decisions and legislative priorities. This generational gap in political leadership can minimize millennial preferences in policy-making arenas. Lastly—and maybe more importantly—is the issue of civic efficacy. Through social media and traditional news outlets, Millennials have been inundated with messages about the institutional levers that prohibit their voices from being heard, such as the Electoral College and filibusters in the United States Senate. Even though he lost the popular vote, President Trump winning the 2016 Presidential Election did not help their perceptions, either.

Naturally, Millennials are poised to gain more control over the political process as they age, accumulate wealth, potentially increase their voter turnout rates, and as older politicians age out of their positions. As more Millennials pursue and achieve political office, there is a strong possibility for a shift in policy priorities that are more reflective of this generation's values and experiences.

Millennials can't leave their work on the table, however! They have to band together and teach each other the important history of America and the world. Our children's futures rely on this. Without an understanding of America's racial history, they will have no compass on forward progression. Without gun violence protection and guidance, they will kill themselves and one another. Without the freedom to make decisions over their bodies and reproductive rights, they are subject to any and all means of oppression. This generation must take the baton and position itself to enforce change by participating in the political process. They must hold elected officials accountable and promote partisan outcomes that benefit the greater good.

Millennials have the potential to reshape the American political landscape. Still, their influence is currently tempered by political disinterest, lower voting rates, and a lack of representation in political office. As they continue to mature into their roles as economic and political actors, their ability to influence policy and elections is set to increase, particularly as they leverage digital tools to mobilize and advocate for their interests. The extent to which they can convert their numerical strength into political power will be one of the defining features of American politics in the decades to come.

THE BLACK AND BROWN VOTE: A CHARGE TO KEEP

There is an old Baptist hymn that was written by Charles Wesley in 1762, "A Charge to Keep I Have." When I was young, I thought many of these old hymns sounded alike and said the same things, but I generally understood the solemness. Wesley's hymn speaks toward our daily living and commands that we walk with purpose each and every day. Further, it explains that we have a responsibility in our actions—greeting a stranger with a smile, completing a task for your boss, prioritizing self-care—that all has an impact. In a society where selfishness and lack of empathy is at an all-time high, we must remember that failing to be responsible for our actions or selfishly believing that our individual indifference will go overlooked produces consequences. These consequences may not only impact you, but the world around you, including the people you love and care for. This sentiment includes so many purposes in our lives, but it especially refers to exercising our right to vote.

When Black and Brown people do not show up to the polls to exercise their right to vote, it is an insult to our elders who put their lives on the line and fought for the opportunity to be a legitimate part of the electoral process. Not exercising your right to vote is essentially a vote against the warriors that came before us and the generations to follow. Further, it is a slap in the face to you personally and all the people you love or care for.

Since the 15th Amendment—which granted Black men the right to vote—was passed by Congress on February 26, 1869 and ratified February 3, 1870, our elders have had to combat numerous other tactics to eliminate the Black vote, i.e., poll taxes, intelligence tests, threats of being fired from their jobs, death threats and acts of violence by the Ku Klux Klan, and more. These barriers overshadow and were much more dangerous than the voter suppression tactics we experience today, yet Black and Brown people still showed up to the polls despite the risk. They knew how important the moment was and they believed their vote would matter. Today, Black and Brown votes matter more than ever before—but only if Black and Brown voters choose not to be disaffected and show up to vote.

The idea that your vote doesn't count or matter is due to a lack of perspective and understanding. If we all decided not to vote, then no percentage of our voices would be represented. During the 2008 presidential election of Barack Obama, voting lines wrapped around city blocks all over this country to elect the first Black president. We stood in long lines because we believed we could have an impact on electing a Black person to the highest office in the land. I believe the phrase was, "Yes, we can"—and we absolutely did. If enough of us believed it then, why didn't that belief system grow and work to create a new narrative that would make the subject matter of this book null and void?

To date, the United States is growing increasingly diverse. According to the 2020 Census data, 57.8% of the population identify as "White, not Hispanic or Latino," as opposed to 63.7% in the 2010 Census, and 69.1% in 2000. It's estimated that by 2045, fewer than 50% of the population will be non-Hispanic White.[193]

Naturally, as the population becomes more diverse, so should the electorate. This country and its ability to maintain democracy belongs to whoever shows up to the polls. And who consistently shows up for every election? The elderly. Only 46% of people 18 to 34 years old voted in the last election. Further, 70% of voters in the last election were White, 10.7% were Hispanic or Latino, 12.2% were Black, and 4.4% were Asian. So, the elderly and individuals who are not people of color have a disproportionate influence on our politics and our country, and many of them would like to keep it that way.

The surge in both registration and voting rates suggest that Latinos are poised to exert political influence in the U.S., commensurate with their share of the population. The midterm elections and the presidential election of 2024 may confirm their readiness to emerge in full force. Even if you believe that your one vote will not have an impact, together, Black and Brown communities can make a difference and possibly create change.

The voting gap across demographic lines has become a self-inflicted wound that hurts all Black and Brown people because it makes it harder to elect candidates committed to fighting for fair elections, racial justice, reproductive rights, fair and affordable housing, accessible healthcare and insurance, public education, minority-business creation, criminal justice reforms, and other goals most people of color support. The voting gap has weakened the Voting Rights Act of 1965, devastated a woman's right to the full range of reproductive healthcare and is likely—as in Florida—to completely gut affirmative action.

It is your responsibility to participate in the electoral process and in politics, because you simply can't arrange for it to not impact your life. To have it any other way would simply leave the political future of minorities, or people in general, up to a minority of people who don't look like you or share your life experiences.

Unfortunately, in most midterm elections, Black and Brown Americans vote at a lower rate than Whites, which weakens our ability to help elect candidates who are committed to our issues (such as eradicating systemic racism or opening the doors of opportunity for everyone, regardless of race).

In 2022, the United States Supreme Court overturned the 1973 ruling on the paradigm-shifting Roe v. Wade case. It lifted any federal protection of rights to abortion access, and the decision has been criticized for harming women's rights across the country, especially for women of color. The importance of voting on a state and national level cannot be overstated enough. The Supreme Court justices who made this decision were appointed by Republican presidents who run on platforms espousing eliminating abortion rights.

Did you think they were joking during their campaigns? No, they were not and guess what? The people who showed up to vote for them were not joking either. The only joke is on the people who decided not to show up and vote for the candidates who believe in the issues they care about.

All these things are connected. I can't and don't blame the people who think differently than I do for showing up to vote. It's their right and they win often because they show up often. You can win too, but you have to show up consistently and intentionally. You have to show up even when it's not easy or it takes a long time to reach the ballot box — because the person on the other side of the issue or supporting another candidate *will show up*. In 2022, it was attacks on abortion rights. In 2023, it was attacks on diversity, equity and inclusion laws as well as limits on what can be taught in our classrooms related to slavery and Black history. Election laws are making it harder for the poor and people of color to vote. Vote anyway! If not for your life, do it for the lives of people you love and care for.

The importance of voting is not a matter of shifting public opinion on a political candidate, but rather making sure the polls represent the public's view. Congressional elections determine who represents your state in the U.S. House of Representatives and Senate. They also decide which political party will hold a majority in each chamber of Congress for the next two years. If we fail to vote, we not only fail to have representation, but we also fail to have a voice.

The least we can do is show up to the polls, but we must also hold our elected officials accountable for eradicating voter suppression. Signature match verification, too few voting precincts in poor and Black communities, voter intimidation by ballot security teams, voter registration over regulation, voter caging and purging, and redistricting tactics—among other things—must be rolled back and/or protected from abuse. Voting is largely a compulsory act and, because of this, these kinds of laws have a direct and dramatic effect that disproportionately disenfranchises people of color.

Cell phone data from every voting precinct in America found that Black and Brown people have to wait to vote for about 30% longer than people in White neighborhoods. If 40% of Black and Brown people in the country live in predominantly Black and Brown neighborhoods, we must be proactive as citizens to vote for elected officials that support efforts like the John R. Lewis Voting Rights Advancement Act. We must combat voter suppression tactics that specifically target Black and Brown districts.

Voting is the absolute best tool we have to create change. In knowing the history of those who came before us, we must use their pain as our power as we consider all the reasons why we should meet at the polls. Your vote matters, and if you want your voice to be heard, you must vote.

JOE BIDEN'S MULTI-ETHNIC COALITION

In the 2020 election primary season, Senator Joe Biden began as the Democratic party front-runner but quickly fell behind. By the end of the Iowa caucuses on February 3, Biden found himself finishing fourth behind Pete Buttigieg, Bernie Sanders, and Elizabeth Warren. In New Hampshire's primary on February 11, Sanders and Buttigieg again virtually tied for the top spot. Biden came in a dismal fifth, the choice of only one out of every 12 voters. In Nevada, he finished second with 20%. This was enough to carry him to South Carolina, the first-in-the-South primary where Black voters carried significant influence.

In a momentous decision, the state's senior officeholder, Rep. James Clyburn, the highest-ranking Black member of Congress, announced his endorsement of Joe Biden. Clyburn's approval gave Biden instant credibility and the first real surge of energy for his campaign. On February 29, Biden won the Black vote in South Carolina, especially among women. Suddenly, he was the candidate to beat. On Super Tuesday, March 3, Biden won 10 of 15 state contests. By April 10, every other candidate had dropped out.

On November 3, Biden won a decisive victory against Trump. According to the AP/Votecast data, he won seven states—Wisconsin, Pennsylvania, Michigan, Virginia, Arizona, Nevada, and Georgia—while *losing* among White voters in those states. In three of those states—Arizona, Nevada, and Georgia—his victory could be linked to the increased racial diversity of the electorate over the last few decades. He could not have won them without long-term increases in *both* non-White voting power and Democratic strength among White voters.

According to Pew Research, Biden's coalition of voters in 2020 vs. the 2016 election included gains in suburban voters and White, non-college voters. Researchers Ruth Igielnik, Scott Keeter, and Hannah Hartig noted that Joe Biden's electoral coalition looked much like Hillary Clinton's, with Black, Hispanic, Asian, and those of other races casting about 40% of his votes. Black voters remained overwhelmingly loyal to the Democratic candidate, voting 92% for Biden and 8% for Trump.

At the last moments before this book went to press, the increased and consistent scrutiny of Biden's performance during the debate led the party to deter from the incumbent strategy leading to a Kamala Harris Presidential nomination and campaign. As the first biracial woman to lead a Presidential ticket, a Harris properly executed campaign has the potential to energize the Democratic base, bringing out many previously disaffected voters.

I mention earlier in the book that over 70 percent of voters indicated that they did not want a rematch of Biden and Trump. With the Harris candidacy in mind, echoing the sentiments of former Republican Presidential candidate Nikki Haley, I believe the first of the two parties to give the people what they want, will galvanize a coalition of support that will win the moment and the White House. We will all find out come November.

ERIC ADAMS WINS IN NEW YORK CITY

While New York City remains heavily Democratic, the office of mayor can go to a Republican—most recently Rudy Giuliani (1994-2001) and Michael Bloomberg (2002-2013). In the 2020 election to choose a successor to Bill de Blasio, Democratic voters chose Eric Adams. He had served as an officer in the New York City Transit Police and then in the New York City Police Department for more than 20 years, retiring at the rank of captain. He entered politics, and in November 2013, was elected Brooklyn borough president—the first African American to hold the position. He was reelected in November 2017.

In the general election for mayor in 2021, he defeated Republican Curtis Sliwa in a landslide victory. While Sliwa was considered by most to be a low-quality candidate, Adams's victory can also be attributed to the multi-ethnic coalition he put together during his primary campaign.

As Nathaniel Rakich wrote in FiveThirtyEight.com, Adams campaigned as a law-and-order candidate opposed to "defunding the police" (a stance usually held by Republicans) while positioning himself as a crusader for New York City's large non-White working class. He used Manhattan's "ivory tower" and its "fancy candidates" as a punching bag.

As one might expect, Adams scooped up votes in predominantly Black neighborhoods. But he was the first choice of 47% of voters in the Bronx, which is mostly Hispanic (57%) plus a sizable non-Hispanic Black population (29%). This included significant numbers of Hispanic voters in districts like Belmont and Fordham Manor's, where the population is 73% Hispanic and 16% non-Hispanic Black.

In New York City's most conservative areas—made up mostly of White, Asian-American, and Hispanic voters—Adams received 25% of first-place votes. As Rakitch noted, Adams was able to extract enough votes from all ethnic groups to seal his primary victory. His path to the nomination circumvented the city's predominantly White cultural trendsetters and power brokers.

THE FORMULA FOR DEMOCRATIC PARTY VICTORY

The Democratic Party is larger and more diverse than the Republican Party. This can be a source of great strength, but only if Democrats consistently work together to achieve common goals and agree to take steady, measured steps.

Michael Kazin—one of Georgetown University's professors of history—wrote in *The New Republic*, "Any serious political mobilization within the Democratic Party entails a willingness to compromise with centrists who can win elections in parts of the country where the GOP frightens voters by quoting members of the Squad and labeling every Democrat a stalking horse for 'socialism.' For their part, centrists need to realize that leftists now make up one of the largest and most committed cohorts of party activists...Each camp of Democrats thus has a responsibility to learn from, if not gratify, the other."

Over and over again, political analysts repeat the same refrain: if you want to win in the long run, you need to form a coalition balancing the interests of radicals and centrists. "Movements always have their radicals and their moderates," wrote Daniel Schlozman, Associate Professor and Director of Graduate Studies at Johns Hopkins University, "and they may need both ... I would say that people in movements should be aware of where they are in that spectrum and figure out how to support one another, and not eat each other alive. Because when they can't work together, that's really bad."

The key is to focus on what unites us. As Pew Research points out, the areas of general agreement within the Democratic coalition are numerous and potent. They include: the government should do more to solve problems. The economic system unfairly favors powerful interests. Tax rates on large businesses and corporations—and on households with incomes over $400,000—should be raised, as should the federal minimum wage. More needs to be done in the country to achieve racial equality. Women continue to face significant obstacles in society that make it harder for them to get ahead than men. Voting is a fundamental right that cannot be restricted.

These and other issues are both rational and emotional. They should be placed front and center, arouse strong emotions, and serve as the point around which all progressive-minded people can rally and move ahead.

CONCLUSION

A Call to Action

As we delve into the issues surrounding the American electoral system and the exclusion of marginalized communities from the voter process, it's crucial to acknowledge the elephant in the room. In November, the American public will participate in a historic election: Vice President Kamala Harris and former President Donald Trump.

For many of us, the 2020 presidential election and its aftermath were some of the most painful memories in our nation's history. The election was marked by conspiracy theories, accusations of fraud, and culminated in supporters of former President Trump storming the U.S. Capitol in an attempt to disrupt the transition of power articulated in our Constitution. At the time of this writing, Donald Trump has been found guilty in a hush money case in New York, while being embroiled in three other criminal trials surrounding his involvement and efforts to overturn the results of the 2020 election, as well as his concealment of classified documents.

Following the election, Republicans at the federal, state, and local levels pushed for policies promoting "election integrity" and safeguards in response to Trump's grievances. According to the Brennan Center for Justice, at least 404 voting restriction bills were introduced in 48 state legislatures in 2021 following the presidential election. These bills focused on issues such as mail-in ballots, voter identification, and restrictions on early voting.

And the rhetoric hasn't died down since then. As he's campaigned nationwide, the former President has warned voters to be on the lookout for irregularities and election interference leading up to the 2024 rematch.

Outside of the legislative voting restrictions, this upcoming election also has the potential to turn off voters due to the candidates on the ballot. Polls show that President Biden and former President Trump are some of the most unpopular presidential candidates in American history. Anecdotally, there have been countless articles leading up to the November election with interviews from voters, especially from marginalized communities, who have voiced their displeasure with the dichotomous choice and said they plan not to vote for either candidate.

Whatever the result, this election can alter the American electoral structure for generations to come. Trump has already mentioned that he plans to implement sweeping changes to our political system if re-elected. Meanwhile, Republicans have warned that another four years of President Biden could send the United States down a path that will forever change the Republic.

For the purposes of this book, the biggest takeaway from whatever happens in November will be: the turnout rate of Black voters and other marginalized communities and how it affects their electoral participation in future elections. As individuals work to see these populations more engaged in the political process, the idea of fielding two candidates whom a large swatch of the country doesn't want to see running might be devastating. How can we tell voters that we hear their concerns and prioritize their issues when the two major parties won't even hear their calls for better candidates to serve in the highest elected office in the country?

If we want to welcome these voters back into the fold, we must engage them during the candidate selection process and avoid the coronation of certain political figures, which has been prevalent in both the 2016 and 2024 presidential elections.

I admit, in recent years, I've seen incredible resilience, activism, and a renewed sense of purpose from people who feel disaffected from voting. I've seen a younger generation attempt to step up, take charge, and carry the torch of progress. But I have also seen a growing apathy towards voting, one that will be exacerbated by growing and deliberate limitations to voting access.

We've come a long way since the days when African Americans were denied the right to vote. Yet, we must remember that progress isn't inevitable. It's the result of candidate selection, the choices we make, the paths we take, and the values we uphold.

If it's hard or difficult for some people to access a ballot box, low turnout will always be the result. One can't address the issue of turnout and civic participation without acknowledging the real disparity between Democrat and Republican turnout rates. According to the Pew Research Center, 76% of Republican registered voters reported voting compared to 72% of Democrats in the 2020 presidential election. In races often decided by the margins, and with the existence of the electoral college, a 4% difference can be enormous in determining the trajectory of this nation.

What's the cause of this difference? Republican voters tend to be older, with 76% of citizens aged 65 and older reporting voting, compared to just 51% of those aged 18-24, according to the Pew Research Center. As many of us know, the Republican Party enjoys a larger share of older American voters compared to Democrats. The Republican Party also benefits from an ideologically aligned electorate, which generally enjoys higher levels of wealth. According to a Columbia University study, since 2000, Republicans have tended to do five to 20 percentage points better than Democrats with voters in the upper third of America's income distribution. Studies have shown that those with higher wealth levels are more engaged in the political process and have more time in their daily lives to participate and vote during the election season.

To boost voter turnout amongst our most vulnerable people and other populations, we must ensure voting is equally accessible for all voters. We must meet the voters where they are and show that casting a ballot can bring the changes they desire in this country. We must add more polling places to eliminate long lines. We should make election day a work holiday, so everyone has real-time voting opportunities. Mobilization and creative messaging via social media and other emerging technologies are critical to communicating to these hard to reach constituencies. We must also emphasize how their vote can enact the reforms necessary to level the playing field of voting in the United States.

WHAT ARE WE PRETENDING NOT TO KNOW?

Whenever I had a difficult issue in my life, I often sat down with my unofficial therapist and best friend, the late Dr. Ken Fowler. Whenever the conversation got tough, he always asked me a thought-provoking question: "What are you pretending not to know?" I can still hear him in my head whenever I'm in a tough moment and I need to make decisions. It was always a valuable (albeit infuriating) inquiry that forced me to face my fears and deal with realities.

Looking back on it, I believe Ken was asking about the inconvenient truths many of us ignore or brush aside to paint ourselves a rosier picture. We always know what we want to hear, but not always what we *need* to hear. What was I pretending to be naive about to help me make the easy decisions or take the easier way out?

I've been thinking about Dr. Fowler's words more and more as they relate to voting, parties, and politics. What are we all pretending not to know? More specifically, for this book, what are the political parties and elected officials pretending not to know about people who choose not to participate or who cannot participate in our electoral process?

WE ARE PRETENDING NOT TO KNOW ELECTION DENIERS ALSO LEAD TO VOTER APATHY

Election deniers can contribute to voter apathy by spreading misinformation and casting doubt on the integrity of the electoral process. This in return can have a negative impact on democracy in America and undermine confidence in election outcomes. When people think the system is rigged or that their votes won't count, they may become disaffected and less likely to participate in elections to come. It's important to fight against misinformation and work to grow trust in the democratic process in order to promote and encourage voter participation. If we allow election deniers to control the narrative, voter apathy will weaken our foundation of democracy. Even Donald Trump has recognized that he can't keep calling elections rigged if he wants people to show up and vote for him. The 2022 midterms are a great example, as the red wave promised didn't materialize because so many MAGA republicans were convinced that the elections were rigged and decided not to show up. During the 2024 election cycle and his re-run for the highest office in the land, Trump changed his tone on mail-in ballots and other forms of early voting and released an ad to correct the narrative and to encourage republicans to use VBM and to vote.

WE ARE PRETENDING NOT TO KNOW DEMOCRATS TALK TOO LONG AND INVEST TOO LATE

Most Black people who don't vote have a feeling that their vote won't bring about meaningful change or won't count. Some may express disillusionment or skepticism towards the political system due to historical disenfranchisement and systemic racism. For years, the Democratic Party has positioned itself as an ally to Black Americans, advocating for issues such as civil rights, criminal justice reform, and economic mobility for the, often, marginalized demographic. However, look no further than news coverage of the 2024 presidential election to see growing criticism that the party takes these voters for granted, as a small percentage of Black men, in particular, have been reported to be moving away from Democrats and toward former President Donald Trump, even though his policies remain contrary to their interest.

A constant criticism is that Democratic outreach and resources in Black communities and to Black candidates usually ramps up shortly before an election, if at all. During these times, candidates and their surrogates appear in Black neighborhoods, participate in Black churches and community events, and increase outreach efforts. This trend gives the appearance of a transactional approach—it's as if the party is assuming that, so long as they show up and shake hands, they'll earn the support of this critical base.

But Black Americans face systemic issues around education, healthcare, economic opportunities, and criminal justice that they struggle with daily. Democrats showing up a few months before an election not only feels like pandering but also indifferent to these critical challenges. Furthermore, after elections, Democrats and Republicans alike are often accused of ignoring this consistency until the next election cycle.

For the Democratic Party to stay in the good graces of Black voters and grow upon the voting block the party has enjoyed, a change is required. This includes having the party maintain a year-round presence with Black voters, listening to their concerns, including them at the decision-making tables during campaigns, and creating a platform that prioritizes their issues and problems.

On a parallel track with these possible solutions, recruiting and adequately funding Black candidates for higher offices is paramount. These candidates need money early to define themselves and their positions before the opposition does it. The goal has got to be to maintain a consistent presence in Black communities to increase confidence in the political process and to eventually drive up voter turnout for a population that has historically supported the democratic agenda. In addition to recruiting Black candidates for higher office, we need to hire and support Black operatives who not only understand best practices for Black candidates and communities of color, but who have, by no fault of their own, worked and understand every job in a campaign from top to bottom.

I have personally witnessed the talent, work ethic, and ability to organize from Black operatives like Quentin Faulk, Jasmine Burney-Clark, Maya Brown, Vince Evans, Kristen Broner, Reggie Cardoza, Rosy Gonzales, Karen Andre, Meredith Lillly, Tharon Johnson, Raymond Paultre, Phillip Jerez, Nadia Garnett, Fred Hicks, Don Callaway, Jasmyne Henderson, Alain Jean, Davicka Thompson, Stephanie James, Quentin James, Darryl Banks, Brandon Davis, Lindsay Pollard, Katia Saint Fleur, Tammy Jackson-Moore, Kamiron Pittman, Roosevelt Holmes, Jerome Maples, Michael Carter, Nick Fryson, Omar Khan, Jasmine Rogers, Kirsten Allen, Janee Murphy, Nikki Barnes, and so many more I don't know personally. These operatives have, time and time again, led candidates to higher office while navigating complex and challenging races. Not only are these individuals incredible political minds, but they also have a unique ability to communicate with hard-to-reach communities and develop strategies that result in people showing up to vote who have been disaffected and ignored for generations.

So, how do we support minority operatives? Hire them for bigger jobs.

Compensate them at the same level as their White counterparts. Pay the women operatives at the same level as their male peers. Give them the chance to lead high-profile campaigns.

WE ARE PRETENDING NOT TO KNOW THE "BIG TENT" CATERS TO THE FEW

The Democratic Party, often touted as the "big tent" party, has fallen victim to being overly reactive to the louder minority of its base. This imbalance has come at the expense of its broader voting base. This shift has influenced policy, campaign strategies, and messaging, leading to difficulties in maintaining a united party and courting moderate Republicans and Independents. This vocal minority leverages new technologies and grassroots strategies to amplify their preferences and voices—disproportionately influencing the Democratic Party's direction and platform.

Polling and recent elections highlight this phenomenon. For example, in the 2020 general elections, several Democratic-elected officials, such as Minnesota Attorney General, Keith Ellison, and South Carolina Congressman, James Clyburn, raised the alarm that slogans and policies such as defunding the police had scared off Moderate and Conservative voters who might have considered voting for Democrats.

To re-balance this overcorrection to the far left, the Democratic Party could benefit from prioritizing better and returning to the days of developing a more integrated and cohesive platform and messaging strategy that appeals to the broader electorate. Engaging in constant communication with the various Democratic factions and focusing on common ground issues such as healthcare, jobs, and safe neighborhoods would provide the party with a more cohesive approach to bringing together all aspects of the "big tent" and appeal to the broader electorate.

This is not to say that these minority positions don't matter. They do, and they are important, but the best opportunity to make changes is when you control the agenda. To control the agenda, you have to win elections. By managing the passions of the fringes and harnessing the progressive wing's energy with its moderates' pragmatic issue preferences, the Democratic Party can strengthen its position as a big-tent party capable of delivering meaningful improvements to the lives of all Americans—not just those at the vocal edges.

WE ARE PRETENDING NOT TO KNOW HOW TO OPTIMIZE OPPORTUNITIES TO EXCITE THE BASE

Far too often, we fall into the trap of not speaking what we know to be true regarding issues and how they will affect voters and—equally as important—non-voters. Even though we know specific topics will move people to the ballot box, we stay silent so as not to seem brash or stereotypical in today's hyper-sensitive world. If we want to capitalize when opportunities arise and drum up voter turnout, we must not shy away from issues and the constituencies for whom they impact.

For example, in Florida, those in the political space, Democrats in particular, are pretending not to know that a real opportunity to increase voter turnout is the ballot initiative that will ask voters to decide whether to legalize adult-use marijuana (Amendment 3). There are passions on both sides of this issue. Polling has consistently and overwhelmingly favored the initiative, but opponents have a strong message to move their voters to action. The referendum on legalizing marijuana and its potential for 1) decriminalization and 2) product safety through regulation and quality controls, will be a massive motivation for young, independent, Black and many other Floridians to show up to the polls. Decriminalization and Safety both poll extremely high in all demographics. The Democratic Party in particular and their candidates should not hesitate to tell it how it is—namely, that the passing of adult-use marijuana will pave the way to correct decades of systemic oppression through the arrests of millions of black and brown Americans over small amounts of marijuana. Hard to reach communities are not so hard to reach when there is a reason to rush to the polls. Adult use marijuana seems to be the kind of issue that can enthusiastically draw new and infrequent voters to the ballot box.

One of the most significant factors contributing to disaffected voters is that we're simply not discussing specifics on how the issues that matter most impact our everyday lives. And, maybe more importantly, we are not dedicating the required resources to communicate our message to more voters. Elected officials in Florida who support adult-use Marijuana and Amendment 3, should not hesitate to mobilize resources to speak directly and frequently to voters.

Florida also has an initiative on the November 2024 ballot establishing a constitutional right to abortion (Amendment 4). While I think Amendment 4 has a strong base to excite and follow to the ballot box, I strongly believe that Amendment 3 has a larger tent and more runway of persuadables. Democrats and Amendment 4 supporters need to optimize the reliable, new, and infrequent voter opportunities that Amendment 3 brings to the table.

WE ARE PRETENDING NOT TO KNOW CULTURE WARS NEED AN EXPIRATION DATE

American politics have seen a dramatic shift in messaging from kitchen-table issues to perceived culture war topics, such as immigration, gun rights, and LGBTQ+ rights, to name a few. This trend occurred even before the Trump administration, with the Tea Party movement holding town halls and rallies nationwide around the immigration issue back in 2009. Since then, politicians and campaigns on both sides of the aisle have only amplified these issues in the public square.

Engaging in the culture wars is an easy trap to fall into if you're a politician. These topics generate massive engagement on social media, energize the base and those most likely to volunteer for your campaign, and serve as lightning rods for engaging grassroots donors and driving up ever-important fundraising dollars. Additionally, when you spend your time talking about cultural issues, you're absolved from coming up with real policy solutions that are much more nuanced and complex. That is to say: if you're spending your days talking about the need to ban books from classrooms, you do not have to explain your position on Social Security and how you plan to fix a welfare system that is expected to be insolvent in the next fifteen years.

While these controversial topics still dominate national headlines and cable news panels, this trend has turned off large swaths of voters who are more concerned about how they will pay rent and buy groceries than which pronouns are allowed to be used in the workplace. These voters see the political landscape and what's being discussed as lacking, regarding the issues that affect them. As one can expect, if none of your choices on the ballot talk about issues that impact you, you're much more likely to stay home on Election Day.

Voter turnoff and depressed turnout are natural symptoms of a culture war that seems never-ending. Furthermore, these issues have a shelf life from a political and candidate perspective. While it may seem far away now, there will soon be a day when voters are simply exhausted from these issues and turn off entirely from the political process. When that becomes the case, how will Republicans and Democrats reach these voters and earn their support?

Suppose we want to drive up voter turnout and sustain political engagement, particularly from our most vulnerable populations. In that case, we must speak to the issues that affect Americans everyday rather than those that energize the fringes of our political parties.

WE ARE PRETENDING NOT TO KNOW THE AMERICAN DREAM IS EASILY ACCESSIBLE TO THE FEW

The United States was founded on the principle that anyone from anywhere could have an opportunity—not just to live in this country but to *thrive* in it. This central tenet was enshrined in our constitution and has been used as a beacon for nations looking to create more representative forms of government. However, since this country's inception, this notion of everyone having a fair shot has only ever been an illusion. I need not remind us that, when this country was created, only White, property-owning men were given a seat at the electoral table to vote.

Fast forward to today, and the notion of the American Dream seems even farther away than it did in the 18th century. According to the Federal Reserve Bank of St. Louis, the top 10% of households by wealth have $6.5 million on average. As a group, they hold 66.6% of total household wealth. The bottom 50% of households, by wealth, have $50,000 on average. As a group, they hold only 2.6% of total household wealth. This gap has only widened in recent years. During the COVID-19 pandemic, income gains were most prominent among the highest-earning families and fastest among White families, while incomes at the median registered slight declines for Hispanic and Black families; this was discovered by the Fed in its latest Survey of Consumer Finances, which is conducted every three years.

This wasn't by accident. Policies and institutions have been erected to maintain levers of power for those who have wielded it for centuries. Mechanisms such as the Electoral College, voter ID restrictions, the filibuster, and other legislative tools have been utilized to stymie change while protecting those who stand to lose the most if everyone in this country had the relative levels of access and influence.

To put it bluntly, we are pretending not to know that our American Democracy was never built to be truly democratic. As I mentioned, the country began by limiting who could vote and thus who had a voice.

That said, we can all vote now and we need to endure the difficulties and the hardship to access the polls so a difference can be made, and so the American Dream can be realized through people who believe in our constitution and governments. We need to stop pretending not to know that we are systematically working against the dream.

WE ARE PRETENDING NOT TO KNOW EVERY ELECTION IS LITERALLY THE ELECTION OF A LIFETIME

Every election cycle, media pundits and campaigns alike issue the warning that "this election is the election of a lifetime." Voters and non-voters have grown desensitized to this statement as an exaggeration or a campaign tactic. However, the reality is that every election really is the election of OUR lifetime. The issues discussed in this book quite literally have life-or-death implications. Topics such as public safety, including criminal justice and law enforcement, reproductive rights, and housing will shape the course of America and the lives of those who call it home.

In an era of hyper-partisanship and media coverage reporting on every moment of political discourse, our politicians and political systems are incentivized to campaign and legislate on the most controversial of subjects. These issues drum up support from base voters, generate fundraising dollars, and lift individuals into national spotlights where they'd otherwise be unknown.

While candidates and many of us who operate in this space try to say that there will always be another election and more time to enact reforms, which we believe to be of existential importance, we know better. In even one four-year cycle, our nation could be irrevocably altered to where certain rights or values will cease to exist, for example, Roe v. Wade. If we want to engage current and future voters and illustrate to them just how important every election is, we have to be honest and clear in explaining how every election is the most important and is not just a campaign slogan but a reality that we have to confront. Today more than ever before, electing people who understand your life needs and struggles is paramount to the promotion of policies and dollars addressing your livelihood. Its incumbent upon everyone, not just democrats or republicans or independents alone, to speak loudly through their votes so that communities and governments are a true reflection of the people they represent.

CLOSING THOUGHTS – THINKING OUT LOUD

I'm often reminded of the brave men and women who marched in Selma, facing down hatred and violence for the right to vote. Their courage, their sacrifice, and their belief in a better America should inspire us all—and not just some of us. Being bolstered by their actions is a testament to the enduring spirit of our nation, a spirit that says we rise or fall as one people.

Disaffected! is my written scream to the country that we must not be complacent. We must not allow cynicism and apathy to win the day. Our democracy requires us to be vigilant, engaged, and, above all, to believe in the possibility of change. When the bus boycotts began because of racial segregation on the public transit system in Montgomery, Alabama, our people had to get uncomfortable to make a change. Black people walked miles to work and schools in protest of the inequality of being forced to sit in the back of the bus. We have to emulate that kind of sacrifice when it comes to voting. When the government passes laws to make it harder and inconvenient to vote, vote anyway! It may be uncomfortable for a while, but vote anyway!

Our votes are not just a statement of our preferences; our votes are a declaration of our power. It's a way of saying that we believe in an America where everyone has a seat at the table, where everyone gets a fair shot, and where we lift each other up.

In America, our democracy lives and thrives, not in spite of our differences, but because of them. The right to vote is at the heart of this extraordinary experiment we call the United States. It's a right that represents our shared belief in equality, our faith in one another, and our commitment to a more perfect union.

ACKNOWLEDGMENTS

I was motivated to write this book because I'm a girl dad, and at some point, I started to wonder what kind of world Paloma, Pilar, and Phoebe would have to navigate and raise their families. I believe showing up at the ballot box is the one thing we can all do that will contribute to the world, the country, the state, the county, the cities, and the communities we leave behind.

President John F. Kennedy said, "One person can make a difference, and everyone should try." That said, we can all, at least at some point in our lives, vote.

So many people helped me get this book out of my head, onto paper, and into a manuscript. My wife, Dr. Audra Pittman, encouraged me to put the time in and be more committed to the process throughout the journey. Because of her words, I eventually committed to the process without being attached to the outcome. That's not easy. Audra's general support and encouragement of me is multilayered because she is more than a wife and, more importantly, has never stopped being my girlfriend. And after all these years, I still look for ways to impress her just like I did when we were dating. Mostly because on a regular basis she impresses me, and that alone challenges me to be the best partner I can be. I thank her parents, the recently late Otis Price and Dr. Willena Price for raising such a strong and amazing woman and allowing her to pursue her Ph.D. at Florida State University where I was blessed to meet her. And her brother, the also recently late Coach Terry Price, for being Audra's lifetime role model and being the example of what she looked for in a husband. In that regard, the influence of Audra's family on who she ultimately is as a person, contributed greatly to the work and completion of this book. Audra would say she was simply my personal spellcheck and my Webster dictionary, but indeed, she was so much more than that and I thank her.

I do very few things in life without considering whether it would make my mother proud. I think all momma's boys are like that. That litmus test has always led me in the right direction. So many people and things in my life benefit from my love for Wilhelmina Pittman and her life that I always wished had more of the finer things she deserved. Anything she did not have as a daughter or I did not have as a son, my kids enjoy. Any way she wasn't supported as a mother, my wife has an unconditional partner in me. Any pain she experienced as a wife and protector, my own family never fears. For every college textbook she could not afford to buy me, now hundreds of college freshmen each year in Florida receive a book stipend from the foundation named in her honor, The Wilhelmina Foundation. I hope this book project adds to her believing that the sacrifices she made and endured as a mother, have a real chance of positive change and it all begins with her.

Hard truth. Finishing this project is not the same without my best friend and hype man Ken Fowler alive and here to share in the moment. Becoming an author is the first milestone in the last 30 years of my life that Dr. Ken Fowler wasn't by my side. It's bittersweet. But mostly bitter because I kept this book a secret from pretty much everybody, including Ken who died suddenly and before completion. Ken knew I wanted to be an author one day, but he died without knowing it was becoming a reality. And what is worse is that I did not share with him or most people in my life because I wasn't confident that I would accomplish the goal. I didn't realize it before he passed, but I have significantly relied on his feedback and encouragement throughout most of my adult life.

My fraternity brother Jwyanza Watt reminded me of a quote from the book "The Prophet", by Kahlil Gibran, which says "love know not its own depth until the hour of separation." Now that Ken is gone, I understand fully that he was that friend who gave me the confidence I needed to take leaps. As scary as that is to face as a new reality, I am, however, confident that Ken is in heaven, proud that I took this leap without him, and that I pushed through the pain of his loss to get this project over the finish line. Ken Fowler is partially responsible for this work because for over 20 plus years, he would periodically ask (and even more profoundly after his death), "What are you pretending not to know?" No pretending. I must carry on and Leap!

My friend and fraternity brother John Charles Thomas was the first person outside of my house with whom I shared the idea of Disaffected. John is a brutally honest person like Brandon Stark in Game of Thrones and is indeed the Three Eyed Raven in my life. I knew I would leave his house either moving forward with the project or getting considerable time back on my schedule because he said not to do it. John told me if it's done right, this book could find the appropriate words to speak clearly and strongly about our sacred right to vote during a pivotal and important time in our history. I don't know many people wiser than John Charles Thomas, so I strived to meet his direction and expectations. I hope I did.

Ted Thomas has been a blessing in my life since I met him in 2003. He has been a father figure who helped bridge the gaps between my underprivileged upbringing and the life I could develop with proper mentorship, knowledge, and information. Ted has been a consistent beacon of knowledge, guidance, and support. Despite my background, he has generously shared his wisdom and taught me invaluable lessons I didn't have access to growing up or during my early adult life. Unbeknown to Ted, Disaffected is one of many seeds planted by his kindness, patience, and belief in my potential.

What Ted added to my personal journey, Attorney Ron Book added similarly in my business and professional life. Ron is a true friend and his mentorship and guidance has been a significant impact on my career and this effort.

Our Pittman Law Group family goes hard in the paint in general, and their support of this project was no exception. I kept the project from them until I knew it was worth asking for their input. This team of professionals, especially Sam Peltier, Dana Dudley, Opal McKinney Williams, and the incomparable Horace Jackson, helped push me to the finish line with countless hours of editing, proofreading, and making sure I allocated time to meet important deadlines (Horace would wake me up during our road travels with the charge, "time to write boss!") The weekly prayers and encouragement by Dana to stay focused and diligent on completing this project was impactful at all the right moments. Sam and his interest and research capabilities were a significant blessing to this project. Opal's early feedback was pivotal to moving forward. I could not have completed this project on time or probably ever without my colleagues, and I hope you all know that means the world to me.

The amazing friends who leaned in with their credibility and added subject matter quotes to the back of the book are very special intervenors in this important conversation. I know Disaffected will support the work they are already doing to protect and promote our sacred right to vote in America. Thank you Joanna, Aaron, Allan and Ben!

It's impossible to complete a project like this with any success without being surrounded by a village of achievers who walk with purpose and have high expectations of each other like my amazing Siblings Tera and Lorenzo Hands, Larry Smith and partner Stephanie Patterson, my Auntie Norma Williams and family, Uncle Herman Sawyer and family, close friends who are more like family including our Tribe Kim Rivers, JT Burnette, Michelle Personette, Greg Garrett, & Jen Anderson, Da FAMUly Andrew and R.Jai Gillum, Opal McKinney Williams, Anita Favors, Darryl Jones, and Alan Williams, Rhonda Fowler, Ahli Moore, Sam Oliver, Davin and Angela Suggs, John and Jane Marks, Adrian and Wendy Crawford, Charlie and Tonja Ward, Eric and Andrea Friall, Edrick and Sia Barnes, Jim and Beth Clements, Stephan and Devona Thompson, Talethia Edwards, Marc and Carla Mentry, Danielle Cohen-Higgins, Byron and Melissa Daub, Ben and Genae Crump, Cedrick and Tamika Thomas, Brenda Williams, Temple Robinson, Todd and Rachael Bonlarron, Angelo and Kim Crowell, Melissa McKinlay, Corey and Charisse Fuller, Fitz and Camille Blake, Roderick Milton, Kevin Price, Imani Sampson, James White, Chris Smith, Rod West, Warde Manuel, Benjamin Macfarland, Rocky Hanna, Joe York, Gaston Cantens, Emmett Reed, Joan Thomas, Big Bend Minority Chamber family Antonio Jefferson, Lila Jaber, Monesia Brown, ShaRon James, Marcus Nicolas, Sheriff Walt McNeil, Jim Murdaugh, Harold Knowles, John Grayson, Rod McQueen, Christie Henry and Laurise Thomas, my co-hosts on Usual Suspects Gary Yordon and Steve Vancore and my amazing friends on the Orange Bowl Committee (too many to mention individually). I have always strived to develop relationships built on genuine purpose and trust. As my amazing and talented friend Oliver Gilbert says, "there's no singular path to success." I'm blessed that my path has so far led to an incredibly diverse silo of remarkable friendships and kinships. I thank God for you all and in advance for your support of Disaffected and the messages within.

Florida State University saved my life several times, and much of that was due to the village created around me. From my first days on campus, to law school, to now serving on significant boards, and contributing as a donor, booster, and alumni. All of which impacted my journey and my ability to complete this project. The late Dr. Bob Leach, The late Dr. Sandra Rackley, Dr. Freddie Groomes McLendon, Sherrill Ragans, Dr. John Dalton, My fraternity Theta Eta of Kappa Alpha Psi, Mathew Bahl, Donald West, Vince Campbell, Lance Tomlin, Anthony Moore, Student Body Presidents before me like Zelda Zarco and Tricia Haisten or after me like Trey Traviesa, Kim Fedele Rivers and Brett Cook or way way way after me like Nastassia Janvier, Evan Steinberg and Jonathan Levin. Deans Erin O'Hara O'Connor, Randy Hanna and Susan Fiorito, Amy Hecht Macchio, Athletic Director Michael and Laura Alford, Peter and Jennifer Collins, Corey Simon, Malikah Nash, Selina Nevin, and John JD Davis. Burning Spear siblings like Liza Park, Ben Crump, Daryl Parks, Julie Dunn Eichenberg, Randall Vitale, Eric Carr, Louis Dilbert, Alisia Adamson Profit, Wayne Messam, Nan Rothstein, Chris Chestnut, Rueben Stokes II, Jalicia Lewis, Brandon Brown,

Dustin Daniels, Wesley Sapp, Bruce Suarez, Amber Johnson, Chris Hall, Scott Vedder and Stephen A. Smith, and more, all had a small hand in preparing me for this moment.

Andrew Gillum made history in Florida by becoming the first black person to become a major party gubernatorial nominee in the state. And he almost won. In fact, many believe he actually did win. I thank Andrew for allowing me to be a close advisor, Finance Chair, and on the inside of his movement. That experience and his very close defeat indeed catalyzed this book. If the equivalent of six more people per precinct across Florida had shown up and voted for Andrew Gillum, this book would not exist or would have a different title and subject matter (perhaps on something a little sexier than civic participation). But his courage and willingness to speak truth to power forced me to see the electoral process and this thing we call democracy through a different lens. I began to see, hear, and feel the difference between people fighting to keep hope and those fighting to keep power. Fighting to keep power seems easier to motivate action. I wanted to write about why fighting to keep hope is equally as important. Like Gillum, there are other friends who helped inspire me and motivate Disaffected, like Ben Crump, Angela Rye, and Bakari Sellers. While there are others for sure, the people above have been examples of people in my life who use their national platforms to speak what they know to be true, even if these truths are uncomfortable. We all have a part to play in leaving the world better than we found it, and we all have different approaches to that end. While I am often very careful with my thoughts and words (and how and who I share them with), I would like to think that there is a little Andrew, Ben, Angela, Bakari; moreover, Marcus, Frederick, Harriet, Martin, and Malcolm inside of me when necessary. I believe Disaffected is necessary. The courage and fortitude to advocate for what's right is inherent in all of us. I'm grateful for their examples.

I work daily with amazing leaders who tirelessly encourage people to vote. Past and present members of the Florida Conference of Black State Legislators understand what I mean when I say that our ability to vote is a sacred right, and we should treat it as such. They understand that voting is a matter of life and death. These particular leaders see firsthand the struggle with adequate access and apathy to voting. They are undeterred as they show up daily for their people and constituents even when the odds are stacked against them. They have served as shining examples of how to lead, and what service can mean in each of our communities. This project is encouraged by their struggle to make apathy and abstaining from voting a thing of the past, and I hope it helps.

Thank you to Art Collins, Willie Logan, and John Thrasher for taking a chance on me when no one else would. You collectively set the stage for this book because my time as a Staff Attorney in the Florida House of Representatives afforded me the opportunity to work on and against election legislation that, we know now, was the beginning of many changes that would impact access and apathy related to voting in Florida.

When Attorney Carlos Moore was President of the National Bar Association (NBA), he nominated me as the General Counsel for this esteemed organization. During my time as General Counsel, President Moore assigned me to Capitol Hill, where I worked with him to secure the passage of the John Lewis Voting Rights Act. Named in honor of the late Congressman and civil rights leader, the bill would restore and strengthen parts of the Voting Rights Act of 1965, including requiring certain jurisdictions to seek federal approval before enacting changes to their voting laws. In retrospect, this work on behalf of the NBA and the frustrations associated with arguing for these fundamental rights further convinced me to write Disaffected. Although the John Lewis Voting Rights Act still languishes in both federal chambers with no clear path to passage, I appreciate Carlos for putting me on this path to speak on a national level about the importance of voting in America.

Dot Ealy, The Almighty Joe Bullard and Torrey "Spreedracer" Ford of Cumulus Broadcasting gave me a voice through the broadcast of the Sean Pittman Show which, similar to Usual Suspects, provided me an additional platform to discuss issues of importance to those who need to hear them the most. They guided me as I discovered my voice in the public arena and were always encouraging of the topics I needed to discover, explore and discuss. The weekly support of their entire team including Victor Duncan and DJ Edwin "Ezone" Correa and the content direction of our production team (past and present) of Sam Peltier, Tre Hands, Jessica Lumpkin and Jamie Van Pelt has made the Sean Pittman Show one of the most listened to and anticipated on the station's regional platform, with the best jingle ever produced by Darius Baker at D-Ree Productions.

Throughout my professional career, I've been blessed to have the opportunity to work for some incredible candidates (mentioned earlier in the book) and work with amazing clients across the country. To those individuals who were brave enough to step up and serve their communities through public office, I'm grateful they entrusted me to guide and advise their journeys. Those experiences were what provided me a front row seat to see the challenges associated with convincing people that their vote matters and is necessary. I'm equally grateful for all my local government, corporate and philanthropic clients that engage in public policy and rely on good government to transform communities and our lives. I also appreciate them helping me to keep the lights on so I could write this book!

To my Riviera Beach family, thank you for the life lessons and the hard core that is needed to speak confidently in powerful settings. From my upbringing in Broadmoor, to my education at John F. Kennedy Jr. High School and Suncoast High School, each childhood friend and relationship, to my work today as lawyer and lobbyist for the great city I call home, each moment and each obstacle, made me who I am today. My childhood and high school best friends John Lyons, Antonio Johnson, Joe Alston, Edwina Beanie Wade, Brian Taylor, Frank Kendrick, Clifford Wilson, Michael Lynn, Anthony Moore, James Hulk Williams and Keith and Tracy Smith kept it real in The Raw (nickname for Riviera Beach) for me then and now. They always pushed me to rise above our circumstances and without their voices in my head, I'm not sure I would have accomplished very much. Additionally, Marjorie Smith, Dr. Gerald Burke, Coach Bob Traina, Tarra Pressey, Sonya Knighton Dickens, Pam Ryan, Powery Family, Teague Family, Hicks Family, as well as the late Elizabeth Liz Wade were supportive in every way possible for a long time. And to the Riviera Beach City Council members and staff, past and present, who all have worked to make the city the best place to live, work and play, thank you for allowing me to play a small part in that ultimate effort. And to the current city leadership, you know the work that needs to be done and you understand the challenges our people endure. I hope you will use this book to help motivate our community to show up in larger numbers to the polls and vote. Because here is some truth, when the county, the state and the nation see that a community votes in high numbers, politicians pay attention and they are inspired to make a difference there.

At Audra's request, we got married in Atlanta but could not have known at the time what Atlanta would come to mean for us. Atlanta has been a great refuge for me since my wife took a job there as Vice President of SCAD Atlanta (Savannah College of Art and Design). What a great city of amazing people. I appreciate the family of friends we have created in Atlanta in a short period of time. I have been motivated by their individual successes and Audra and I are inspired to strive for more. That is certainly the mentality from which this book was born. Special thanks to Paula Wallace, Tricky and Makeda Stewart, Keisha and Derek Bottoms, Kasim Reed, JJ and Elizabeth Waller, Vicki and John Palmer, Dina Marto, Tim Jones, Chantel Jiroch, Derek Dudley, Gloria and Cristal Cole, John "Tony" Moore, Channa Lloyd, Phillana Williams, Rufus Montgomery, J. Batt, Ramon Rivers, Julius Hollis, Darius Jones, Marvel Joseph, Natalie Knight, Kenyatta Mitchell, John Bey, Joy Rohadfox, Tobey Renee Sanders, Brett Chestnut, Victoria Johnson, Candace and Spencer Kollace, Julie and Bob Eichenberg, Bishop Robert Williams, The Kimpson and Price Families and Mayor Andre Dickens.

I'm thankful to my great friends and brothers Darryl Jones, Nick Maddox, Steve Baker and Rufus Davis. Their help and support of me personally has been lifesaving. When my best friend Ken Fowler died, they individually and collectively leaned in to attempt to fill the void that immediately left a hole in my heart and my daily life. After Kens death, this book took a back seat because I could not find the desire to write for over 3 months. I could not find the words or the interest to do anything that wasn't required by my business and my family. None of these guys knew about Disaffected at the time, but their brotherhood in this tough time contributed greatly to me being able to get back on the saddle and galloping forward with my book project and many other things. Readers, find you a Darry, Nick, Steve or Rufus for your life. I only hope this book makes them, as Darryl Jones would say, deliciously proud and that the best is yet to come.

One of my greatest moments in the Disaffected journey was when Dr. Myron Rolle said YES to writing the forward. I had my speech together and was ready to convince him why he should join this project. He stopped me mid-sentence and said, "Brother you had me at hello, say less, I'm in!" Now, I think he was actually in a rush to get back to a brain surgery (I hope the guy survived), but to have a Dr. Myron Rolle in your life to inspire you every day through his own actions and passions is a blessing straight from God- and I receive it. In his book, "The 2% Way," Myron teaches us all the power of gradual but consistent improvements in our goals and our lives. He teaches us that tiny changes can bring about remarkable results. Myron is younger than me in age, but he is someone I learn from and look up to tremendously. And now, he is more than an athlete, Rhodes Scholar and Brain Surgeon; because he is a husband and father. I know from Myron's own words, that husband and father are the best titles God could ever bestow upon him. If Disaffected has the kind of impact I pray for, the reward would potentially be attracting and electing brilliant and compassionate people like Myron Rolle to get America back to the basics and back for the people again.

Dr. Melanie Hicks and I have deep debates from time to time when she would call to remind me why she moved away from Florida. After one particular conversation, she told me I should start writing my thoughts about voting and the political climate because others need access to what I understand and believe. For anyone who finds Disaffected helpful or motivating, you have Dr. Melanie Hicks to thank, not just for her editorial and literary leadership skills, and abilities, but because she had the right words at an important time to convince me that I had something worth saying and worth sharing. Those sentiments now have a name, it's called Disaffected! Thank you, Dr. Hicks.

Like all projects of importance, it took a team to bring this book to full fruition. I would be remiss to not express my appreciation to the subject matter experts and advocates that lent their expertise to me through interviews and resource suggestions.

- Dr. Myron Rolle, Pediatric Neurosurgeon at Johns Hopkins All Children's Hospital
- Speaker Joanna McClinton, Speaker of the House of Representatives, State of Pennsylvania
- Attorney General Aaron D. Ford, Attorney General, State of Nevada
- Ambassador Allan Katz, Obama appointee and US Ambassador to Portugal
- Attorney Benjamin Crump, Civil Rights Attorney
- Amy Cohen, Co-Founder, Families for Safe Streets
- Arricka Watkins, Arizona Lived Experience Advisory Council
- Ben Dierker, Executive Director, Alliance for Innovation and Infrastructure
- Beth Osborne, Director, Transportation for America
- G.E. Loveless, Community Advisor, Hearts2gether for Equitable Change Project
- Ken Lawler, Chairman of the Board, Fair Districts Georgia Foundation
- Laurie Benner, Associate Vice President of Housing and Community Development, National Fair Housing Alliance
- Liss Smith, Advocacy & Communications Director, Inside Out Youth Services

Again, I want to thank my literary team, Dr. Melanie Hicks for literary guidance on this work, my publisher Inked Elephant Publishing House, my editors Chelsea Beam and my cover art and interior design team Neon Pig Creative.

Next, I would like to thank my ESP Media team for their help and commitment to content, outreach and promotion of this project.

- Dana Dudley, Chief Operating Officer
- Sam Peltier, Chief Content Officer
- Britain Solari, Chief Graphic Designer
- Jessica Lumpkin, Marketing and Content Director
- CydNey Flanagan, Graphic Designer
- Tre Hands, Copywriter

Finally, I could not have pulled together all this deep research data without a quality research team deeply committed to the goals of this project: Michael Reid, Kate Wassel, Erik Ananyan, Thomas Hauck, Rachel Coleman, Emily Boykin, Hawa Ocheni, and Stephanie Ramos.

Most importantly, Paloma, Pilar and Phoebe Pittman, you are my WHY! Daddy loves you!

ABOUT THE AUTHOR

ATTORNEY SEAN PITTMAN is the founder of Pittman Law Group, P.L., which specializes in the areas of government, administrative, education, and corporate law. Sean is also the Founder of a leading public relations and marketing firm, ESPMedia Production, providing strategic communications and messaging expertise. Sean represents a diverse client list of private citizens, local governments, small businesses, and Fortune 500 companies.

Sean received his Bachelor of Science degree in Political Science from Florida State University and earned his Juris Doctor degree from the Florida State University College of Law. While at FSU, Sean's leadership qualities led him to become the Student Body President and two-time Chairman of the Florida Student Association Board of Directors, and Governor appointed member of the Florida Board of Regents. Continuing his leadership at the university level, in 2021 Sean was selected to interview and ultimately named a semi-finalist for the Presidency at Florida State University.

Sean served as a President of the Orange Bowl Committee (OBC) and currently serves on the OBC Board of Directors. Sean also serves on the National Football Foundation's Board of Trustees, the Florida State University Foundation Board of Trustees, the Board of Directors for the College Football Hall of Fame, the American Diabetes Association, the Charlie and Tonja Ward Family Foundation, the Florida State University Law School Board of Visitors, the Big 10 Equality Coalition formed by Commissioner Kevin Warren, is a member of the Florida State University Hall of Fame Committee and is the Founder and Chairman of the Big Bend Minority Chamber of Commerce. Sean served as General Counsel of the National Bar Association (NBA) and was presented the Johnnie L. Cochran, Jr. Lawyer of the Year Award by the NBA.

For his contributions to the Orange Bowl Committee and his tireless efforts to bring Glades Pioneer Park to Palm Beach County, Sean was awarded with special recognition by the Palm Beach County Sports Commission. Sean was also selected to serve on the Jim Moran Institute Advisory Board and was inducted into the Tallahassee Barristers Legal Hall of Fame. He received the Distinguished Member of the Year Award from Leadership Florida and under his leadership, has led the Pittman Law Group and ESPMedia to be multi-year recipients of the Seminole 100 award as one of the fastest-growing alumni owned businesses by the Florida State University Alumni Association. Sean is the recipient of the FSU Alumni Association and Omicron Delta Kappa's Grads Made Good Award and the Tallahassee Community College President's Award. For his outstanding and sustained contribution to the university's academic mission, Sean was awarded the Florida State University Faculty Senate Vires Award.

For his philanthropic endeavors, Sean was presented the Heman Sweatt Award by the National Bar Association, the Tallahassee Servant Leadership Award by the Greater Tallahassee Chamber of Commerce, the Florida Conference of Black State Legislators Joe Lang Kershaw Award, and the Founders Award from the Big Bend Minority Chamber of Commerce. Sean is the former Chairman of the Children's Home Society and has served on the boards of the Apalachee Center, Leon County Civic Center Authority, United Way of the Big Bend, and Children's Campaign. Among his many philanthropic efforts, Sean created an FSU College of Law Scholarship for minority students. Sean also created the Wilhelmina Foundation in honor of his mother to provide textbook stipends to high school graduates.

The Tallahassee Democrat named Sean one of the "Top Twenty-Five Most Influential People in Tallahassee" and featured him in the article, "Capitol Clout" for being a significant political insider within the constantly changing environs of Florida's State Capitol. Sean has been ranked annually as one of the "Top 100 Most Influential People in Florida Politics" by Influence magazine. He has also been included in Florida Trend's "Top 500 Business Leaders in Florida."

Sean is a co-host of the television talk show "The Usual Suspects," airing on one of the highest watched CBS affiliates in the country and hosts his own radio show and podcast series, "The Sean Pittman Show." Sean has also made appearances on MSNBC, CNN and Fox News, while also being published in USA Today, Tallahassee Democrat, the Palm Beach Post, and Miami Herald.

Sean and his wife, Dr. Audra Pittman, reside in Florida raising their three amazing daughters, Paloma, Pilar, and Phoebe.

WANT TO REACH OUT TO SEAN?

Go to **https://seanpittman.com** or scan the QR code below.
For Media Inquiries: sam@espmedia.net
For Personal Inquiries: dana@pittman-law.com
Follow him on social media: @seanpittman

JOIN THE MOVEMENT

---

*"If the United States
believes in the fundamental right
to vote for every citizen, Election Day
should be a federal holiday in this nation."*
- Sean Pittman

Were you inspired by the messages in Disaffected?

Want to be a part of the cause?

Learn more about the difference you can make. Join the movement and help break the cycle of apathy. Sign our petition to support election day becoming a federal holiday so we can all easily enjoy the privilege and sacred right to vote.

Go to or scan the QR code below to learn more.

CITATIONS

1. U.S. Census Bureau (2023) Annual Report.
2. Tallahassee Democrat. *Winners and Losers in the Tallahssee and Leon County primary election.* August 22, 2020. https://www.tallahassee.com/story/news/tlhelections2020/2020/08/22/winners-and-losers-tallahassee-and-leon-county-primary-election/3403297001/
3. State of Florida Elections Data. n.d. https://dos.fl.gov/elections/data-statistics/elections-data/
4. State of Virginia Elections Data n.d. https://www.elections.virginia.gov/resultsreports/election-results/
5. State of Kentucky Elections Data n.d. https://elect.ky.gov/Pages/default.aspx
6. State of Washington Election Data n.d. https://www.sos.wa.gov/elections/data-research/election-data-and-maps/election-results-and-voters-pamphlets
7. State of Georgia Election Results n.d. https://www.sos.wa.gov/elections/data-research/election-data-and-maps/election-results-and-voters-pamphlets
8. State of Florida Elections Data. n.d. https://dos.fl.gov/elections/data-statistics/elections-data/
9. State of Arizona Elections Data n.d. https://azsos.gov/elections/results-data
10. Library of Congress Congressional Elections Data n.d. https://guides.loc.gov/election-statistics/congressional-elections
11. Library of Congress Congressional Elections Data n.d. https://guides.loc.gov/election-statistics/congressional-elections

12. The American Presidency Project. n.d. https://www.presidency.ucsb.edu/statistics/elections

13. Reeve, E. The Atlantic August 30, 2011 *Powell Aide: Cheney was President 'for all Practical Purposes'* The Atlantic. https://www.theatlantic.com/politics/archive/2011/08/powell-aide-cheney-was-president-all-practical-purposes/338526/

14. The American Presidency Project. n.d. https://www.presidency.ucsb.edu/statistics/elections

15. New York Magazine. *For the MAGA Right, Democracy Itself is a Fraud.* August 19, 2022. https://nymag.com/intelligencer/2022/08/trump-maga-democracy-fraud.html

16. Bloomberg. *He's Not Good: Trumps MAGA Creation Takes On Life of Its Own.* June 2, 2022. https://www.bloomberg.com/news/articles/2022-06-08/gop-primary-elections-results-show-trump-s-maga-movement-isn-t-all-about-him

17. Eckart, K.UW News. Feb 5, 2021 *New nationwide survey shows MAGA supporters beliefs about the pandemic, the election and the insurrection.* https://www.washington.edu/news/2021/02/05/new-nationwide-survey-shows-maga-supporters-beliefs-about-the-pandemic-the-election-and-the-insurrection/

18. USAGOV.com Voting and Election Laws. n.d. https://www.usa.gov/voting-laws

19. Fiorina, M. *The Case of the Vanishing Marginals.* Book Chapter in McCubbins, D. and Sullivan, T. (1987) Congress: Structure and Policy.

20. Fact Sheet 2022. n.d. https://www.whitehouse.gov/dpc/fact-sheets/

21. Browne-Marshall, G. J. (2017). The voting rights war : the NAACP and the ongoing struggle for justice. Rowman & Littlefield.

22. Miller, E. (2021, October 4). Voting laws roundup: October 2021 | brennan center for justice. Www.brennancenter.org. https://www.brennancenter.org/our-work/research-reports/voting-laws-roundup-october-2021

23. Lerner, K. (2022, May 2). *Florida gave voting rights to people with felony convictions. Now some face charges for voting.* | NC Policy Watch. https://ncpolicywatch.com/2022/05/02/florida-gave-voting-rights-to-people-with-felony-convictions-now-some-face-charges-for-voting/

24. Soule, D. (n.d.). A 69-year-old Floridian thought she was eligible to vote. Then police came knocking at 3 a.m. Tallahassee Democrat. Retrieved June 20, 2024, from https://www.tallahassee.com/story/news/politics/2023/10/05/69-year-old-arrested-for-voter-fraud-at-3-a-m-in-desantis-florida-tallahassee/71045125007/

25. Cineas, F. (2022b, May 3). *Florida's election police will investigate very rare cases of voter fraud—Vox.* https://www.vox.com/2022/5/3/23048665/florida-election-police-voting-rights

26. https://www.naacpldf.org/press-release/florida-voters-win-case-challenging-suppressive-voting-law-as-judge-rules-s-b-90-violates-voting-rights-act-and-u-s-constitution/

27. Voting Laws Roundup: October 2021 | Brennan Center for Justice. (2021, October 4). Brennan Center for Justice. https://www.brennancenter.org/our-work/research-reports/voting-laws-roundup-october-2021

28. Abrams,S. (2001). OUR TIME IS NOW: power, purpose, and the fight for a fair America. Picador

29. Redistricting Criteria. (2021, July 16). National Conference of State Legislatures. https://www.ncsl.org/research/redistricting/redistricting-criteria.aspx

30. https://redistricting.lls.edu/redistricting-101/who-draws-the-lines/

31. Allen, G. (2022, April 12). Gov. DeSantis takes over congressional redistricting in Florida—Google Search. National Public Radio. https://www.npr.org/2022/04/12/1092414662/gov-desantis-takes-over-congressional-redistricting-in-florida

32. Ellis, D. (2022, April 20). ACLU's brief contends judge erred in dismissing challenge to Arkansas' redistricting map. Arkansas Online. https://www.arkansasonline.com/news/2022/apr/20/aclus-brief-contends-judge-erred-in-dismissal-of/

33. Ramsey, R. (2022, April 20). Analysis: Gerrymandering has left Texas voters with few options. The Texas Tribune. https://www.texastribune.org/2022/04/20/texas-redistricting-elections/

34. Staten, A. (2022, April 27). Democrats at Risk of Losing House Seats After Failed New York Redistricting. https://www.newsweek.com/new-york-redistricting-failure-democratic-house-seats-midterms-1701552

35. McGhee, E. (n.d.). Redistricting Injects Some Uncertainty into the 2022 Elections. Public Policy Institute of California. Retrieved May 31, 2022, from https://www.ppic.org/blog/redistricting-injects-some-uncertainty-into-the-2022-elections/

36. Enten, H. (2017, January 31). Under A New System, Clinton Could Have Won The Popular Vote By 5 Points And Still Lost. FiveThirtyEight. https://fivethirtyeight.com/features/under-a-new-system-clinton-could-have-won-the-popular-vote-by-5-points-and-still-lost/

37. Daily Kos Elections presents the 2016 presidential election results by congressional district. (n.d.). Daily Kos. https://www.dailykos.com/

stories/2017/1/30/1627319/-Daily-Kos-Elections-presents-the-2016-presidential-election-results-by-congressional-district

38. September 29, E. L., 2020October 21, & 2020. (2020, September 29). Stacking the deck: How the GOP works to suppress minority voting. Berkeley News. https://news.berkeley.edu/2020/09/29/stacking-the-deck-how-the-gop-works-to-suppress-minority-voting/

39. Hanna-Attisha, M. (2018). What the eyes don't see: a story of crisis, resistance, and hope in an American city. One World.

40. Gross, T. (2018, June 25). NPR Choice page. Npr.org. https://www.npr.org/sections/health-shots/2018/06/25/623126968/pediatrician-who-exposed-flint-water-crisis-shares-her-story-of-resistance

41. Booker, B. (2021, January 14). NPR Cookie Consent and Choices. Npr.org. https://www.npr.org/2021/01/14/956924155/ex-michigan-gov-rick-snyder-and-8-others-criminally-charged-in-flint-water-crisi

42. Gross, T. (2018, June 25). NPR Choice page. Npr.org. https://www.npr.org/sections/health-shots/2018/06/25/623126968/pediatrician-who-exposed-flint-water-crisis-shares-her-story-of-resistance

43. UCI Law. (2016). Establishing equity in our food system. UC Irvine School of Law, EDU 1111. https://www.law.uci.edu/events/food-equity/2016/

44. Hill, B. E. (2021). Human rights, environmental justice, and climate change: Flint, Michigan. American Bar Association, 46(4). https://www.americanbar.org/groups/crsj/publications/human_rights_magazine_home/the-truth-about-science/human-rights-environmental-justice-and-climate-change

45. Basra, K., Fabian, M. P., & Scammell, M. K. (2018). Consumption of contaminated seafood in an environmental justice community: A qualitative and spatial analysis of fishing controls. Environmental Justice, 11(1), 6-14. https://doi.org/10.1089%2Fenv.2017.0010

46. Rather, I. A., Koh, W. Y., Paek, W. K., & Lim, J. (2017). The sources of chemical contaminants in food and their health implications. Frontiers in Pharmacology, 8, 830. https://doi.org/10.3389/fphar.2017.00830

47. Dorman, B. & McCullough, S. (2021, December 14). Frozen food and pizza are on the menu at 3 local schools due to fuel-contaminated water. Hawaii Public Radio. https://www.hawaiipublicradio.org/the-conversation/2021-12-14/frozen-foods-local-schools-due-to-navy-military-fuel-contaminated-water

48. Mueller, T. & Gasteyer, S. (2021). The widespread and unjust drinking water and clean water crisis in the United States. Nature Communications, 12(3544). https://doi.org/10.1038/s41467-021-23898-z

49.   About the Office of Water. (2022, July 18). United States Environmental Protection Agency. https://www.epa.gov/aboutepa/about-office-water

50.   Enforcement (2021, November 4). Safe Drinking Water Act (SDWA) and Federal Facilities. United States Environmental Protection Agency. https://www.epa.gov/enforcement/safe-drinking-water-act-sdwa-and-federal-facilities

51.   Enforcement. (2022, April 13). National Compliance Initiative: Reducing Significant Non-Compliance with National Pollutant Discharge Elimination System (NPDES) Permits. United States Environmental Protection Agency. https://www.epa.gov/enforcement/national-compliance-initiative-reducing-significant-non-compliance-national-pollutant

52.   Mueller, T. & Gasteyer, S. (2021). The widespread and unjust drinking water and clean water crisis in the United States. Nature Communications, 12(3544). https://doi.org/10.1038/s41467-021-23898-z

53.   About the Office of Water. (2022, July 18). United States Environmental Protection Agency. https://www.epa.gov/aboutepa/about-office-water

54.   Laws & Regulations. (2022, July 6). Summary of the Clean Water Act. United States Environmental Protection Agency. https://www.epa.gov/laws-regulations/summary-clean-water-act

55.   News Releases. (2022, February 10). EPA Region 10 Clean Water Act enforcement actions in 2021. United States Environmental Protection Agency. https://www.epa.gov/newsreleases/epa-region-10-clean-water-act-enforcement-actions-2021

56.   Bryan, D. W. (2021). United States Fines BNSF $1.5 Million for Alleged Clean Water Act Violations. United States Environmental Protection Agency. https://www.epa.gov/newsreleases/united-states-fines-bnsf-15-million-alleged-clean-water-act-violations

57.   Padilla, M. (2022). Western Timber Products pays $222,400 EPA penalty for Clean Water Act violations. United States Environmental Protection Agency. https://www.epa.gov/newsreleases/western-timber-products-pays-222400-epa-penalty-clean-water-act-violations

58.   Freeman, A. (2013). The unbearable whiteness of milk: Food oppression and the USDA. UC Irvine Law Review, 3(4). https://scholarship.law.uci.edu/ucilr/vol3/iss4/16

59.   University of Michigan. (2021). Environmental justice factsheet. Center for Sustainable Systems, CSS17-16. https://css.umich.edu/publications/factsheets/sustainability-indicators/environmental-justice-factsheet

60.   Fitzpatrick, K. M., Harris, C., Drawer, G., & Willis, D. E. (2020). Assessing food insecurity among US adults during the COVID-19 pandemic. Journal

of Hunger & Environmental Nutrition, 16(1), 1-18. https://doi.org/10.108
0/19320248.2020.1830221

61. U.S. Department of Agriculture. (2022). Food security in the US: Key statistics & graphics. Economic Research Service. https://www.ers.usda. gov/topics/food-nutrition-assistance/food-security-in-the-u-s/key-statistics-graphics/

62. Feeding America. (n.d.). Hunger in America. Retrieved July 25, 2022. https://www.feedingamerica.org/hunger-in-america

63. University of Michigan. (2021). Environmental justice factsheet. Center for Sustainable Systems, CSS17-16. https://css.umich.edu/publications/ factsheets/sustainability-indicators/environmental-justice-factsheet

64. Donley, N., Bullard, R.D., Economos, J., Figueroa, I., Lee, J., Liebman, A. K., Martinez, D. N., & Shafiei, F. (2022). Pesticides and environmental injustice in the USA: root causes, current regulatory reinforcement and a path forward. BMC Public Health 22, 708. https://doi.org/10.1186/ s12889-022-13057-4

65. Pugh, M. (2017). A recipe for justice. Food and Drug Law Journal, 72(2), 341-360. https://www.jstor.org/stable/26661139

66. Erickson, J. (2019, April 23). Five years later: Flint water crisis most egregious example of environmental injustice, U-M researcher says. Michigan News. https://news.umich.edu/five-years-later-flint-water-crisis-most-egregious-example-of-environmental-injustice-u-m-researcher-says/

67. Supplemental Nutrition Assistance Program (SNAP). (n.d.). Benefits.gov. Retrieved 25 July, 2022. https://www.benefits.gov/benefit/361

68. Food and Nutrition Service. (n.d.a). Special Supplemental Nutrition Program for Women, Infants, and Children (WIC). USDA. Retrieved 25 July, 2022. https://www.fns.usda.gov/wic

69. Food and Nutrition Service. (2018, January 1). FDPIR Program Fact Sheet. USDA. https://www.fns.usda.gov/fdpir/fdpir-fact-sheet

70. Food and Nutrition Service. (n.d.b). The Emergency Food Assistance Program. USDA. https://www.fns.usda.gov/tefap/emergency-food-assistance-program

71. Food and Nutrition Service. (n.d.c). Commodity Supplemental Food Program. USDA. https://www.fns.usda.gov/csfp/commodity-supplemental-food-program

72. Supplemental Nutrition Assistance Program (SNAP). (n.d.). Benefits.gov. Retrieved 25 July, 2022. https://www.benefits.gov/benefit/361

73. Food and Nutrition Service. (n.d.a). Special Supplemental Nutrition Program for Women, Infants, and Children (WIC). USDA. Retrieved 25

July, 2022. https://www.fns.usda.gov/wic

74. Food and Nutrition Service. (2018, January 1). FDPIR Program Fact Sheet. USDA. https://www.fns.usda.gov/fdpir/fdpir-fact-sheet

75. Food and Nutrition Service. (n.d.b). The Emergency Food Assistance Program. USDA. https://www.fns.usda.gov/tefap/emergency-food-assistance-program

76. Food and Nutrition Service. (n.d.c). Commodity Supplemental Food Program. USDA. https://www.fns.usda.gov/csfp/commodity-supplemental-food-program

77. Environmental & Energy Law Program. (2022). Environmental Justice at the Department of Energy. Retrieved 25 July, 2022. https://eelp.law.harvard.edu/ej-tracker-doe/

78. Callahan, C., Coffee, D., DeShazo, J. R., & González, S. R. (2021). Making Justice40 a reality for frontline communities: Lessons from state approaches to climate and clean energy investments. Luskin Center for Innovation. https://innovation.luskin.ucla.edu/wp-content/uploads/2021/10/luskin-justice40-final-web-1.pdf

79. Surrusco, E. K. (2021, October 1). Tribes Defend Minnesota Waterways From Dangerous Line 3 Pipeline. Earthjustice. https://earthjustice.org/article/tribes-defend-minnesota-waterways-from-dangerous-line-3-pipeline

80. Laws & Regulations. (2021c, October 22). Summary of the Toxic Substances Control Act. United States Environmental Protection Agency. https://www.epa.gov/laws-regulations/summary-toxic-substances-control-act

81. Laws & Regulations. (2021d, September 28). Summary of the Resource Conservation and Recovery Act. United States Environmental Protection Agency. https://www.epa.gov/laws-regulations/summary-resource-conservation-and-recovery-act

82. Laws & Regulations. (2021b, September 28). Summary of the Food Quality Protection Act. United States Environmental Protection Agency. https://www.epa.gov/laws-regulations/summary-food-quality-protection-act

83. CBS/AP. (2019, May 8). California bans chlorpyrifos pesticide as largest agriculture state claims it harms child brain development. Cbsnews.com. https://www.cbsnews.com/news/california-bans-chlorpyrifos-pesticide-agriculture-state-child-brain-development/

84. Laws & Regulations. (2021b, September 28). Summary of the Food Quality Protection Act. United States Environmental Protection Agency. https://www.epa.gov/laws-regulations/summary-food-quality-protection-act

85. Donley, N., Bullard, R.D., Economos, J., Figueroa, I., Lee, J., Liebman, A. K., Martinez, D. N., & Shafiei, F. (2022). Pesticides and environmental injustice in the USA: root causes, current regulatory reinforcement and a path forward. BMC Public Health 22, 708. https://doi.org/10.1186/s12889-022-13057-4

86. White, K. & Todrys, K. (2021, September 1). 5 years after Standing Rock, the Dakota Access pipeline continues operating — illegally. Grist. https://grist.org/fix/opinion/dakota-access-pipeline-operating-illegally-shut-it-down-for-good/

87. Brower, S. (2021). Environmental [in]justice: Why Executive Order 12898 falls short in creating environmental equity for vulnerable communities. Minnesota Journal of Law & Inequality, 4(1). https://lawandinequality.org/2021/05/18/environmental-injustice-why-executive-order-12898-falls-short-in-creating-environmental-equity-for-vulnerable-communities/

88. Brown, A. (2018, January 9). Five spills, six months in operation: Dakota Access track record highlights unavoidable reality - pipelines leak. The Intercept. https://theintercept.com/2018/01/09/dakota-access-pipeline-leak-energy-transfer-partners/

89. Sowerwine, J., Mucioki, M., Sarna-Wojcicki, D., & Hillman, L. (2019). Reframing food security by and for Native American communities: A case study among tribes in the Klamath River basin of Oregon and California. Food Security. https://doi.org/10.1007/s12571-019-00925-y

90. Jernigan, V. B. B., Huyser, K. R., Valdes, J., & Simonds, V. W. (2017). Food insecurity among American Indians and Alaska Natives: A national profile using the current population survey–food security supplement. Journal of Hunger & Environmental Nutrition, 12(1), 1-10. https://doi.org/10.1080/19320248.2016.1227750

91. Climate Change Indicators. (2022, August 1). Climate change indicators: Weather and climate. United States Environmental Protection Agency. Retrieved 1 August, 2022. https://www.epa.gov/climate-indicators/weather-climate

92. EPA. (2021). Climate change and social vulnerability in the United States: A focus on six impacts. U.S. Environmental Protection Agency. https://www.epa.gov/system/files/documents/2021-09/climate-vulnerability_september-2021_508.pdf

93. Williams, J. (2022, January 26). Why climate change is inherently racist. BBC. https://www.bbc.com/future/article/20220125-why-climate-change-is-inherently-racist

94. Davies, I. P., Haugo, R. D., Robertson, J. C., & Levin, P. S. (2018). The

unequal vulnerability of communities of color to wildfire. PLoSONE 13(11), e0205825. https://doi.org/10.1371/journal.pone.0205825

95. Masri, S., Scaduto, E., Jin, Y., & Wu, J. (2021). Disproportionate impacts of wildfires among elderly and low-income communities in California from 2000–2020. International Journal of Environmental Research and Public Health, 18(8), 3921. https://doi.org/10.3390/ijerph18083921

96. Tippet, B. (2020, October 8). Burning injustice: why the California wildfires are a class crisis. OpenDemocracy. https://www.opendemocracy.net/en/burning-injustice-why-california-wildfires-are-class-crisis/

97. Fears, D. & Grandoni, D. (2021, September 2). EPA just detailed all the ways climate change will hit U.S. racial minorities the hardest. It's a long list. The Washington Post. https://www.washingtonpost.com/climate-environment/2021/09/02/ida-climate-change/

98. Frank, T. (2020, June 2). Flooding disproportionately harms Black neighborhoods. Scientific American. https://www.scientificamerican.com/article/flooding-disproportionately-harms-black-neighborhoods/

99. Williams, J. (2022, January 26). Why climate change is inherently racist. BBC. https://www.bbc.com/future/article/20220125-why-climate-change-is-inherently-racist

100. Gronlund, C. J., Sullivan, K. P., Kefelegn, Y., Cameron, L., & O'Neill, M. S. (2018). Climate change and temperature extremes: A review of heat-and cold-related morbidity and mortality concerns of municipalities. Maturitas, 114, 54-59. https://doi.org/10.1016/j.maturitas.2018.06.002

101. Benz, S. A. & Burney, J. A. (2021). Widespread race and class disparities in surface urban heat extremes across the United States. Earth's Future, 9(7), e2021EF002016. https://doi.org/10.1029/2021EF002016

102. McCarthy, J. (2021, April 20). Why is climate change a racial justice issue? Global Citizen. https://www.globalcitizen.org/en/content/why-is-climate-change-a-racial-justice-issue/

103. Kinney, P. L. (2018). Interactions of climate change, air pollution, and human health. Current Environmental Health Reports, 5, 179-186. https://doi.org/10.1007/s40572-018-0188-x

104. Gardiner, B. (2020, June 9). Unequal impact: The deep links between racism and climate change. Yale Environment 360. https://e360.yale.edu/features/unequal-impact-the-deep-links-between-inequality-and-climate-change

105. Romney, L. (2020, August 4). Wildfire smoke and environmental justice: One little girl's story. KALW. https://www.kalw.org/show/crosscurrents/2020-08-04/wildfire-smoke-and-environmental-justice-

one-little-girls-story

106. Laws & Regulations. (2021a, September 28). Summary of Executive Order 12898 - federal actions to address environmental justice in minority populations and low-income populations. United States Environmental Protection Agency. https://www.epa.gov/laws-regulations/summary-executive-order-12898-federal-actions-address-environmental-justice

107. Brower, S. (2021). Environmental [in]justice: Why Executive Order 12898 falls short in creating environmental equity for vulnerable communities. Minnesota Journal of Law & Inequality, 4(1). https://lawandinequality.org/2021/05/18/environmental-injustice-why-executive-order-12898-falls-short-in-creating-environmental-equity-for-vulnerable-communities/

108. Donley, N., Bullard, R.D., Economos, J., Figueroa, I., Lee, J., Liebman, A. K., Martinez, D. N., & Shafiei, F. (2022). Pesticides and environmental injustice in the USA: root causes, current regulatory reinforcement and a path forward. BMC Public Health 22, 708. https://doi.org/10.1186/s12889-022-13057-4

109. Columbia Law School. (2022). President issues Executive Order revoking Federal sustainability plan. https://climate.law.columbia.edu/content/president-issues-executive-order-revoking-federal-sustainability-plan-0

110. The White House (2021a). Executive Order on tackling the climate crisis at home and abroad. https://www.whitehouse.gov/briefing-room/presidential-actions/2021/01/27/executive-order-on-tackling-the-climate-crisis-at-home-and-abroad/

111. NOAA. (2022a). Coastal resilience interagency working group. https://www.noaa.gov/coastal-resilience-interagency-working-group

112. The White House (2022). Fact sheet: Readout of the April National Climate Task Force meeting. https://www.whitehouse.gov/briefing-room/statements-releases/2022/04/18/fact-sheet-readout-of-the-april-national-climate-task-force-meeting/

113. Bryan, B. & Smith, M. E. (2021) Looking to expand your existing facility or renew your permits? Here's what may be different under Washington's new climate change policies. The National Law Review, XI(265). https://www.natlawreview.com/article/looking-to-expand-your-existing-facility-or-renew-your-permits-here-s-what-may-be

114. Fears, D. & Grandoni, D. (2021, September 2). EPA just detailed all the ways climate change will hit U.S. racial minorities the hardest. It's a long list. The Washington Post. https://www.washingtonpost.com/climate-environment/2021/09/02/ida-climate-change/

115. The White House. (2021b). Executive Order on advancing racial

equity and support for underserved communities through the Federal Government. https://www.whitehouse.gov/briefing-room/presidential-actions/2021/01/20/executive-order-advancing-racial-equity-and-support-for-underserved-communities-through-the-federal-government/

116. Environmental & Energy Law Program. (2022). Environmental Justice at the Department of Energy. Retrieved 25 July, 2022. https://eelp.law.harvard.edu/ej-tracker-doe/

117. The White House. (n.d.a). White House Environmental Justice Interagency Council. https://www.whitehouse.gov/environmentaljustice/white-house-environmental-justice-interagency-council/

118. Young, S., Mallory, B., & McCarthy, G. (2021, July 20). The path to achieving Justice40. The White House. https://www.whitehouse.gov/omb/briefing-room/2021/07/20/the-path-to-achieving-justice40/

119. Rosenbaum, D., Neuberger, Z., Keith-Jennings, B., & Nchako, C. (2021, May 7). Food Assistance in American Rescue Plan Act Will Reduce Hardship, Provide Economic Stimulus. Center on Budget and Policy Priorities. https://www.cbpp.org/research/food-assistance/food-assistance-in-american-rescue-plan-act-will-reduce-hardship-provide

120. NOAA. (2022b). Infrastructure law: Climate ready coasts. https://www.noaa.gov/infrastructure-law/infrastructure-law-climate-ready-coasts

121. NOAA. (2022c). Habitat restoration. https://www.noaa.gov/infrastructure-law/infrastructure-law-climate-ready-coasts/habitat-restoration

122. NOAA. (2022d). National estuarine research reserve system. https://www.noaa.gov/infrastructure-law/infrastructure-law-climate-ready-coasts/national-estuarine-research-reserve-system

123. The White House. (n.d.b). President Biden's Bipartisan Infrastructure Law. https://www.whitehouse.gov/bipartisan-infrastructure-law/

124. The White House. (n.d.c). National Climate Task Force. https://www.whitehouse.gov/climate/

125. Office of Electricity. (2021). Energy Storage for Social Equity Initiative. Department of Energy. https://www.energy.gov/oe/articles/energy-storage-social-equity-initiative

126. Murray, C. (2022, March 21). US Department of Energy, PNNL to help 14 underserved communities with energy storage needs. Energy Storage News. https://www.energy-storage.news/us-department-of-energy-pnnl-to-help-14-underserved-communities-with-energy-storage-needs/

127. Assistant Secretary for Health. (2022). About the Office of Climate Change and Health Equity (OCCHE). Department of Health and Human Services. https://www.hhs.gov/ash/ocche/about/index.html

128. USDA. (2022a). USDA to invest $1 billion in climate smart commodities, expanding markets, strengthening rural America. https://www.usda.gov/media/press-releases/2022/02/07/usda-invest-1-billion-climate-smart-commodities-expanding-markets

129. USDA. (2022b). In major step to implement American Rescue Plan, USDA announces membership of newly formed Equity Commission. https://www.usda.gov/media/press-releases/2022/02/10/major-step-implement-american-rescue-plan-usda-announces-membership

130. Office of Environmental Justice. (n.d.). Environmental justice at the Department of Justice. U. S. Department of Justice. https://www.justice.gov/oej

131. Climate Action Tracker. (2022, July 6). USA. https://climateactiontracker.org/countries/usa/

132. National Conference of State Legislatures. (2022, January 1). State and Federal environmental justice efforts. https://www.ncsl.org/research/environment-and-natural-resources/state-and-federal-efforts-to-advance-environmental-justice.aspx

133. Growing Food Connections. (n.d.). Local government food policy database. http://growingfoodconnections.org/tools-resources/policy-database/

134. Commonwealth of Virginia. (n.d.). 2021 Interagency Environmental Justice Working Group: A guide for 2022. Retrieved 25 July 2022. https://www.naturalresources.virginia.gov/media/governorvirginiagov/secretary-of-natural-resources/pdf/2021-Interagency-EJ-Report-FINAL.pdf

135. Office of Community Services. (2022a). LIHEAP fact sheet. Administration for Children & Families. https://www.acf.hhs.gov/ocs/fact-sheet/liheap-fact-sheet

136. Howard, L. (2021). LIHEAP IM-2021-01 heat stress flexibilities and resources. Administration for Children & Families. https://www.acf.hhs.gov/ocs/policy-guidance/liheap-im-2021-01-heat-stress-flexibilities-and-resources

137. Howard, L. (2022a). LIHEAP IM-2022-06 heat stress flexibilities and resources FY2022. Administration for Children & Families. https://www.acf.hhs.gov/ocs/policy-guidance/liheap-im-2022-06-heat-stress-flexibilities-and-resources-fy2022

138. Office of Community Services. (2022b). LIHWAP fact sheet. Administration for Children & Families. https://www.acf.hhs.gov/ocs/fact-sheet/lihwap-fact-sheet

139. Howard, L. (2022b). LIHWAP DCL 2022-15 LIHWAP emergency and disaster flexibilities FY2022. Administration for Children & Families.

https://www.acf.hhs.gov/ocs/policy-guidance/lihwap-dcl-2022-15-lihwap-emergency-and-disaster-flexibilities-fy2022

140. Office of Community Services. (2022c). RCD fact sheet. Administration for Children & Families. https://www.acf.hhs.gov/ocs/fact-sheet/rcd-fact-sheet

141. Office of Community Services. (2022d). CED fact sheet. Administration for Children & Families. https://www.acf.hhs.gov/ocs/fact-sheet/ced-fact-sheetCooper, C. R. (2019). Financial Inclusion and Credit Access Policy Issues (p. 25). https://crsreports.congress.gov/product/pdf/R/R45979

142. FACT SHEET: HUD Year 1. (2022a, January 20). HUD.Gov / U.S. Department of Housing and Urban Development (HUD). https://www.hud.gov/press/press_releases_media_advisories/hud_no_22_011

143. Wynn, C. (2021, October 5) More than a Home: Housing is a Human Right. US News https://www.usnews.com/news/health-news/articles/2021-10-05/more-than-a-home-housing-is-a-human-right

144. Schaeffer, K. (2022, January 18). Affordable housing is a major local problem, more Americans now say | Pew Research Center. https://www.pewresearch.org/fact-tank/2022/01/18/a-growing-share-of-americans-say-affordable-housing-is-a-major-problem-where-they-live/

145. Corporation, n.d. Opportunity Atlas shows the effect of childhood zip codes on adult success. https://www.lisc.org/our-resources/resource/opportunity-atlas-shows-effect-childhood-zip-codes-adult-success/ Accessed August 19, 2022.

146. Kalugina, A. (2016). Affordable housing policies: An overview.

147. Singer, J. (2022). There Are No Accidents. Simon and Schuster.

148. Singer, J. (2022). There Are No Accidents. Simon and Schuster.

149. DANGEROUS BY DESIGN 2022 National Complete Streets Coalition. (n.d.). https://smartgrowthamerica.org/wp-content/uploads/2022/07/Dangerous-By-Design-2022-v3.pdf

150. Weller, Z. D., Im, S., Palacios, V., Stuchiner, E., & von Fischer, J. C. (2022). Environmental Injustices of Leaks from Urban Natural Gas Distribution Systems: Patterns among and within 13 U.S. Metro Areas. Environmental Science & Technology, 56(12), 8599–8609. https://doi.org/10.1021/acs.est.2c00097

151. Crump, B. (2019). Open season : legalized genocide of colored people. Amistad, An Imprint Of HarperCollins publishers.

152. Rice, G. E., Nozicka, L., & Moore, K. (2022, March 22). Racism in the KCPD: There's no thin blue line for Black officers, Star investigation finds [Review of Racism in the KCPD: There's no thin blue line for Black

officers, Star investigation finds]. The Kansas City Star. https://www.kansascity.com/news/local/article259140453.html

153. Thrush, G. (2022, September 20). U.S. Investigates Racial Bias Claims in Kansas City Police Employment. The New York Times. https://www.nytimes.com/2022/09/20/us/politics/justice-dept-racial-bias-police.html

154. https://www.census.gov/programs-surveys/decennial-census/decade/2020/2020-census-results.html

155. jarchibald @al.com, J. A. |. (2022, April 26). Inside the remarkable rise and fall of Alabama's most predatory police force. Al. https://www.al.com/news/2022/04/inside-the-remarkable-rise-and-fall-of-alabamas-most-predatory-police-force.html

156. Shoub, K., Christiani, L., Baumgartner, F. R., Epp, D. A., & Roach, K. (2020). Fines, Fees, Forfeitures, and Disparities: A Link Between Municipal Reliance on Fines and Racial Disparities in Policing. Policy Studies Journal. https://doi.org/10.1111/psj.12412

157. DeSilver, D., Lipka, M., & Fahmy, D. (2020, June 3). 10 things we know about race and policing in the U.S. Pew Research Center. https://www.pewresearch.org/short-reads/2020/06/03/10-things-we-know-about-race-and-policing-in-the-u-s/#:~:text=In%20a%202019%20Center%20survey

158. https://naacp.org/

159. Rehavi, M. M., & Starr, S. B. (2014). Racial Disparity in Federal Criminal Sentences. Journal of Political Economy, 122(6), 1320–1354. https://doi.org/10.1086/677255

160. Berdejó, C. (2017, September 13). Criminalizing Race: Racial Disparities in Plea Bargaining. Ssrn.com. https://papers.ssrn.com/sol3/papers.cfm?abstract_id=3036726#paper-citations-widget

161. https://www.census.gov/en.html

162. Carson, E. A. (2021). Bureau of Justice Statistics · Statistical Tables Prisoners in 2020 -Statistical Tables. U.S. Department of Justice. https://bjs.ojp.gov/content/pub/pdf/p20st.pdf

163. Foucault, M. (1995). Discipline and Punish: The Birth of the Prison (A. Sheridan, Trans.). New York: Vintage Books.

164. Davis, A. Y. (2003). Are Prisons Obsolete? New York: Seven Stories.

165. Alexander, M. (2010). The New Jim Crow: Mass Incarceration in the Age of Colorblindness. New York: New Press.

166. Alexander, M. (2010). The New Jim Crow: Mass Incarceration in the Age of Colorblindness. New York: New Press.

167. Bauer, S. (2018, March 23). Private prisons are shrouded in secrecy. I

took a job as a guard to get inside—then things got crazy. Mother Jones. https://www.motherjones.com/politics/2016/06/cca-private-prisons-corrections-corporation-inmates-investigation-bauer/

168. CoreCivic Inc | AFSC Investigate. (2018). Afsc.org. https://investigate. afsc.org/company/corecivic

169. Alexander, M. (2010). The New Jim Crow: Mass Incarceration in the Age of Colorblindness. New York: New Press. P.138

170. Solis, J. (2018, June 5). Fines & fees sent nursing mother to jail for traffic tickets, Nevada Current. Nevada Current. https://nevadacurrent. com/2018/06/05/system-of-fines-and-fees-sent-nursing-mother-to-jail-for-traffic-tickets/

171. https://www.nytimes.com/interactive/2019/08/14/magazine/1619-america-slavery.html

172. https://www.edweek.org/leadership/two-okla-districts-get-downgraded-accreditations-for-violating-states-anti-crt-law/2022/08#:~:text=The%20 state%20board%20of%20education,claimed%2-0%E2%80%9Cshamed%20white%20people.%E2%80%9D

173. Frankovic, K. (2021, November 16). Critical race theory: Who believes it is being taught in their schools? YouGov https://today.yougov.com/politics/ articles/39456-critical-race-theory-who-believes-being-taught?redirect_fr om=%2Ftopics%2Fpolitics%2Farticles-reports%2F2021%2F11%2F16% 2Fcritical-race-theory-who-believes-being-taught

174. Kohli, R. (2021). TEACHERS OF COLOR: resisting racism and reclaiming education. Harvard Education Press.

175. Lewis, A. E. (2017). Despite the best intentions: how racial inequality thrives in good schools. Oxford University Press.

176. Tikkanen, M. (2005) Invisible Children. Expert Pub, Inc.

177. Goodman, S. (2018). It's Not About Grit. Teachers College Press.

178. Kozol, J. (2005). The shame of the nation : the restoration of apartheid schooling in America. Three Rivers Press.

179. Anthony Abraham Jack. (2019). The privileged poor : how elite colleges are failing disadvantaged students. Cambridge, Mass. Harvard University Press.

180. Ginwright, S. (2015). Hope and Healing in Urban Education How Urban Activists and Teachers are Reclaiming Matters of the Heart. Routledge.

181. Cornell Law School. (2018). Roe v. Wade. LII / Legal Information Institute; Cornell Law School. https://www.law.cornell.edu/supremecourt/ text/410/113

182. Cornell Law School. (2018). Roe v. Wade. LII / Legal Information

Institute; Cornell Law School. https://www.law.cornell.edu/supremecourt/text/410/113

183. Northup, N. (2018, March 19). Supreme Court Case: Dobbs v. Jackson Women's Health Organization. Center for Reproductive Rights. https://reproductiverights.org/case/scotus-mississippi-abortion-ban/

184. https://www.pewresearch.org/religion/fact-sheet/public-opinion-on-abortion/

185. https://www.census.gov/en.html

186. Colvin, J. (2021, July 17) GOP eyes Latinos in South Texas in effort to regain Congress. AP News. https://apnews.com/article/republicans-hispanic-voters-south-texas-2022-elections-e3de8f8ed98262f8f9e64dcd0a2a997f

187. Herrera, J. (2021, October) Why Democrats Are Losing Texas Latinos. Texas Monthly. https://www.texasmonthly.com/news-politics/democrats-losing-texas-latinos-trump/

188. https://apnews.com/article/abortion-incest-rape-louisiana-exception-846480b677fbc6fbe60d18ca13572899

189. Bluestein, G. (2022). Flipped. Penguin.

190. Bluestein, G. (2022). Flipped. Penguin.

191. Bluestein, G. (2022). Flipped. Penguin.

192. https://www.aei.org/research-products/report/the-democratic-partys-transformation-more-diverse-educated-and-liberal-but-less-religious/

193. https://www.census.gov/programs-surveys/decennial-census/decade/2020/2020-census-results.html

www.ingramcontent.com/pod-product-compliance
Lightning Source LLC
Chambersburg PA
CBHW031151270326
41931CB00006B/225